Cyber Forensics

Founded in 1807, John Wiley & Sons is the oldest independent publishing company in the United States. With offices in North America, Europe, Asia, and Australia, Wiley is globally committed to developing and marketing print and electronic products and services for our customers' professional and personal knowledge and understanding.

The Wiley Corporate F&A series provides information, tools, and insights to corporate professionals responsible for issues affecting the profitability of their company, from accounting and finance to internal controls and performance management.

Cyber Forensics

From Data to Digital Evidence

ALBERT J. MARCELLA, JR., PhD, CISA, CISM
FREDERIC GUILLOSSOU, CISSP, CCE

WILEY

John Wiley & Sons, Inc.

Published by John Wiley & Sons, Inc., Hoboken, New Jersey.
Published simultaneously in Canada.

For general information on our other products and services or for technical support, please contact our Customer Care Department within the United States at (800) 762-2974, outside the United States at (317) 572-3993 or fax (317) 572-4002.

Wiley also publishes its books in a variety of electronic formats. Some content that appears in print may not be available in electronic books. For more information about Wiley products, visit our web site at www.wiley.com.

Library of Congress Cataloging-in-Publication Data:

Marcella, Albert J.
    Cyber forensics : from data to digital evidence / Albert J. Marcella, PhD, CISA, CISM, Frederic Guillossou, CISSP, CCE.
        pages   cm.— (The Wiley Corporate F&A series)
        Includes index.
    ISBN 978-1-118-27366-1 (hardback); ISBN 978-1-118-28268-7 (ebk);
    ISBN 978-1-118-28505-3 (ebk); ISBN 978-1-118-28731-6 (ebk)
        1. Forensic sciences—Technological innovations.   2. Electronic evidence.   3. Evidence, Criminal.   4. Criminal investigation.   5. Computer crimes—Investigation. I. Guillossou, Frederic, 1970 -   II. Title.
    HV8073.5.M168   2012
    363.250285—dc23
                                                                        2011048568

Printed in the United States of America

10 9 8 7 6 5 4 3 2 1

Al Marcella

To my wife

Diane . . . .

A sunbeam to warm you,

A moonbeam to charm you,

A sheltering angel, so nothing can harm you.

May you always know how happy you make me, and how much I love you! Love doesn't make the world go round; love is what makes the ride worthwhile.

Thank you for sharing with me, the ride of a lifetime.

∞ + 1

Fredric Guillossou

To my wife and daughter

Alexandra and Nathalie

The happy memories of the past, the joyful moments of the present, and the hope and promise of the future.

Contents

Preface

THE ROLE AND RESPONSIBILITY of a cyber forensic investigator is to accurately report upon actions taken to expertly identify, extract, and analyze those data that will ultimately represent evidential matter as part of an investigation of an individual who is suspected of engaging in unauthorized activities.

As an expert, a cyber forensic investigator who heavily relies upon the automated, generated results of a forensic software tool, without an intimate knowledge of how the results have been achieved, is risking not only his or her professional reputation but also the potential of a successful outcome to an investigation.

Data, the primordial building blocks of information as we know it, begins life as nothing more than electrical impulses representing an existence or lack thereof, of an electrical charge. Knowing just how these pulses end up as data, and how these data then end up as potential evidence, is an essential skill for a cyber forensic investigator.

The evolution of bits and bytes into data and finally into human-understandable text is not rocket science; somewhat technical yes, but not beyond the reach or understanding of the professional looking to gain a greater understanding of HOW data become digital forensic evidence, WHERE to look for this evidence, buried beneath hundreds of millions of bytes of data, and WHY specific data may lead the investigator to the proverbial "smoking gun."

In communicating the results of a cyber forensic investigation, responding to the question "How did you identify the specific data you examined to reach your conclusion?" by eluding to your use of a specific cyber forensic tool without a thorough understanding of how that tool "achieved" its answer, could be professionally dangerous.

Reliance on the software to produce an answer, without a solid understanding of the HOWs, WHATs, WHYs, and the theory and logic behind *how* the answer was attained is akin to submitting all of the correct answers to a mathematics exam and failing, because you did not show your work. Knowing the answer without knowing how you achieved the answer or how to explain how the answer was achieved is having only half of a solution.

The book you are about to read will provide you with the specific knowledge to speak confidently about the validity of the data identified, accessed, and analyzed as part of a comprehensive cyber forensic investigation.

We start small, in fact very small . . . bits and bytes small, explaining the origins of data and progressing onward, addressing concepts related to data storage, boot records, partitions, volumes, and file systems, and how each of these are interrelated and essential in a cyber forensic investigation. The role each plays in an investigation and what type of evidential data may be identified within each of these areas.

Also addressed are two often overlooked topics which impact almost every cyber-based investigation: endianness and time. Each of these topics rightly deserve their own chapter and are discussed in-depth with respect to their impact and influence on data and ultimately on the identification of digital evidence.

In an effort to more effectively introduce specific information technology (IT) and cyber forensic concepts and discuss critical cyber forensic processes, we proudly introduce Ronelle Sawyer and Jose McCarthy, employees who become involved in the theft of intellectual property.

Ronelle and Jose's activities and actions are discussed throughout the book as an ongoing case, designed to provide the reader with specific examples of the application of the cyber forensic concepts discussed throughout the 12 primary chapters of this book. Although the case and characters are fictitious, the scenario presented is not.

Along with this case, we have developed and present an exemplar forensic investigation report (Forensic Investigations, ABC Inc.), which appears as an Appendix to this book. This exemplar report provides the reader with a basic forensic report template, which summarizes the forensic investigation and case data as it would be compiled for submission to a respective authorized recipient. We realize that there are many varied ways in which the results of an investigation may be compiled and presented; the report included herein is an example of one such way.

While each investigation is unique, there will be similarities and as each case is unique on to itself, a generalized investigation approach can be constructed. We have provided you, the reader, with generalized Investigative Smart Practices (ISPs) as you hone and develop your individualistic investigative processes. These are not "best practices," but "smart practices" steps, procedures, and actions, which in general, can be applied to most cyber forensic case/investigations.

It would be illogical to try to present an investigative procedure or methodology and claim that it is universal, that it can be applied in all instances under all circumstances. As such, our ISPs cast the widest net and are applicable to most general investigative cases. It is up to you the reader to add to this base, adding specific, specialized company, department, or agency steps and procedures, which will result in a uniquely identifiable case-by-case investigative process.

Regardless of your confidence in the data identified via your investigative efforts or through the use of any specific or generalized cyber forensic software, take to heart the Russian proverb, "doveryai, no proveryai," made famous by the late Ronald Reagan: "trust but verify!"

This book will provide you with a comprehensive examination and discussion of the science of cyber forensic investigations, what is happening behind the scenes to data and why, what to look for and where to find it . . . progressing logically, from data to digital evidence.

Al Marcella and Fred Guillossou

Acknowledgments

A S AUTHORS, LET'S be frank: It is almost impossible to be fully honest when assessing one's own work. It's also impossible to be fully independent or even neutral when attempting to assess or evaluate what one has written, no matter how hard one tries.

Thus, to remedy this truism, we, as most dedicated authors, reach out to colleagues, peers, and sometimes even to strangers (well, the publisher does) to provide us with a truly independent assessment and review of what we have written.

This assessment can occur at various stages of the development of a book, such as the one you are about to read, in segments or chapters, during its formative development stages, as a completed, draft manuscript or even once the last keystroke has been struck and development is finalized.

To achieve this sought after assessment, we have reached out to individuals whom we respect, asking them to critically review our work and to provide us with the benefit of their expertise and extensive knowledge in the fields of cyber forensics, audit, information technologies, e-discovery, and investigative sciences, as they critiqued the book you are about to read.

We are thankful for their assessment and suggestions for improvement, as they have provided us with valuable insights into refining our text and providing you the reader, with the most accurate and technically current material related to the emerging and evolving field of cyber forensic investigation and analysis.

While it is not possible to individually acknowledge all of the reviewers who have assessed our work, as some will forever remain anonymous, the authors would like to personally thank the following individuals for their insights, time, and involvement in making our development efforts result in a better overall examination and presentation of the science of cyber forensics.

To the following professionals, we say a heartfelt thank you . . .

Don Caniglia, CEGIT, CISA, CISM, FLMI
President
IT Risk Management Services, LLC

Richard J. Dippel, JD, MBA, CPA
Assistant Professor of Accounting
George Herbert Walker School of Business & Technology
Webster University

Linda C. Ertel, CISA
Security Compliance Analyst
Independent Reviewer

Steve Grimm
Webster Groves Police Department Detective
The Greater St. Louis Regional Computer Crime Education and
    Enforcement Group

Detective Andy Hrenak, CFCE/A+/ACE/DFCB
Hazelwood Police Department
RCCEEG Forensic Examiner

Jeff Lukins, CISSP, CEH, MCSE, MSE
Deputy IT Sec. Mgr., NASA MITS
Dynetics Technical Services, Inc.

Doug Menendez, CISA, CIA
Audit Manager
Graybar Electric Company

Bruce Monahan, CIA, CISA, CFE, CPCU
Chief Audit Executive
Selective Insurance Group, Inc.

Greg Strauss, CCE
Computer Forensics Expert
Independent Reviewer

Although not reviewers, we also wish to thank Ronelle and Jose, for providing us with a more personal means by which we were able to convey technical, cyber forensic concepts through a realistic case example. Thank you both!

Sincerely,
Al Marcella, Ph.D., CISA, CISM
Frederic Guillossou, CISSP, CCE

Cyber Forensics

CHAPTER ONE

The Fundamentals of Data

THIS BOOK IS DESIGNED to address the fundamental concepts found in the emerging and rapidly evolving field of cyber forensics.

Before one can profess to be knowledgeable and fully cognizant of the breadth encompassing the professional discipline of cyber forensics, a foundation, rooted in the basics of information technology, data storage, handling, and processing, as well as how data is moved and manipulated, is essential.

For the cyber forensic investigator, data is evidence. Understanding how evidence emerges from data is pivotal; however, more important is being able to confidently articulate how evidential data was identified, collected, and processed.

As a cyber forensic investigator, simply pressing buttons or checking off options in a forensic software suite, without the knowledge of what is happening behind the scenes, creates a potential liability. Understanding the "life cycle" of data is pivotal, from its humble beginnings as electronic *bits*, evolving into bytes, characters, then words, finally emerging as a language, as information, and perhaps eventually as evidence.

This book will provide a platform for both broadening as well as enhancing your skills in the basic elements of information technology as the technology supports and is embedded within the science of cyber forensic investigations.

As you read this book, you will encounter words that have been *italicized*. These words represent key concepts and are more fully defined by a working definition, which is included within a glossary at the end of the book. Should you desire an explanation of any *italicized* word, please refer to this glossary.

As with most tasks, one must crawl prior to walking and certainly before dashing off in a full run. Therefore, our first chapter begins naturally, at the beginning, with a discussion of the prime building blocks of data and how as a society we carbon-based humans have learned to communicate with a silicon-based technology—computers.

BASE 2 NUMBERING SYSTEM: BINARY AND CHARACTER ENCODING

Modern humans use character sets (or alphabets) to represent written sounds and words. In many alphabets, including Latin-based alphabets, each symbol or letter has its own phonetic sound.

The letter (or combination of letters, such as "ph") is paired to its corresponding sound, forming a character code. It is through the combination of these symbols or letters that humans generate words, then phrases, and ultimately complex communication.

Symbolic characters, such as alphanumeric symbols found in Latin-based languages, work reasonably well for the complex computing power of the human brain. Computers, however, have yet to evolve to a level capable of exactly duplicating the complex processing—consistently, seamlessly, and reliably—of the human brain. Currently, computers can best communicate with other computers, in a manner based upon the principles of fundamental mathematics. Computer-to-human communication, while having evolved to a certain degree of voice replication, is still based, again, upon the principles of fundamental mathematics.

The current methodology for digital data transfer is called binary, and it is the basis for all computing technology. In order to understand how computers handle, move, store, access, save, delete, or otherwise manipulate data, it is essential to first understand the concepts of the *binary system*.

Binary is a name given to a Base 2 numbering system or encoding scheme. As the name Base 2 implies, there are two and only two possible states. In fact, a Base 2 encoding scheme is the only option of communication when only two possible states exist. Such an encoding scheme works well with electronic communication.

Consider electricity, where only two states are present. Electricity is either on or off; there exists no other possible option or state. A circuit is either open or closed. So, if we were to attach a light bulb to an electrical circuit we could visually see when the circuit is open or closed, as the light would either be off or on, respectively (remember, a closed circuit implies closed loop, and is therefore on).

COMMUNICATION IN A TWO-STATE UNIVERSE

Communication in a two-state environment is now possible; the light is either on, equal to "yes," or it is off, equal to "no." The potential to answer rudimentary, close-ended questions simply by indicating a response as either "yes" (1) or "no" (0) is entirely feasible.

This is important, being that presently, computers essentially can pass or store information as either electrical or magnetic states. Remember our light bulb can be "on" or "off" only.

Without going into great detail on the basics of electricity or magnetism, perhaps it is necessary to delve ever so gently into the very basic concepts of magnetism and electricity, and their relationship to data construction, storage, mobility, and processing.

ELECTRICITY AND MAGNETISM

Magnetism is the force whereby objects are attracted to or repelled by one another. Usually these objects are metals such as iron. (See Figure 1.1.)

Magnetism can store electricity, as in a battery, for example. Magnetism can also generate electricity (e.g., a generator). Magnetism, as with electricity, has only two states or opposing poles, positive and negative. Magnetic states can also be contained or preserved; for example, the direction of an iron oxide shaving can be manipulated by a magnet. This is called a magnetic domain, which is a series of atoms that point their poles in the same direction. A bar magnet is made up of a group of domains.

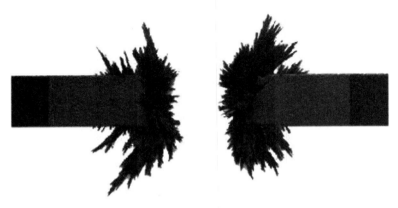

FIGURE 1.1   Magnetic Force

The most common source of magnetic fields is the electric current loop. Electricity is a type of activity arising from the existence of charge. The basic unit of charge is that on the proton or electron. The proton's charge is called positive while the electron's is negative.

Electricity tends to move or flow in its active state. This being the case, electricity is good at representing data in motion and magnetism is good at representing data at rest. Both, however, have two separate and opposing states, and as discussed, having two separate states allows for Base 2 digital communication.

With computers, the movement of digital data is easily represented by the two states of electricity or magnetism, and is conveniently presented by 1 and 0, respectively. Therefore, as the technology used to communicate and to represent data currently exists, this representation is accomplished through a two-state or binary numbering system.

BUILDING BLOCKS: THE ORIGINS OF DATA

A single zero (0) or a single one (1) is equal to what is called a bit. This representation of the two possible states of digital data is the smallest unit of data recognized or processed by a computer.

Therefore, in a one-bit, Base 2 encoding scheme (or as it is usually called, binary), we have the basic building blocks of a communication system: an ability to communicate through and between silicon-based technologies.

To communicate, for example, that the status of a light is on, we can assign the value of one (1). To communicate that the light is turned off, we can just as easily set the value to zero (0). For more complex situations, to indicate on or off (yes or no), we can assign similar values: yes/on equals one (1), or no/off equals zero (0).

As communications grow in breadth and complexity, we are constrained by a single-bit, Base 2 encoding scheme. Essentially, we have two and only two possible outcomes of communication when constrained to a single bit (e.g., yes or no, on or off, 1 or 0).

Communication is possible, then, when only two states or conditions are required. Once we desire to expand the possibilities of communication options to a broader lexicon beyond a two-option state, one bit falls short, severely limiting communication possibilities.

GROWING THE BUILDING BLOCKS OF DATA

As you connect consecutive 0s and 1s (or bits), however, the ability to represent an increasingly larger set of characters, words, communication, and messaging possibilities increases geometrically. Just by adding another bit we double the potential outcomes or states (from two to four).

There are two possible states with one bit: one (1) or zero (0). Add another bit and now the number of possible states doubles: 00, 01, 10, and 11. Armed with such a system we can now represent more complex ideas or those conditions requiring more than a simplistic, on/off, yes/no, two-state description. For example, the four seasons could now be depicted with two bits, for example, 00 = winter, 01 = spring, 10 = summer, and 11 = fall.

To better understand the geometric growth of possible outcomes attained by combining bits, let's look at a few examples. The following discussion might send shivers down the spines of many readers, harking back to younger days and thoughts that math challenges were all behind us; however, an understanding of this basic math principle is critical in understanding the finer working details of data storage and ultimately data extraction using forensic software.

What is 2 to the 0 power?

A short explanation, which requires us to use the law of exponents, may be helpful to fire up those math synapses. One of the laws of exponents is:

$$\frac{n^{\wedge}x}{n^{\wedge}y} = n^{\wedge}(x - y)$$

for all n, x, and y. So, for example,

$$\frac{2^{\wedge}4}{2^{\wedge}2} = 2^{\wedge}(4 - 2)$$

$$\frac{2\wedge4}{2\wedge3} = 2\wedge(4-3)$$

Now suppose we have the fraction:

$$\frac{2\wedge4}{2\wedge4} = 1$$

This fraction equals 1, because the numerator and the denominator are the same. If we apply the law of exponents, we get:

$$1 = \frac{2\wedge4}{2\wedge4} = 2\wedge(4-4) = 2\wedge0$$

$$\text{So, } 2\wedge0 = 1$$

We can plug in any number in the place of 2, and that number raised to the zero power will still be 1. In fact, the whole proof works if we just plug in x for 2:

$$x\wedge0 = x\wedge(4-4) = \frac{x\wedge4}{x\wedge4} = 1$$

Wow, math flashbacks—we proved that $2\wedge0$ equals 1, so what about the following:

What is 2 to the first power? Second power? Third power?

Well, naturally, then we would answer $2 \times 1 = 2$, $2 \times 2 = 4$, and $2 \times 2 \times 2 = 8$!

Why is this important? It provides us with a better way to understand the geometric growth of possible states or outcomes attained by combining bits.

The following is a small example of the power of 2 and the exponential growth of increasing the bit combination possibilities:

```
2^0  =  1
2^1  =  2
2^2  =  4
2^3  =  8
2^4  =  16
2^5  =  32
2^6  =  64
2^7  =  128
2^8  =  256
2^9  =  512
2^10 =  1,024
```

From our previous question, "What is 2 to the third power?" we find the answer in our encoding scheme. The number 2 represents our encoding scheme, Base 2 or binary; the power (third) represents how many bits will be strung together.

The answer 8 is how many outcomes or combinations are possible when we can string together three bits: 000, 111, 001, 010, 100, 110, 101, 011. That's it! There are 8 possible outcomes, thus 2 to the third = 8.

MOVING BEYOND BASE 2

Eight possible outcomes or combinations is still fairly limiting for complex human communications, as necessary in today's global business economy. As we continue to add 0s and 1s, the potential for very complex digital signaling or communication is increased, as stated exponentially. In fact, if we string together enough bits, we will be able to represent complete alphabets, alphabets of more than one language, and alphabets to even represent graphical concepts and expressions.

In order to represent the English alphabet (A–Z) and the numbers 1 through 10, we would need 26 unique representations for letters and 10 for numbers (0–9). Thus, we need 36 unique identifiers. How many bits would be needed to represent 36 unique identifiers or outcomes?

Well, from our earlier math lesson, 6 bits would easily cover our needs, resulting in 2 to the sixth or 2^6, represented as a result of $2 \times 2 = 4 \times 2 = 8 \times 2 = 16 \times 2 = 32 \times 2 = 64$.

This six-bit combination not only produces the necessary 36 unique identifiers required, but also gives us some unique identifiers to spare, 28 to be specific, which we can use to represent special symbols such as (!, @, #, $, %, ^, &,*) and so forth. In fact, 64 unique characters, while significant in the amount of combinations possible, do not suffice. In representing most basic characters of the English language, we use 7 bits or 2^7, resulting in 128 unique characters to be identified or mapped.

AMERICAN STANDARD CODE FOR INFORMATION INTERCHANGE

The history of the American Standard Code for Information Interchange (ASCII) and its development is a long story and will only be briefly touched upon in this chapter. The characters identified by $2 \wedge 7$, or the 128-bit unique characters to be identified or mapped, are known as American Standard Code for Information Interchange/extended ASCII or just ASCII.

English-language personal computers used in America employ a seven-bit character code called American Standard Code for Information Interchange (ASCII), which allows for a character set of 128 items of upper- and lower-case Latin letters, Arabic numerals, signs, and control characters (i.e., $2 \wedge 7 = 128$ code points). ASCII also serves as the foundation of the Universal Character Set (UCS), containing 0–9, A–Z, a–z, and special characters).

When an eighth bit is used as a "parity bit," with its value used for checking whether or not data have been transmitted properly, then ASCII becomes an eight-bit, or one-byte (eight bits = one byte), character code. A true eight-bit character code allows for up to 256 items to be encoded ($2^8 = 256$ *code points*).[1]

ASCII is a character-encoding scheme based on the ordering of the English alphabet. ASCII codes represent text in computers, communications equipment, and other devices that use text. Most modern character-encoding schemes, which support many more characters than did the original, are based on ASCII.

Tables 1.1 and 1.2 highlight the ASCII coding scheme and associated binary equivalents. Table 1.1 presents the numbers 0–9 and Table 1.2 depicts a list of special characters.

Alphabetic characters from the English language have similar representations in the ASCII coding scheme, as represented in Table 1.3.

TABLE 1.1 The Numbers Represented by 0–9

Character	ASCII	Binary
0	chr(48)	110000
1	chr(49)	110001
2	chr(50)	110010
3	chr(51)	110011
4	chr(52)	110100
5	chr(53)	110101
6	chr(54)	110110
7	chr(55)	110111
8	chr(56)	111000
9	chr(57)	111001

TABLE 1.2 Special Character Representation

Character	ASCII	Binary
!	chr(33)	100001
"	chr(34)	100010
#	chr(35)	100011
$	chr(36)	100100
%	chr(37)	100101
&	chr(38)	100110
'	chr(39)	100111
(	chr(40)	101000
)	chr(41)	101001
*	chr(42)	101010
+	chr(43)	101011

TABLE 1.3 English-Language Representations in the ASCII Coding Scheme

Character	ASCII	Binary
A	chr(65)	1000001
B	chr(66)	1000010
C	chr(67)	1000011
D	chr(68)	1000100
E	chr(69)	1000101
F	chr(70)	1000110
G	chr(71)	1000111
H	chr(72)	1001000
I	chr(73)	1001001
J	chr(74)	1001010
K	chr(75)	1001011
L	chr(76)	1001100
M	chr(77)	1001101

CHARACTER CODES: THE BASIS FOR PROCESSING TEXTUAL DATA

Many people are unaware of the fact that to a computer, textual data is also numerical data.

In modern computer systems, the individual characters of the scripts that humans use to record and transmit their languages are encoded in the form of binary numerical codes, just as are the Arabic numerals used in calculation programs. (See Tables 1.1, 1.2, and 1.3.) This is because the circuitry of the microprocessor that lies at the heart of a modern computer system can only do two things—calculate binary arithmetic operations and perform Boolean (i.e., true or false) logic operations.[2]

A *character code* pairs a character set, such as an alphabet, with something else, in this case with a decimal and/or binary system. An example most would be familiar with is the Braille Encoding System. While some of us may not know what the Braille encoded dots translate to, we have seen them, as many elevators display the floor number along with its Braille counterpart. This combination of information would be considered a character code.

The maximum characters possible in a character code depend upon the numbering system (Base 2 for Binary) and the number of bits. As demonstrated previously, the more bits in the character code, the bigger the character set.

In regard to character codes, it should also be noted that computers operate most efficiently when they process data in bytes. This is because their internal circuitry is usually designed with data pathways that are 8, 16, 32, or 64 bits wide. For that reason, a 10-bit or a 15-bit character code is clumsy and inefficient to handle inside a personal computer.

On the other hand, if too many bytes are used for encoding characters, computers will tend to process data inefficiently. For example, a three-byte character code could encode almost 17 million characters ($2 \wedge 24 = 16{,}777{,}216$ code points), which would cover all known historical and currently used character sets throughout the world. But the majority of the world's languages only need a one-byte (eight bits) code for character encoding, since they are alphabetical scripts.[2]

 ## EXTENDED ASCII AND UNICODE

As people gradually required computers to understand additional characters, the ASCII set became restrictive. Extended ASCII is an eight-bit encoding scheme that includes the standard seven-bit ASCII characters as well as others.

Unicode is an industry standard developed by the Unicode Consortium. The Unicode Standard is a character coding system designed to support the worldwide interchange, processing, and display of the written texts of the diverse languages and technical disciplines of the modern world. In addition, it supports classical and historical texts of many written languages.

Unicode (or Universal Character Set) is another binary mapping scheme intended to be more universal, and includes a wider array of characters, which helps to accommodate a truly global character set. UCS incorporates the initial ASCII character mapping scheme, allowing for backward compatibility.

Unicode could be roughly described as "wide-body ASCII" that has been stretched from 8 bits to 16 bits. Unicode also allows for 8-, 16-, or 32-bit binary formats. A 16-bit coding scheme will allow for 65,536 potential outcomes. It is these 65,536 potential bit outcomes that allow Unicode to encompass most of the characters of all the world's living languages.

Figure 1.2 shows the first 20 values from the Unicode Arabic character set, with the Arabic letter THAL highlighted.

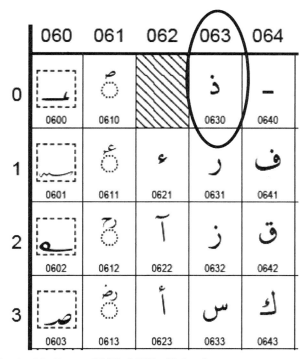

FIGURE 1.2 Arabic Range 0600–06FF—Unicode

Arabic Range 0600–06FF, Unicode Standard 5.2, www.unicode.org/charts/PDF/U0600.pdf, Copyright © 1991–2009 Unicode, Inc. All rights reserved.

FIGURE 1.3 The Arabic Letter THAL: Unicode Value 0630

Thus, if the user desired to generate the Arabic letter THAL, the individual would use the Unicode value 0630. This specific numeric value (0630) has a unique and special meaning when used in electronic, computational communications, and effectively represents the Arabic character THAL (see Figure 1.3) to a computing device, which currently can only interpret and calculate numeric values.

 ## SUMMARY

This first chapter began with a brief introduction and discussion on how computational communication systems have evolved and how we attempt to codify our ability to communicate in a world with only two possible states, a binary existence.

We moved on to a further discussion, not only of the role that a binary numbering systems plays in our ability to represent the most basic patterns of human communication, but also how this binary system has allowed us to expand into producing complex alphabetic patterns, character sets, and ultimately a method that enables us to represent entire languages.

From primary states of existence to representation of complex language patterns, carbon-based communication, like that of silicon-based communication, began with primary building blocks. For computers, that is the bit, represented by either a one (1) or a zero (0).

The combination and pairing of these 1s and 0s allows computational machines to communicate and in the end, to perform complex data manipulation. Representing complex textual words or graphics to a mechanical device is now possible simply by arranging and rearranging the pairings and groupings of 1s and 0s.

Establishing a method of pairing alphabetic characters with the characters' binary equivalents produced character codes (which have evolved into more complex character sets), allowing us to expand our ability to represent a greater range of characters and also control how computers store, manipulate, and transmit data.

Binary representation of numbers and characters is required when working in a world restricted to only two states of description or existence (e.g., electrical or magnetic). Fortunately for us, our human world is more robust, more colorful, and exists in many states, well beyond that of a binary life. It would also be more difficult and time-consuming if we were required to perform all of our figuring, communicating, and similar functioning with numbers or letters represented by groups and pairings of 1s and 0s (e.g., the statement, "Hi, my name is Tom" would be represented by a string of ones and zeroes 144 characters long, 01001000 01101001 00101100 00100000 01101101 01111001 00100000 01101110 01100001 01101101 01100101 00100000 01101001 01110011 00100000 01010100 01101111 01101101).

Luckily, only silicon-based computational devices have to process data in this binary fashion. Humans, on the other hand, have a more convenient method. Humans work more effectively and more efficiently representing numbers in a Base 10 or decimal equivalent to the computer's binary representation, making life a tad bit easier.

In Chapter 2 we discuss how to convert a binary number into its decimal equivalent, and why this knowledge is also essential for gaining a greater depth of understanding of how data is stored, moved, manipulated, and processed and how this treatment of data is critical to a better understanding of cyber forensics.

 ## NOTES

1. Searle, S. "A Brief History of Character Codes in North America, Europe, and East Asia," TRON Web, Sakamura Laboratory, University Museum, University of Tokyo, August 6, 2004, retrieved October 2009, http://tronweb.super-nova.co.jp/characcodehist.html.
2. Ibid.

CHAPTER TWO

Binary to Decimal

I N CHAPTER 1 WE INTRODUCED the basic concepts of numbering systems and how data is moved and manipulated. The life cycle of data, from its humble beginnings as electronic bits and bytes, evolving into characters, then words, finally emerging as a language, then as information and eventually into potential evidence. Understanding how evidence emerges from data, is pivotal in successful forensic investigations.

We continue now in the next step of our cyber forensic learning process, moving from our humble binary beginnings of our two-state world, growing now beyond binary to decimal and back again, gaining a deeper understanding of the math behind the forensics and how a knowledge of the math is essential in understanding even the most basic cyber forensic investigation.

So, as we probe deeper into an understanding of what happens behind the flash and sizzle of forensics, let's begin where we left off.

AMERICAN STANDARD CODE FOR INFORMATION INTERCHANGE

The history of *ASCII* and its development were discussed at length previously, and we now know that the characters identified by 2^7 or 128-bit unique characters are known as American Standard Code for Information Interchange/extended ASCII or just ASCII.

ASCII characters are assigned a decimal value because binary cannot be directly converted to ASCII, and silicon-based computing devices can only compute in binary math. However, binary can be converted into a decimal value, and this decimal value is assigned an ASCII character, thereby completing the cycle.

The first 32 characters in the ASCII-table are unprintable control codes and are used to control peripherals such as printers. Codes 32-127 are common for all the different variations of the ASCII table; they are called printable characters, representing letters, digits, punctuation marks, and a few miscellaneous symbols. You will find almost every character on your keyboard. Character 127 represents the command DEL.

In Table 2.1 we see a sample of binary values, their decimal equivalent, and the ASCII character assigned to that binary value.

COMPUTER AS A CALCULATOR

A computer bases its functions on mathematics, thus in reality, the computer's *microprocessor* (its brain) is essentially a glorified calculator. It is the computer's microprocessor which performs the mathematical calculation from binary to decimal (doing so at a rate of millions of calculations a second), and it does this "behind the scenes," meaning we do not actually see this function occurring when we are using a computer. Computer instruction speeds fall into various ranges, as shown in Table 2.2.

Binary values and numbers (decimals) are capable of having mathematics operations performed on them. Since they have this in common, one can be derived from another. Binary cannot be mathematically computed into a letter "A" or an Arabic character, for example. ASCII or *unicode* characters are symbols conceived by man; they are little more than pictograms as far as the microprocessor is concerned.

TABLE 2.1 Binary Values, Their Decimal Equivalent, and ASCII Code

Binary	Decimal	ASCII Symbol	Description
110000	48	0	Zero
110001	49	1	One
110010	50	2	Two
110011	51	3	Three
110100	52	4	Four
110101	53	5	Five
110110	54	6	Six
110111	55	7	Seven
111000	56	8	Eight
111001	57	9	Nine
111111	63	?	Question mark
1000000	64	@	At symbol
1000001	65	A	Uppercase A
1000010	66	B	Uppercase B
1000011	67	C	Uppercase C
1111011	123	{	Opening brace
1111100	124			Vertical bar
1111101	125	}	Closing brace
1111110	126	~	Equivalency sign – tilde
1111111	127		Delete

TABLE 2.2 Microprocessor Speeds

Millisecond	one thousandth (10^{-3}) of a second
Microsecond	one millionth (10^{-6}) of a second
Nanosecond	one billionth (10^{-9}) of a second
Picosecond	one trillionth (10^{-12}) of a second
Femtosecond	one quadrillionth (10^{-15}) of a second

A binary value can be mathematically computed into a decimal value. And a decimal value can be assigned to an ASCII value as seen in Table 2.1. The decimal value is referenced by the corresponding value in the character chart (ASCII or UniCode) by the *Operating System* (OS) and/or software being used. Ultimately it is software that translates the information into something useful: pictures, words, video, and so on.

Referencing a chart to convert a decimal value to an ASCII character code is a simple concept to grasp; however, we will need to go into further detail to explain the complexities involved with converting binary to decimal.

WHY IS THIS IMPORTANT IN FORENSICS?

Data are not always complete. Most of the time, in fact, data are incomplete or don't exist at all. Evidence is found in bits of data which do not reside in their *native format* or visible in an ASCII character code.

Data are not easily discernable when they cannot be reassembled into their "native format" by software designed to read the data. This happens when the *headers* or other pieces of the original document get overwritten or otherwise erased. Imagine removing the ".doc" from a word document, and then trying to open that document. What happens? A lot of error messages for one. A computer has great difficulty opening up (processing or acting upon) something (a file, folder, instruction, etc.) that it does not recognize.

Forensically, in order to extract only the necessary, critical bits and pieces of data (representing perhaps a document) relative to an investigation, we need to be able to view the data contained within the document, regardless of the software used to generate the document or the document's "native file type."

DATA REPRESENTATION

As identified in Chapter 1, the smallest unit of data is a *bit*. Eight bits form one *byte*. Eight bits is the binary representation of a byte that has been assigned a corresponding character code or symbol, whether that character or symbol is in English, Urdu, Chinese, or Sanskrit. So, the eight bits representing a byte must be mathematically "translated" into a representative decimal equivalent to be understood by us humans.

The decimal values of eight bits are shown in Table 2.3.

This table shows Base 2 to the nth power. The mathematical outcome (or the decimal value) of each power is presented in the second row. This decimal value represents the total possible outcomes (or states) of Base 2 to the *n*th power. It is a mathematical constant, 2^7 will always equal 128.

TABLE 2.3 Decimal Values of Eight Bits

Power	2^7	2^6	2^5	2^4	2^3	2^2	2^1	2^0
Decimal Equivalent	128	64	32	16	8	4	2	1

CONVERTING BINARY TO DECIMAL

Since a computer cannot recognize or process the character "&" in its native form, and only processes binary stored bits, and since we humans do not process binary information, how do we convert a binary value into a decimal value?

Let's take, for example, converting the binary value 01011000 into its decimal equivalent. Using the information in Table 2.3, we add another row to the table for our binary value, 01011000, which gives us Table 2.4.

The key to converting the binary value to its decimal equivalent is the existence (or lack thereof) of a "current" represented by the binary value of a "0" or a "1" switch or binary character.

If a binary value is present in the placeholder, the value is turned on, represented by the value of one (1). If no binary value occupies the place holder, then the value is turned off, which is represented by the value zero (0).

If the binary switch (or value) is ON (a "1") then the decimal value is ON, meaning it is added or counted when determining the total decimal value. If the binary switch is OFF (a "0"), then the decimal value is not counted or added when determining the total decimal equivalent.

To complete our conversion process, we add a final row to our table to represent the decimal value of our converted binary value. (See Figure 2.1.)

The only binary values turned "on" and represented by the value one, are the fourth, fifth, and seventh bits, with decimal equivalents of 8, 16, and 64 respectively. Simply adding up these decimal values (8 + 16 + 64) gives us the decimal value 88, and the decimal equivalent of the binary value 01011000.

TABLE 2.4 Binary to Decimal Conversion

Power	2^7	2^6	2^5	2^4	2^3	2^2	2^1	2^0
Decimal Equivalent	128	64	32	16	8	4	2	1
Binary Value	0	1	0	1	1	0	0	0

Power	2^7	2^6	2^5	2^4	2^3	2^2	2^1	2^0		Adding the decimal values
Decimal Equivalent	128	64	32	16	8	4	2	1		
		↓		↓	↓					
Binary Value	0	1	0	1	1	0	0	0		
		↓		↓	↓					**Adding the decimal values**
Decimal Value	0	64	0	16	8	0	0	0		$0+64+0+16+8+0+0+0 = 88$

The "switch" is ON = 1, bring down the decimal value
The "switch" is OFF = 0, value = zero (0)

FIGURE 2.1 Binary to Decimal Conversion

CONVERSION ANALYSIS

Count the number of digits in the binary number. For each digit, list the powers of 2 from right to left in order, starting with 1 until you have one power of 2 for each digit. In our example, for an eight-digit binary number 01011000, you would list 128, 64, 32, 16, 8, 4, 2, and 1.

Connect the binary digits with their corresponding powers of 2 with a straight line.

Go through the binary numbers and if the binary number is 1, bring down the power of 2 and write it in the corresponding box on the decimal value line. If the binary number is 0, put a 0 in the box.

Convert the binary number to decimal by adding up the decimal value you entered into each box.

The sum of the numbers is the decimal equivalent of the binary number.

Binary 01011000 equals a decimal value of 88.

A FORENSIC CASE EXAMPLE: AN APPLICATION OF THE MATH

Mrs. Ronelle Sawyer, a cyber forensic investigator is looking for evidence of communications between Mr. Jose McCarthy, a research scientist at ABC Inc., and Ms. Janice Witcome, managing director of the XYZ Company, a competitor, in a case involving the potential theft of *intellectual property* (IP).

The question then is, "How can Ronelle identify any occurrences of the company name 'XYZ' when examining the contents of Jose's hard drive?" An initial answer, the "human view" of the data sought by Ronelle, is already known. Ronelle would begin looking for any occurrences or references to either "Witcome," "Janice," or "XYZ" that may exist on Jose's hard drive.

From any ASCII table, such as the one partially reproduced in Table 2.5, Ronelle would identify the ASCII characters "X", "Y", and "Z" and in doing so would be able to derive the decimal equivalent of these characters: 88, 89, and 90, respectively.

Ronelle now can determine the binary equivalent of the decimal values 88, 89, and 90, based upon our earlier discussion by turning "on" those bits that will give Ronelle the values 88, 89, and 90, respectively. (See Tables 2.6, 2.7, and 2.8.)

Table 2.9 summarizes the conversion of the decimal values 88, 89, and 90 into their binary equivalent.

The recognizable ASCII characters "X," "Y," and "Z" are stored and "viewed" as binary values by the computer. To the computer, the combined characters "X," "Y," and "Z," would simply "look" like this: 010110000101100101011010.

TABLE 2.5   Decimal and ASCII Values

Decimal	ASCII Symbol	Description
83	S	Uppercase S
84	T	Uppercase T
85	U	Uppercase U
86	V	Uppercase V
87	W	Uppercase W
88	X	Uppercase X
89	Y	Uppercase Y
90	Z	Uppercase Z

TABLE 2.6   88 Decimal to Binary

Power	2^7	2^6	2^5	2^4	2^3	2^2	2^1	2^0
Decimal Equivalent	128	64	32	16	8	4	2	1
Binary Code	0	1	0	1	1	0	0	0
Decimal Value	0	64	0	16	8	0	0	0

TABLE 2.7 89 Decimal to Binary

Power	2^7	2^6	2^5	2^4	2^3	2^2	2^1	2^0
Decimal Equivalent	128	64	32	16	8	4	2	1
Binary Code	0	1	0	1	1	0	0	1
Decimal Value	0	**64**	0	**16**	**8**	0	0	**1**

TABLE 2.8 90 Decimal to Binary

Power	2^7	2^6	2^5	2^4	2^3	2^2	2^1	2^0
Decimal Equivalent	128	64	32	16	8	4	2	1
Binary Code	0	1	0	1	1	0	1	0
Decimal Value	0	**64**	0	**16**	**8**	0	**2**	0

TABLE 2.9 Binary Value of Characters X, Y, and Z

Binary	Decimal	ASCII Symbol	Description
1011000	88	X	Uppercase X
1011001	89	Y	Uppercase Y
1011010	90	Z	Uppercase Z

It is pretty easy for a computer to recognize and to make sense of what all those 1s and 0s mean. It is impossible, however, for humans to decipher, especially when looking through thousands of 1s and 0s all strung together!

How will Ronelle determine if Jose is indeed corresponding with Janice? How will Ronelle possibly be able to examine the millions of 1s and 0s filling Jose's hard drive, to identify any occurrences of 010110000101100101011010?

Specific tools used by the cyber forensic investigator can convert the binary code 010110000101100101011010 into a format more easily understood by humans.

This format is called Hexadecimal (HEX), which is strictly a human friendly representation of binary values, and the subject of Chapter 3.

 ## DECIMAL TO BINARY: RECAP FOR REVIEW

A decimal value is a mathematical computation of binary, not a visual representation of binary.

There are 10 unique decimal characters– 0, 1, 2, 3, 4, 5, 6, 7, 8, and 9. Ten unique characters by themselves cannot represent the entirety of the ASCII character set or of Unicode.

Converting binary to decimal, as previously described, is easy when the binary value to be converted is small, but as the binary value increases in size, the numbers can get rather large and tedious.

For example, assume a binary value of 010110000101100101011010. This value may appear daunting, but it is only equivalent to three bytes or 24 bits.

If we were to convert this binary string to its decimal value equivalent by turning "on" position values represented by 1s and leaving "off" those position values represented by 0s, our string of numbers would look like this:

010110000101100101011010

off + 4194304 + off + 1048576 + 524288 + off + off+ off
+ off + 16384 + off + 4096 + 2048 + off + off + 256
+ off + 64 + off + 16 + 8 + off + 2 + off

When finally totaled, this string of binary values would yield a result of 5,787,994.

The process of deciphering binary values into their decimal equivalent can get very tedious, time consuming, and very expensive, especially if the string of binary values is more than three bytes. Imagine converting an entire sentence, or how about an image?

How can we humans better represent binary without the tedium of decimal computation?

Solution: hexadecimal notation and numeric representation.

SUMMARY

Mathematics is perhaps the only universal language, and its principles are based upon inherent truths. Regardless of language or written character representation, 1 + 1 will always equal 2. Mankind may have created the numerals or symbols by which mathematical concepts are expressed; however, mankind did not create math.

Mankind developed character encoding methods based upon symbolic representations including: alphabets, symbols, scripts, punctuation marks, numerals, pictographs, cave drawings, and so on. Written languages continue to evolve and progress; however, as refined as these have become, none have ever been capable of "direct" digital transmittance.

Mathematics' true universal nature is revealed by how well it is suited for the digital representation of written language. In order to communicate electronically, or digitally, a method must exist by which a human character based script can be converted to a mathematical one.

Binary is the mathematical encoding method by which data is sent electronically. Humans prefer a symbol or character encoding paradigm. It is therefore necessary to connect the dots and convert binary to human character sets.

CHAPTER THREE

The Power of HEX

Finding Slivers of Data

RONELLE SAWYER IS INVESTIGATING whether Jose McCarthy has potentially engaged in the unlawful distribution of his organization's intellectual property to a competitor, Ms. Janice Witcome, Managing Director of the XYZ Company.

Ronelle is faced with examining millions of pieces of potential evidential data residing on Jose's hard drive, looking for the proverbial needle in the haystack, a sequential occurrence of the character string "X," "Y," "Z." Ronelle has deciphered the character's decimal equivalent into individual binary values, and now must make sense of this run on string of 1s and 0s in an effort to identify a similar string of 1s and 0s on the hard drive seized from Jose's office.

Our running case is used as a basic illustration of a complex scenario, to communicate to the reader the complexities behind essential building blocks of cyber forensics. It is important for the reader to note that in an actual investigation, searching for a character string of the company name, "XYZ," as in our example case, may not be ideal as it would generate many false positives. The reader should keep in mind that the examples used in this book are utilized to express forensic concepts or ideas, and *not* investigative assistance.

The process of deciphering binary values into their decimal equivalents can become very tedious, time-consuming, and very expensive, especially if the string of binary values is large. Fortunately for Ronelle, the binary string representing the characters "X," "Y," and "Z" is relatively small.

How can Ronelle better represent this binary string without the tedium of decimal computation as discussed previously? The solution, convert the binary string of 1s and 0s into their hexadecimal equivalent notation.

 ## WHAT THE HEX?

Hexadecimal (abbreviated as HEX) is strictly a human friendly representation of binary values. A HEX character is often prefixed with 0x (zero, sub x) to denote it from another encoding system. So, 0x3F tells the reader that 3F is HEX, and not ASCII.

The computer or processor does not calculate in HEX. Software can convert binary to HEX, but the microprocessor itself does not perform its mathematical computations in HEX. HEX is a *base 16 character code*, which, as we will see, works well at representing binary.

Why? The 16 characters representing HEX are the symbols 0–9, representing values 0 to 9, and A, B, C, D, E, and F, representing values 10 to 15. There are thus 16 unique characters, each of which corresponds to a pattern of four bits.

The 16 HEX values along with their assigned decimal and binary conversions can be seen in Table 3.1.

As seen in Table 3.1, the 16 HEX characters can assume all possible 4 bit binary values ($2^4 = 16$).

In order to understand how binary is converted to HEX we need to examine the concept of a *byte* a "bit" more closely.

TABLE 3.1 HEX, Binary, and Decimal Equivalents

Hex	F	E	D	C	B	A	9	8	7	6	5	4	3	2	1	0
Binary	1111	1110	1101	1100	1011	1010	1001	1000	0111	0110	0101	0100	0011	0010	0001	0000
Decimal	15	14	13	12	11	10	9	8	7	6	5	4	3	2	1	0

BITS AND BYTES AND NIBBLES

A byte is split (*for human understanding, again this is not something the processor does when computing*) into two equal halves called *nibbles*. A single HEX character corresponds to one nibble's worth of data, 4 bits. However, a standard encoding character needs a full byte or 8 bits for representation. So, two nibbles need to be paired in order to accomplish this representation.

Thus, we have four (4) bits per nibble (see Figure 3.1), two (2) nibbles per byte (see Figure 3.2), and eight (8) bits per byte (see Figure 3.3).

Thus in Figure 3.3, we see that eight (8) bits equal one (1) byte.

It can also be said then, that eight bits, or two nibbles, equals one byte (see Figure 3.4).

It is important to remember a byte stands alone when representing a character or symbol, whereas a nibble cannot; it needs its other half (or said

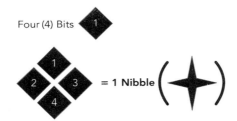

FIGURE 3.1   Four Bits Equals One Nibble

FIGURE 3.2   Two Nibbles Equal One Byte

FIGURE 3.3   Eight Bits Equals One Byte

FIGURE 3.4 Bit, Nibble, and Byte Equivalents

another way—a standard encoding character needs a full byte or eight bits for representation).

Therefore, two nibbles must be paired in order to accomplish this representation. Remember, a HEX character code has 16 unique values—A through F and 0 through 9.

How many binary values (bits) are needed to represent 16 unique values? The answer: 2^4 (2 . . . 4 . . . 8 . . . 16).

It is important to remember that we are dealing with binary values, so any math will need to be base two. So the "base" number of calculation is 2:

$$2 \times 2 \times 2 \times 2 = 16$$

2 to the fourth power.

A HEX value can, therefore, exactly correspond to all 16 values, each four bits in length.

To help understand this further let us revisit a previously asked question, "how many bits would be necessary to represent the four seasons (winter, spring, summer, and fall)?"

One bit gives us only two possible values, 0 or 1. This would be sufficient to represent the state of a light On or Off but not four seasons. Remember, we are looking for binary values, Base 2, so each value will only have two possible states.

Two bits would actually give us the four possible values needed to represent four seasons: 00, 01, 10, and 11, as shown in Table 3.2. This can be done mathematically as well: $2 \times 2 = 4$.

TABLE 3.2 Two Bits Representing Four Possible Values

Bit 1	Bit 2
0	0
0	1
1	0
1	1

A HEX value can therefore exactly correspond to all 16 possible four-bit values. The 16 HEX characters (A–F, 0–9) can be represented by four binary values (e.g., 1101, 0110, 0010) per character, such that the HEX character "A," for example, is represented by the binary value 1010. (See Table 3.3.)

TABLE 3.3 HEX Characters and Binary Equivalents

Hex	F	E	D	C	B	A	9	8	7	6	5	4	3	2	1	0
Binary	1111	1110	1101	1100	1011	1010	1001	1000	0111	0110	0101	0100	0011	0010	0001	0000
Decimal	15	14	13	12	11	10	9	8	7	6	5	4	3	2	1	0

Remember, four bits equals one nibble; therefore, one HEX character represents one nibble.

In summary:

1 bit = binary value of 0 or 1
4 bits = nibble = one HEX character
2 nibbles = 1 byte
8 bits = 1 byte
1 byte = 2 HEX characters

So, to answer the question which led off this discussion, why use HEX to represent binary? Because both a byte and 2 HEX characters represent eight bits, totaling 256 potential values.

 NIBBLES AND BITS

In order to differentiate between two nibbles, one is referred to as the left nibble and the other as the right nibble.

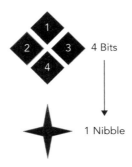

FIGURE 3.5 Four Bits Equal One Nibble

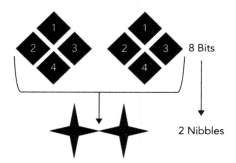

8 Bits

2 Nibbles

FIGURE 3.6 Eight Bits Equals Two Nibbles

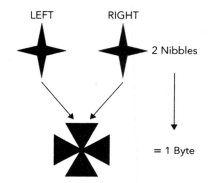

LEFT   RIGHT

2 Nibbles

= 1 Byte

FIGURE 3.7 Two Nibbles Equal One Byte

HEX, as we have demonstrated, uses a base of 16. We can split a byte into two groups of four bits each (e.g., nnnn nnnn). Each individual group is then referred to as a nibble.

The right nibble with all of its bits turned off, or 0000, is equal to a value of 0; with all of its bits turned on, 1111, the right nibble has a value of 15 (8 + 4 + 2 + 1).

Let's summarize (see Figures 3.5, 3.6, and 3.7).

Remember nibbles work in pairs, left and right. See Table 3.4.

BINARY TO HEX CONVERSION

Let's compare a decimal conversion with a conversion to HEX, using Ronelle's relatively small binary string representing the characters "X," "Y," and "Z."

The binary value of the characters "X," "Y," and "Z" equals 010110000101100101011010.

TABLE 3.4 Left and Right Nibble

	Left Nibble					Right Nibble			
Power	2^7	2^6	2^5	2^4		2^3	2^2	2^1	2^0
Decimal Value	128	64	32	16		8	4	2	1
Binary Value	0	1	0	1		1	0	0	0
Decimal Value	0	64	0	16		8	0	0	0

0+64+0+16+8+0+0+0=88   88 =   0101   1000

LEFT   RIGHT

If we split these values into four-bit chunks representing nibbles, and pair them up to form a byte, the result is shown in Table 3.5. Figure 3.8 shows the decomposition of a byte, beginning with the nibble, both the right and left, and the individual bit. We need four (4) bits to make a nibble, and two (2) nibbles to make a byte.

Table 3.6 shows how easily we can convert binary into decimal.

Table 3.7 shows the conversion of binary values into their HEX equivalent. Combining Tables 3.6 and 3.7 produces the results shown in Table 3.8.

TABLE 3.5 Left and Right Nibbles for the Binary Value 010110000101100101011010

Left Nibble	Right Nibble
0101	1000
0101	1001
0101	1010

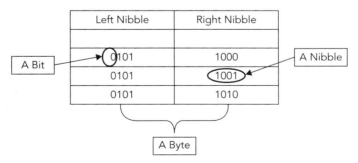

FIGURE 3.8 Data Basics

TABLE 3.6 Binary to Decimal

Binary	1111	1110	1101	1100	1011	1010	1001	1000	0111	0110	0101	0100	0011	0010	0001	0000
Decimal	15	14	13	12	11	10	9	8	7	6	5	4	3	2	1	0

TABLE 3.7 Binary to HEX

Hex	F	E	D	C	B	A	9	8	7	6	5	4	3	2	1	0
Binary	1111	1110	1101	1100	1011	1010	1001	1000	0111	0110	0101	0100	0011	0010	0001	0000

TABLE 3.8 HEX, Binary, and Decimal Equivalent

Hex	F	E	D	C	B	A	9	8	7	6	5	4	3	2	1	0
Binary	1111	1110	1101	1100	1011	1010	1001	1000	0111	0110	0101	0100	0011	0010	0001	0000
Decimal	15	14	13	12	11	10	9	8	7	6	5	4	3	2	1	0

TABLE 3.9 ASCII "X" Converted to Binary Equivalent 01011000

	Left Nibble				**Right Nibble**				
Power	2^7	2^6	2^5	2^4	2^3	2^2	2^1	2^0	
Decimal Value	128	64	32	16	8	4	2	1	
Binary Code	0	1	0	1	1	0	0	0	
Decimal Value	0	64	0	16	8	0	0	0	0 + 64 + 0 + 16 + 8 + 0 + 0 + 0 = 88

TABLE 3.10 ASCII "Y" Converted to Binary Equivalent 01011001

	Left Nibble				**Right Nibble**				
Power	2^7	2^6	2^5	2^4	2^3	2^2	2^1	2^0	
Decimal Value	128	64	32	16	8	4	2	1	
Binary Code	0	1	0	1	1	0	0	1	
Decimal Value	0	64	0	16	8	0	0	1	0 + 64 + 0 + 16 + 8 + 0 + 0 + 1 = 89

To continue using Ronelle's binary string representing the characters "X," "Y," and "Z" as part of her search strategy to determine Jose's culpability, Ronelle first converts the ASCII values to their binary equivalent as shown in Tables 3.9, 3.10, and 3.11.

TABLE 3.11 ASCII "Z" Converted to Binary Equivalent 01011010

	Left Nibble				Right Nibble				
Power	2^7	2^6	2^5	2^4	2^3	2^2	2^1	2^0	
Decimal Value	128	64	32	16	8	4	2	1	
Binary Code	0	1	0	1	1	0	1	0	
Decimal Value	0	64	0	16	8	0	2	0	0 + 64 + 0 + 16 + 8 + 0 +2 + 0 = 90

Summarized, Ronelle's data is shown in Table 3.12.

TABLE 3.12 Decimal to Binary Conversion

ASCII	Decimal Value	Binary Value
X	88	0101 1000
Y	89	0101 1001
Z	90	0101 1010

Next, Ronelle converts the binary values to their HEX equivalent, as shown in Tables 3.13, 3.14, and 3.15.

TABLE 3.13 Binary 01011000 Converted to HEX

Hex	F	E	D	C	B	A	9	8	7	6	5	4	3	2	1	0
Binary	1111	1110	1101	1100	1011	1010	1001	1000	0111	0110	0101	0100	0011	0010	0001	0000

TABLE 3.14 Binary 01011001 Converted to HEX

Hex	F	E	D	C	B	A	9	8	7	6	5	4	3	2	1	0
Binary	1111	1110	1101	1100	1011	1010	1001	1000	0111	0110	0101	0100	0011	0010	0001	0000

TABLE 3.15 Binary 01011010 Converted to HEX

Hex	F	E	D	C	B	A	9	8	7	6	5	4	3	2	1	0
Binary	1111	1110	1101	1100	1011	1010	1001	1000	0111	0110	0101	0100	0011	0010	0001	0000

Table 3.16 summarizes Ronelle's conversion efforts to give her the HEX values of the ASCII characters she must search for on Jose's hard drive.

Thus, Ronelle must search for the HEX string 58595A, which represents the ASCII characters "X," "Y," and "Z."

TABLE 3.16 HEX Equivalent of ASCII Characters "X," "Y," and "Z"

ASCII	Decimal Value	Binary Value	HEX Equivalent
X	88	0101 1000	58
Y	89	0101 1001	59
Z	90	0101 1010	5A

Using a *HEX editor*, Ronelle looks for the very distinguishable 58595A HEX value representation to uncover the occurrence of any reference to the XYZ Company on Jose's hard drive.

BINARY (HEX) EDITOR

A HEX editor is a program which allows you to view and or edit *compiled programs* and binary data files.

These editors are called HEX editors because they most often present data in hexadecimal format. Hexadecimal is used because it is easier for most humans than working in binary. In addition, hexadecimal is frequently useful because computers tend to work with eight-bit bytes of information and because ASCII is an 8-bit code.

You can't see all the bytes stored in a file using a regular application to open the file, and there are no applications available to view deleted items. Sometimes, part of the file is missing, including the piece that contains the executable code launching the application needed to open it in the first place.

A cyber forensic investigator needs a binary/HEX editor for analyzing file structures. Viewing HEX allows Ronelle to go beyond the application or file, and it will allow for the viewing of all data contained within a file, including remnants of old files or even deleted files, which may exist on Jose's hard drive.

Figure 3.9 is a representative example of the output view of a HEX editor.

A HEX editor consists of four distinct display areas, or panels, each having its own significance and conveying specific information relative to the editor itself, as well as providing essential information to the investigator.

The four distinct display areas are:

1. Header Panel (A)
2. Address Panel (B)
3. HEX-data Panel (C)
4. Character Panel (D)

These four panel areas of the HEX editor are identified in Figure 3.10.

Offset	0C	0D	0E	0F	00	01	02	03	04	05	06	07	08	09	0A	0B	
0001ef80	55	52	4C	20	03	00	00	00	00	1D	16	CB	42	51	C1	01	URL......BQ...
0001ef90	20	0C	17	F1	39	3B	C3	01	80	4A	73	3C	35	3B	C3	01	..9...Js<5..
0001efa0	D2	04	00	00	00	00	00	00	00	00	00	00	00	00	00	00	....
0001efb0	00	00	00	00	48	01	00	00	68	00	00	00	00	00	00	00	.......h.........
0001efc0	A4	00	00	00	01	2E	00	00	B8	00	00	00	BC	00	00	00	....
0001efd0	00	00	00	86	D9	2E	00	86	01	00	00	00	00	00	00	00	....[.........
0001efe0	D9	2E	5B	58	59	5A	00	73	68	74	74	70	3A	2F	2F	77	...[..http://w
0001eff0	77	77	2E	2F	73	69	74	68	61	72	58	59	77	72	65	2E	ww.XYZ-produ
0001f000	63	6F	6D	2F	01	00	00	65	2F	69	6D	61	BC	00	00	C3	ct-site.com/da
0001f010	A4	00	00	00	69	63	24	5F	77	61	80	4A	F1	D9	2E	00	ata....compan
0001f020	66	74	75	1D	39	4C	3C	3A	51	C1	42	D1	00	00	2E	C3	y...directory/w
0001f030	6E	74	00	00	01	00	00	00	B8	00	00	00	BC	00	00	00	itcome.Dir.....
0001f040	A4	00	00	00	01	00	00	00	B8	00	42	00	00	00	00	00	....
0001f050	D2	E2	F1	34	51	80	4A	73	2F	2E	67	73	77	58	59	5A	info..interest...
0001f060	00	00	00	00	00	00	00	00	00	00	00	00	00	58	59	00	.........XYZ
0001f070	D2	04	00	00	00	00	00	00	00	00	00	00	00	00	00	00	....
0001f080	D2	04	00	00	00	4C	3C	3A	51	C1	42	D1	00	00	00	00	....
0001f090	C3	74	75	1D	39	6C	30	31	6C	37	51	D1	0D	71	00	00	Witcome.Dir...
0001f0a0	41	41	41	41	4F	6C	30	31	6C	37	51	22	0D	0A	43	6F	AAAA010117Q
0001f0b0	67	20	3A	71	80	2F	5C	00	00	00	00	65	2F	6C	6E	22	ABC_product.
0001f0c0	A4	00	00	45	01	6C	00	00	B8	00	00	51	BC	20	6E	00	...to....sell.inter
0001f0d0	64	6D	68	71	D9	6E	4A	72	57	37	34	51	20	D9	00	00	ested?..........
0001f0e0	A4	00	00	00	01	00	00	00	B8	00	00	00	BC	00	00	00	....

FIGURE 3.9 HEX Editor (sample view)

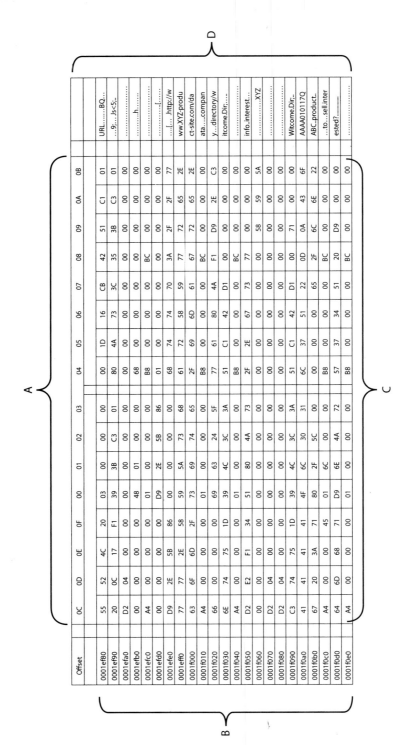

FIGURE 3.10 The Four Panel Areas of the HEX Editor

Header Panel (A)

The header panel displays the headers of any of the other three panels (see Figure 3.11). Among them, HEX-data panel (C) uses the *byte offsets* relative to the beginning of the line as its header.[1]

Address Panel (B)

Every byte in a file is assigned a number, called its *address*, starting at 0 for the first byte of the file, 1 for the second byte, and so on. See Figure 3.12.

The address panel displays the address of the byte at the beginning of the line.[2]

Offset		0C	0D	0E	0F	00	01	02	03		04	05	06	07	08	09	0A	0B		

FIGURE 3.11   Header Panel

Offset	
0001ef80	
0001ef90	
0001efa0	
0001efb0	
0001efc0	
0001efd0	
0001efe0	
0001eff0	
0001f000	
0001f010	
0001f020	
0001f030	
0001f040	
0001f050	
0001f060	
0001f070	
0001f080	
0001f090	
0001f0a0	
0001f0b0	
0001f0c0	
0001f0d0	
0001f0e0	

FIGURE 3.12   Address Panel

HEX-Data Panel (C)

The middle hexadecimal area is the most commonly used area of a HEX editor. It lists each byte of the file in a table, usually 16 bytes per line.

In Figure 3.13, the first eight bytes of the file are "55-52-4C-20-03-00 00 00." The HEX-data panel lists the hexadecimal value of each file byte; default is 24 bytes per line. It works in the HEX editing mode, and displays the hexadecimal value of each byte as a two-character field.[3]

Character Panel (D)

Figure 3.14 shows the details of the character panel.

The character panel displays the ASCII value of each file byte. It only provides the view of printable characters; non-printable characters are shown as a period character (".") or with another user-defined character.[4]

Ronelle will now search the HEX editor looking for any occurrence of the HEX value 58595A, as she knows that this value represents the characters "X, Y, and Z."

55	52	4C	20	03	00	00	00	00	1D	16	CB	42	51	C1	01
20	0C	17	F1	39	3B	C3	01	80	4A	73	3C	35	3B	C3	01
D2	04	00	00	00	00	00	00	00	00	00	00	00	00	00	00
00	00	00	00	48	01	00	00	68	00	00	00	00	00	00	00
A4	00	00	00	01	00	00	00	B8	00	00	00	BC	00	00	00
00	00	00	00	D9	2E	5B	86	01	00	00	00	00	00	00	00
D9	2E	5B	86	00	00	00	00	68	74	74	70	3A	2F	2F	77
77	77	2E	58	59	5A	73	68	61	72	58	59	77	72	65	2E
63	6F	6D	2F	73	69	74	65	2F	69	6D	61	67	72	65	2E
A4	00	00	00	01	00	00	00	B8	00	00	00	BC	00	00	00
66	00	00	00	69	63	24	5F	77	61	80	4A	F1	D9	2E	C3
6E	74	75	1D	39	4C	3C	3A	51	C1	42	D1	00	00	00	00
A4	00	00	00	01	00	00	00	B8	00	00	00	BC	00	00	00
D2	E2	F1	34	51	80	4A	73	2F	2E	67	73	77	00	00	00
00	00	00	00	00	00	00	00	00	00	00	00	00	58	59	5A
D2	04	00	00	00	00	00	00	00	00	00	00	00	00	00	00
D2	04	00	00	00	00	00	00	00	00	00	00	00	00	00	00
C3	74	75	1D	39	4C	3C	3A	51	C1	42	D1	00	71	00	00
41	41	41	41	4F	6C	30	31	6C	37	51	22	0D	0A	43	6F
67	20	3A	71	80	2F	5C	00	00	00	00	65	2F	6C	6E	22
A4	00	00	45	01	6C	00	00	B8	00	00	00	BC	00	00	00
64	6D	68	71	D9	6E	4A	72	57	37	34	51	20	D9	00	00
A4	00	00	00	01	00	00	00	B8	00	00	00	BC	00	00	00

FIGURE 3.13 HEX-Data Panel

URL.......BQ...
...9;... Js<5;..
....
...........h........
....
..............[......
....[... .http://w
ww.XYZ-produ
ct-site.com/da
ata.....compan
y...directory/w
itcome.Dir;.....
....
info..interest...
...............XYZ
....
....
Witcome.Dir;..
AAAA010117Q
ABC..product..
...to...sell.inter
ested?..............
....

FIGURE 3.14   Character Panel

If Ronelle finds the HEX sequence 58595A within the data retrieved from Jose's hard drive, then this is likely stronger evidence, which might further implicate Jose in the potential theft of intellectual property and involvement between Jose and the XYZ Corporation.

HEX Value 58595A

In Figure 3.15, we see a representative example of how the HEX value 58595A might appear to Ronelle as she examines the HEX editor data panel.

 ## THE NEEDLE WITHIN THE HAYSTACK

Why do humans need a friendly way to view binary? Most humans will have a very difficult time attempting to make sense out of long strings of 1s and 0s, end to end, for more than, say, eight positions. Quick, what does this say: 0110100001100101011011000110110001101111?

Offset	00	01	02	03	04	05	06	07	08	09	0A	0B	0C	0D	0E	0F	ASCII
0001ef80	55	52	4C	20	03	00	00	00	00	1D	16	CB	42	51	C1	01	URL....BQ...
0001ef90	20	0C	17	F1	39	3B	00	01	80	4A	73	3C	35	3B	C3	01	..9;..Js<5;..
0001efa0	D2	04	00	00	00	00	00	00	00	00	00	00	00	00	00	00	...........h......
0001efb0	00	00	00	00	48	01	00	00	68	00	00	00	00	00	00	00	....
0001efc0	A4	00	00	00	01	00	00	00	B8	00	00	00	00	00	00	00	....
0001efd0	00	00	00	00	D9	2E	5B	86	01	00	74	74	70	3A	2F	77	.........[...
0001efe0	D9	2E	5B	86	00	00	68	74	74	70	3A	2F	77	74	74	70	...[. .http://w
0001eff0	77	77	2E	58	59	5A	73	2D	70	72	6F	64	75	65	68	68	ww.XYZ-produ
0001f000	63	6F	6D	73	69	74	65	2E	63	6F	6D	2F	64	61	00	00	ct-site.com/da
0001f010	A4	00	00	01	00	00	00	00	B8	00	00	00	D9	00	00	C3	ata.....compan
0001f020	66	00	00	00	69	63	24	5F	77	61	80	4A	F1	00	2E	C3	y...directory/w
0001f030	6E	74	75	1D	39	4C	3C	3A	51	C1	42	D1	00	00	00	00	itcome.Dir,......
0001f040	A4	00	00	01	00	00	00	00	B8	00	00	BC	00	00	00	00	....
0001f050	D2	E2	F1	34	51	80	4A	73	2F	2E	67	00	00	00	00	00	info..interest...
0001f060	00	00	00	00	00	00	00	00	00	00	00	00	00	58	59	5A	.............XYZ
0001f070	D2	04	00	00	00	00	00	00	00	00	00	00	00	00	00	00	....
0001f080	D2	04	00	00	00	00	00	00	00	00	00	00	00	00	00	00	....
0001f090	C3	74	75	1D	39	4C	3C	3A	51	C1	42	D1	00	71	00	00	Witcome.Dir;...
0001f0a0	41	41	41	41	4F	6C	30	31	6C	37	51	22	0D	0A	43	6F	AAAA010117Q
0001f0b0	67	20	3A	71	80	2F	5C	00	00	00	65	2F	6C	6E	22	22	ABC..product..
0001f0c0	A4	00	00	45	00	6C	00	00	B8	00	00	BC	BC	6C	00	00	...to...sell.inter
0001f0d0	64	6D	68	71	D9	6E	4A	72	57	37	34	51	20	D9	00	00	ested?............
0001f0e0	A4	00	00	00	01	00	00	00	B8	00	00	BC	00	00	00	00	....

FIGURE 3.15 HEX Value 58595A as It Appears in the HEX Editor

Cyber forensic investigators MUST have a thorough understanding of the process by which raw bits of data are turned into information, and how complex silicon devices interpret pulses of energy, assigning these pulses the computable values of one and zero, and then into higher order numerical values, and eventually into characters that are understood by their carbon-based handlers. This provides Ronelle and cyber forensic investigators a means to find the sliver of data they are looking for, amid potentially billions of bytes of extraneous data.

 ## SUMMARY

A document or file has what is sometimes called headers or supplemental data, placed at the beginning of a block of data. In data transmission, the data following the header are called the body. The header in effect binds the body to the software needed to open it or otherwise access it.

For example, a document created with Microsoft (MS) Word may have difficulty being opened using Adobe Acrobat Reader/application. This is because there is code embedded within any document created using MS Word, which tells the operating system that MS Word (or other compatible software) is needed in order to open the document.

If the code which binds the document to its native software is somehow overwritten or "erased," the software will not be able to reassemble the document into its native format or into a format readable by the user, thereby causing the document to be inaccessible and unreadable by the user.

Some of these data, such as incriminating text (the occurrence of "XYZ" for example), may however still reside in a document, on a disk, within the hard drive. Ronelle would not want to miss this potentially incriminating evidence and would need a verifiable way to cull through the millions of bytes of data on Jose's hard drive. Finding such evidence could substantiate or refute the claims brought by ABC Inc. against its employee Jose, in the theft of ABC's intellectual property.

For a cyber forensic investigator to properly search for a keyword contained within data seized from an entire hard drive (or even from data narrowed down to a specific folder or specific image within a user's hard drive), it is best to use HEX to assist in accomplishing this herculean task.

Viewing HEX allows an investigator to go beyond the application or file. It allows for the viewing of all the data contained within a file including remnants of old or even deleted files.

With this introduction of the basics of "computer math," we are ready to kick it up a level in Chapter 4 to working in the world of HEX, the cyber forensic investigator's best friend.

 NOTES

1. "What Is a Hex Editor?" Hexprobe, retrieved December 10, 2009, www.hexprobe .com/hexprobe/hex_editor.htm.
2. Ibid.
3. Ibid.
4. Ibid.

4

Files

A S WE MOVE FURTHER ALONG, as we dive deeper into exploring and gaining an understanding of the science behind cyber forensics, our goal is to provide useable materials to the reader, materials that will sustain the evolutionary creep of technology, materials that will not become dated or obsolete before they are published.

In order to accomplish our goal, it is necessary to explore general or broad concepts (although perhaps complex) while refraining from addressing specific software, programs, or even generalized forensic tools, which can quickly become dated and obsolete over time.

As we examine further the building blocks of cyber forensics, special attention has been made to focus on tools that will not quickly become dated, expire, or no longer be vendor supported. We spend more time, for example, discussing a tool such as a HEX editor, versus discussing the Windows NT operating system. A HEX editor has been around for as long as well—since HEX itself—whereas Windows NT is quickly becoming less and less relevant.

Read on as we continue with our exploration of the science behind cyber forensics, focusing here on files, file signatures, and their role and relevancy in cyber forensic investigations.

OPENING

In Chapter 3 the following topics were addressed:

1. Discussed HEX and the steps involved with converting this binary representation to ASCII.
2. Covered the actual conversion process in an effort to better understand the HEX character representation.
3. Went into some detail discussing the nuts and bolts of HEX.
4. Referred to HEX editors and their function, but stopped short of probing deeply into the functionality and usefulness of a HEX editor when viewing files (or pieces of files). This discussion is saved for a later chapter.

HEX, as was discussed, is useful when attempting to view a file that is partially deleted. This begs the questions:

1. Why would a partially deleted file have difficulties being opened or viewed normally?
2. What parts of a file does a HEX editor allow us to see, which otherwise would not be visible?

FILES, FILE STRUCTURES, AND FILE FORMATS

To answer the questions posed above, we need to further investigate the basics of a *file*, *file structures*, and *file formats*. A partially deleted file in many cases may be missing part of its formatting data, the data that identifies the file.

It is this formatting information that identifies the file to its parent or native software. If a file does not contain this formatting information, the software or *operating system* (OS) will most likely not be able to access or execute the file. It is this formatting information that uniquely identifies a file.

There are hundreds of different formats for data (databases, word processing, spreadsheets, images, video, etc.). There are also formats for executable programs on different platforms (Windows, Mac, Linux, Unix, etc.). Each format defines how the sequence of bits and bytes are laid out, with the ASCII based text file being one of the simplest formats for humans to decipher.

Some file formats are designed to store very particular sorts of data: the JPEG format, for example, is designed only to store static photographic images. Other file formats, however, are designed for storage of several different types of data: the GIF format supports storage of both still images and simple animations, and the QuickTime format can act as a container for many different types of multimedia.

A text file is simply one that stores any text, in a format such as ASCII or UTF-8, with few if any *control characters*. Some file formats, such as HTML, or the source code of some particular programming language, are in fact also text files, but adhere to more specific rules which allow them to be used for specific purposes.[1]

There are a wide variety of digital file types in our ever expanding electronic universe. These various file types contain specific formatting information which allows for file access, storage, or "manipulation." This "manipulation" may occur via the operating system itself, or it may occur via a "parent" program installed on the operating system.

Parent program, meaning the program and possibly proprietary software, is used to create, execute, or otherwise access the file. In most cases a file will contain data, its *file signature*, from which its parent software (or the operating system) will be able to identify and handle its operation.

This file signature information is contained in what is sometimes referred to as a *file header*. The data contained within a file header is not seen by the casual user, yet is very important for the file to function as designed. It is this data contained within the file header that is used to identify the format of the file.

File headers may also contain data regarding the integrity of the file as well as information about itself and its contents. This data is often referred to as *metadata*.

There is no one specific file format structure that fits all file types. File formats will vary as does file content. The contents of an image, as well as its format, for example, will be different from the contents and format of a word processing document.

A summary of some more common file formats along with their Windows file extensions can be found in Appendix 4A.

FILE EXTENSIONS

Within the Windows Operating System environment, file formats are easily identified by *file extensions*.

The Windows Operating System uses file extensions to "bind" an application to a specific file type. For example, Windows will bind Adobe Reader software to the .PDF file extension, or MS Word to the .DOC (or .DOCX) file extension.

File extensions are specific to the Windows Operating System and without an extension the Windows Operating System would not know how to open, process, or handle a file. The Windows Operating System looks at the extension when binding a file to an application.

Question: What would occur if the file extension of an executable (.EXE) file was changed to that of an Adobe file extension (.PDF)?

Answer: Windows would look at the file extension and see that it's a .PDF; it would therefore hand that file over to Adobe to open. Adobe would attempt to launch or open the file and report an error since the file, regardless of its name, is not actually an Adobe file.

Windows stores this application binding information in a section of the *Operating System* (OS) called the *registry*.

Each file type contains a corresponding file extension; this correlation stored within the registry tells the OS what type of program is needed to access a certain file type. This is Window's way of organizing the many different types of files to their corresponding software.

When the OS identifies an extension, say .CSV (Comma Separated Values), the OS looks to the registry and finds which application is bound to this extension. It most cases, MS Excel is bound to CSVs, so Windows will hand that file over to Excel to open and process. A file extension and/or its corresponding registry information can be manipulated by a savvy user.

For example, suppose a change was made to the registry so that the .CSV file extension was associated to and therefore opened with an image viewer such as Windows Picture Viewer. If a user were to click on an actual CSV file, Windows would hand that file over to Windows Viewer instead of the logical application (e.g., Excel); the image viewer would then attempt to open the file. If the file was an actual CSV file, a "no preview available" message or an error would be displayed, as the Windows Viewer application would not be able to process a file with the .CSV file format extension.

Say the file was an image, which had been renamed with a .CSV extension. Windows would hand that CSV file over to the image viewing software and the image would be displayed. A file with an incorrect file extension would open as long as the Windows Registry had that "incorrect" file extension associated with the correct software. Remember, changing or renaming a file's extension does not change the content of the file; it only changes the way in which Windows OS handles the file (i.e., which application the file is sent to).

So why is the way the OS handles the interpretation of a file's extension important to the cyber forensic investigator?

What if a cyber forensic investigator receives a *forensic image* of a suspected child molester's hard drive, and searches the drive's contents for image files (e.g., JPGs). Let's say that the investigator is unable to find the existence of files with image extensions such as .JPG. Is this case closed? Is the suspected child molester innocent and free to go?

Hardly; there could be plenty of images on this hard drive that have just been renamed. The fact that Windows uses file extensions creates a means by which a user can hide information by renaming file extensions.

 ## CHANGING A FILE'S EXTENSION TO EVADE DETECTION

The process to change a file's extension to evade detection is quite simple, as shown in the following steps.

Step 1

Create a legitimate looking folder into which you wish to place your files (see Figure 4.1).

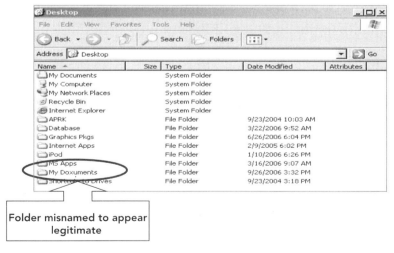

FIGURE 4.1 Creating a Misnamed but Legitimate Looking Folder

Step 2

Open the misnamed but legitimate looking folder called My Doxuments (see Figure 4.2).

Step 3

Open the Tools tab and select Folder Options (see Figure 4.3).

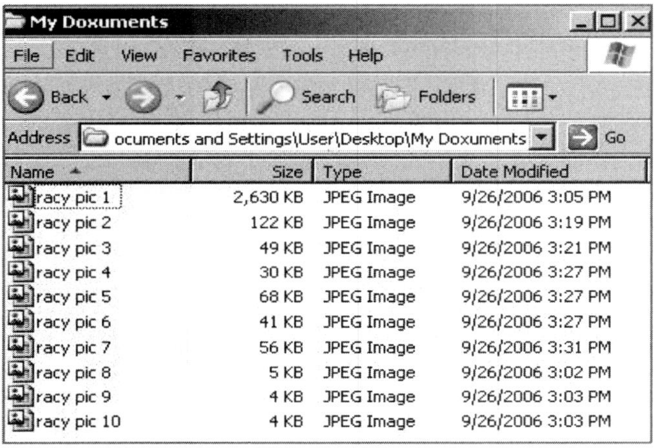

FIGURE 4.2 Contents of My Doxuments Folder

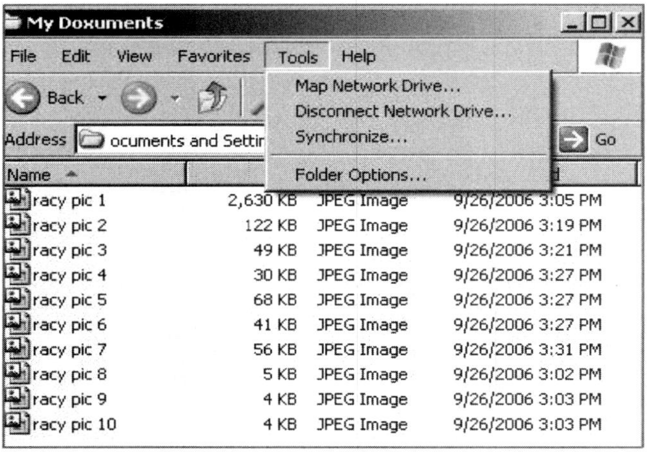

FIGURE 4.3 Preparing to Change a File's Extension

Step 4

Open the View tab (see Figure 4.4).

Step 5

Uncheck "Hide extensions for known file types" (see Figure 4.5).

Step 6

File extension type is revealed (see Figure 4.6).

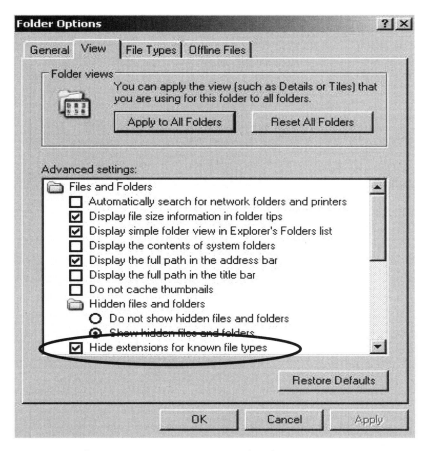

FIGURE 4.4   File Management Option to Hide File Extensions

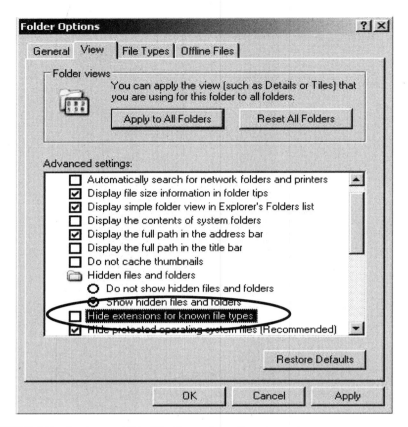

FIGURE 4.5 Option to Hide File Extensions Deselected

Step 7

Right-click on the file name to Rename the file, including providing any valid file extension type.

The file type is changed based upon the extension provided (see Figure 4.7).

Step 8

Click Hide extensions for known file types, to hide the new file extensions (see Figure 4.8).

Where there were once 10 JPEG image files there are now only six (see Figure 4.9). Scanning simply for image files will result in missing the four files with modified extensions!

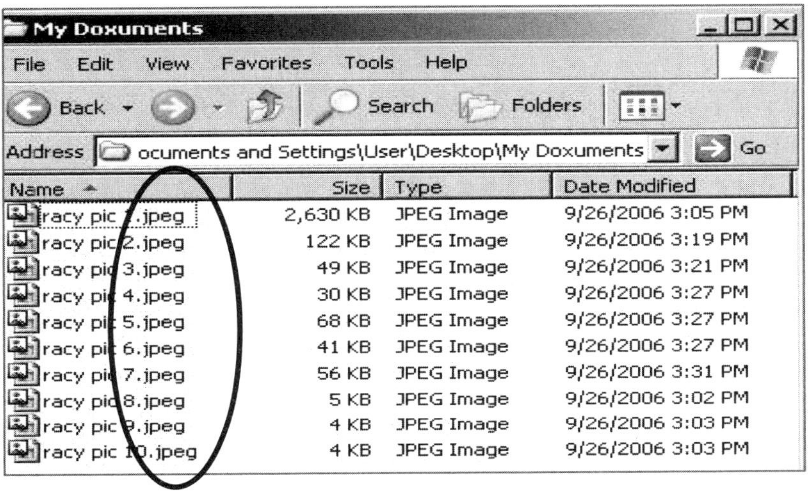

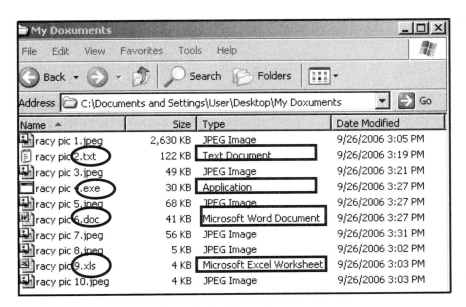

FIGURE 4.6 Individual File Extension Types Revealed

FIGURE 4.7 Renaming File and File's Extension

Name ▲	Size	Type	Date Modified
racy pic 1	2,630 KB	JPEG Image	9/26/2006 3:05 PM
racy pic 2	122 KB	JPEG Image	9/26/2006 3:19 PM
racy pic 3	49 KB	JPEG Image	9/26/2006 3:21 PM
racy pic 4	30 KB	JPEG Image	9/26/2006 3:27 PM
racy pic 5	68 KB	JPEG Image	9/26/2006 3:27 PM
racy pic 6	41 KB	JPEG Image	9/26/2006 3:27 PM
racy pic 7	56 KB	JPEG Image	9/26/2006 3:31 PM
racy pic 8	5 KB	JPEG Image	9/26/2006 3:02 PM
racy pic 9	4 KB	JPEG Image	9/26/2006 3:03 PM
racy pic 10	4 KB	JPEG Image	9/26/2006 3:03 PM

BEFORE

Name ▲	Size	Type	Date Modified
racy pic 1	2,630 KB	JPEG Image	9/26/2006 3:05 PM
racy pic 2	122 KB	Text Document	9/26/2006 3:19 PM
racy pic 3	49 KB	JPEG Image	9/26/2006 3:21 PM
racy pic 4	30 KB	Application	9/26/2006 3:27 PM
racy pic 5	68 KB	JPEG Image	9/26/2006 3:27 PM
racy pic 6	41 KB	Microsoft Word Document	9/26/2006 3:27 PM
racy pic 7	56 KB	JPEG Image	9/26/2006 3:31 PM
racy pic 8	5 KB	JPEG Image	9/26/2006 3:02 PM
racy pic 9	4 KB	Microsoft Excel Worksheet	9/26/2006 3:03 PM
racy pic 10	4 KB	JPEG Image	9/26/2006 3:03 PM

AFTER

FIGURE 4.8 Original Files and Extensions and the Files after Changing Their Extensions

Name	Size	Type ▲	Date Modified
racy pic 4	30 KB	Application	9/26/2006 3:27 PM
racy pic 1	2,630 KB	JPEG Image	9/26/2006 3:05 PM
racy pic 3	49 KB	JPEG Image	9/26/2006 3:21 PM
racy pic 5	68 KB	JPEG Image	9/26/2006 3:27 PM
racy pic 7	56 KB	JPEG Image	9/26/2006 3:31 PM
racy pic 8	5 KB	JPEG Image	9/26/2006 3:02 PM
racy pic 10	4 KB	JPEG Image	9/26/2006 3:03 PM
racy pic 9	4 KB	Microsoft Excel Worksheet	9/26/2006 3:03 PM
racy pic 6	41 KB	Microsoft Word Document	9/26/2006 3:27 PM
racy pic 2	122 KB	Text Document	9/26/2006 3:19 PM

FIGURE 4.9 Results of Changes to a File's Extension

Advice to the potential criminal: It may be wise to rename the file names from "racy pic" to something more inconspicuous! Also, using or renaming a less well-known folder buried further down in the directory tree may be advantageous.

Remember Windows looks at a file's extension first, and hands that file over to the appropriate application to open. A Microsoft Word application attempting to open a .JPEG or .TIF file would attempt to launch or open the file and report an error since the file, regardless of its name, is not actually a Microsoft Word file.

FILES AND THE HEX EDITOR

In our intellectual property theft case, Ronelle Sawyer is investigating whether Jose McCarthy has potentially engaged in the unlawful distribution of his organization's intellectual property to a competitor, Janice Witcome, Managing Director of the XYZ Company.

Ronelle is faced with examining millions of pieces of potential evidential data residing on Jose's hard drive, such as any occurrence of the character string "X," "Y," and "Z." To add to the complexity of Ronelle's task, these files could have easily been renamed and moved to locations buried deep within the *logical folder structure* of the computer.

Figure 4.10 displays the contents of a folder (7.0.6000.374) buried within the Windows folder structure, a location which would normally contain system files such as .*DLLs*. The folder's name is [C:\WINDOWS\system32\SoftwareDistribution\Setup\ServiceStartup\wups2.dll\7.0.6000.374]

Windows Folder 7.0.6000.374 contains two files: file #1, wups2.dll, and file #2, systemm32.dll.

Remember, there can be hundreds if not thousands of folders and even more files, all of which may seem inconsequential as they are scattered and stored throughout an individual's hard drive.

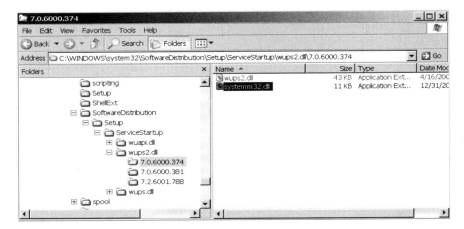

FIGURE 4.10 Windows Folder 7.0.6000.374

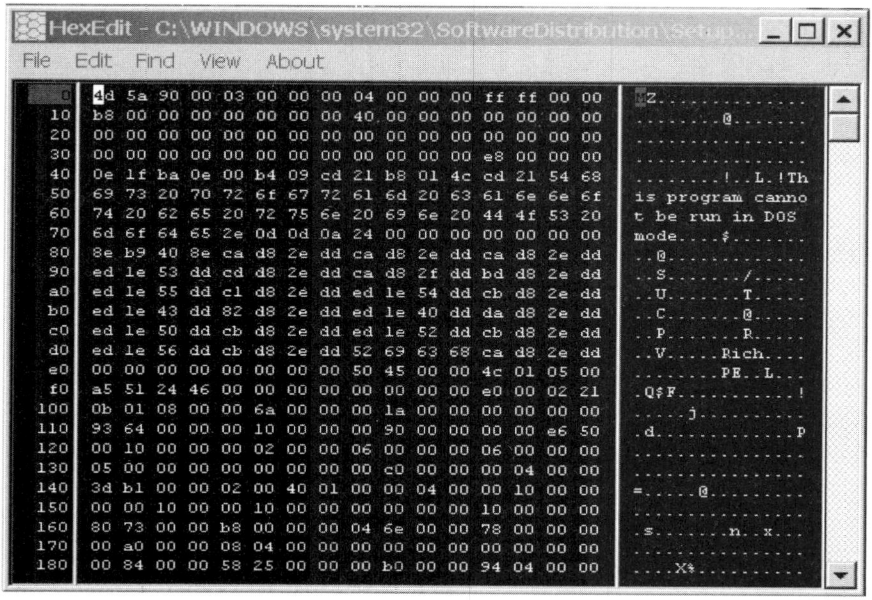

HexEdit - C:\WINDOWS\system32\SoftwareDistribution\Setup... _ □ ×

File   Edit   Find   View   About

```
  0  4d 5a 90 00 03 00 00 00 04 00 00 00 ff ff 00 00   MZ..............
 10  b8 00 00 00 00 00 00 00 40 00 00 00 00 00 00 00   ........@.......
 20  00 00 00 00 00 00 00 00 00 00 00 00 00 00 00 00   ................
 30  00 00 00 00 00 00 00 00 00 00 00 00 e8 00 00 00   ................
 40  0e 1f ba 0e 00 b4 09 cd 21 b8 01 4c cd 21 54 68   ........!..L.!Th
 50  69 73 20 70 72 6f 67 72 61 6d 20 63 61 6e 6e 6f   is program canno
 60  74 20 62 65 20 72 75 6e 20 69 6e 20 44 4f 53 20   t be run in DOS
 70  6d 6f 64 65 2e 0d 0d 0a 24 00 00 00 00 00 00 00   mode....$.......
 80  8e b9 40 8e ca d8 2e dd ca d8 2e dd ca d8 2e dd   ..@.............
 90  ed 1e 53 dd cd d8 2e dd ca d8 2f bd d8 2e dd      ..S......./.....
 a0  ed 1e 55 dd c1 d8 2e dd ed 1e 54 dd cb d8 2e dd   ..U.......T.....
 b0  ed 1e 43 dd 82 d8 2e dd ed 1e 40 dd da d8 2e dd   ..C.......@.....
 c0  ed 1e 50 dd cb d8 2e dd ed 1e 52 dd cb d8 2e dd   ..P.......R.....
 d0  ed 1e 56 dd cb d8 2e dd 52 69 63 68 ca d8 2e dd   ..V.....Rich....
 e0  00 00 00 00 00 00 00 00 50 45 00 00 4c 01 05 00   ........PE..L...
 f0  a5 51 24 46 00 00 00 00 00 00 00 00 e0 00 02 21   .Q$F...........!
100  0b 01 08 00 00 6a 00 00 00 1a 00 00 00 00 00 00   .....j..........
110  93 64 00 00 00 10 00 00 00 90 00 00 00 00 e6 50   .d.............P
120  00 10 00 00 00 02 00 00 06 00 00 00 06 00 00 00   ................
130  05 00 00 00 00 00 00 00 c0 00 00 00 04 00 00 00   ................
140  3d b1 00 00 02 00 40 01 00 00 04 00 00 10 00 00   =.....@.........
150  00 00 10 00 00 10 00 00 00 00 00 00 10 00 00 00   ................
160  80 73 00 00 b8 00 00 00 04 6e 00 00 78 00 00 00   .s.......n..x...
170  00 a0 00 00 08 04 00 00 00 00 00 00 00 00 00 00   ................
180  00 84 00 00 58 25 00 00 00 b0 00 00 94 04 00 00   ....X%..........
```

FIGURE 4.11   HEX Editor View of File wups2.dll

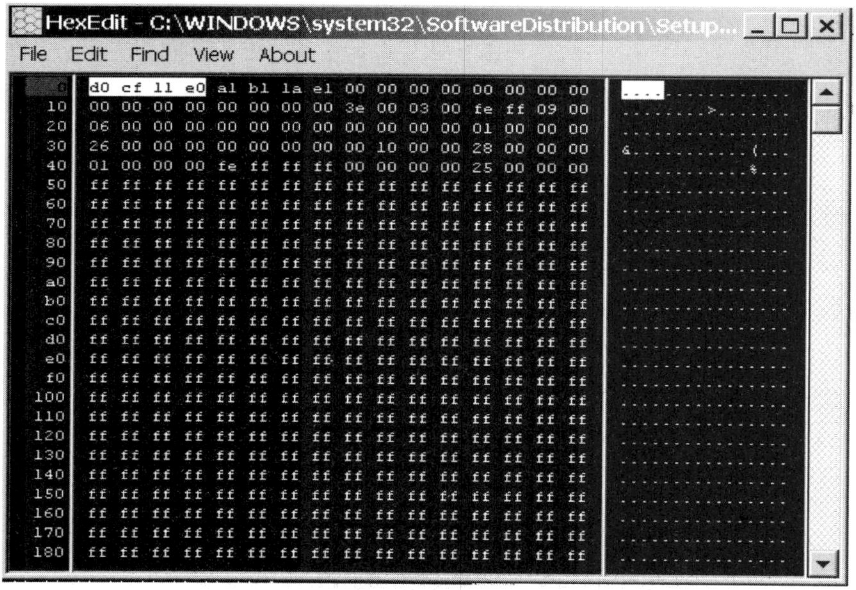

HexEdit - C:\WINDOWS\system32\SoftwareDistribution\Setup... _ □ ×

File   Edit   Find   View   About

```
  0  d0 cf 11 e0 a1 b1 1a e1 00 00 00 00 00 00 00 00   ................
 10  00 00 00 00 00 00 00 00 3e 00 03 00 fe ff 09 00   ........>.......
 20  06 00 00 00 00 00 00 00 00 10 00 00 01 00 00 00   ................
 30  26 00 00 00 00 00 00 00 00 10 00 00 28 00 00 00   &...........(...
 40  01 00 00 00 fe ff ff ff 00 00 00 00 25 00 00 00   ............%...
 50  ff ff ff ff ff ff ff ff ff ff ff ff ff ff ff ff   ................
 60  ff ff ff ff ff ff ff ff ff ff ff ff ff ff ff ff   ................
 70  ff ff ff ff ff ff ff ff ff ff ff ff ff ff ff ff   ................
 80  ff ff ff ff ff ff ff ff ff ff ff ff ff ff ff ff   ................
 90  ff ff ff ff ff ff ff ff ff ff ff ff ff ff ff ff   ................
 a0  ff ff ff ff ff ff ff ff ff ff ff ff ff ff ff ff   ................
 b0  ff ff ff ff ff ff ff ff ff ff ff ff ff ff ff ff   ................
 c0  ff ff ff ff ff ff ff ff ff ff ff ff ff ff ff ff   ................
 d0  ff ff ff ff ff ff ff ff ff ff ff ff ff ff ff ff   ................
 e0  ff ff ff ff ff ff ff ff ff ff ff ff ff ff ff ff   ................
 f0  ff ff ff ff ff ff ff ff ff ff ff ff ff ff ff ff   ................
100  ff ff ff ff ff ff ff ff ff ff ff ff ff ff ff ff   ................
110  ff ff ff ff ff ff ff ff ff ff ff ff ff ff ff ff   ................
120  ff ff ff ff ff ff ff ff ff ff ff ff ff ff ff ff   ................
130  ff ff ff ff ff ff ff ff ff ff ff ff ff ff ff ff   ................
140  ff ff ff ff ff ff ff ff ff ff ff ff ff ff ff ff   ................
150  ff ff ff ff ff ff ff ff ff ff ff ff ff ff ff ff   ................
160  ff ff ff ff ff ff ff ff ff ff ff ff ff ff ff ff   ................
170  ff ff ff ff ff ff ff ff ff ff ff ff ff ff ff ff   ................
180  ff ff ff ff ff ff ff ff ff ff ff ff ff ff ff ff   ................
```

FIGURE 4.12   HEX Editor View of File systemm32.dll

So these file types (i.e., .DLL) seem normal enough, right?

Let's look at the files with a *HEX editor*. There are many HEX editors available, most of which are free to download. Google is your friend; just be sure you are downloading a HEX editor and not a *Trojan*.

Figure 4.11 shows File #1 "wups2.dll" viewed in a HEX editor.

Figure 4.12 shows File # 2, "systemm32.dll" viewed in a HEX editor.

Contained within the file format information is the *file signature*, sometimes referred to as the *"Magic Number."*

Magic numbers are referred to as magic because the purpose and significance of their values are not apparent without some additional knowledge. The term *magic number* is also used in programming to refer to a constant that is employed for some specific purpose but whose presence or value is inexplicable without additional information.[2]

 ## FILE SIGNATURE

A file signature is the binary that identifies a particular file: the data that will aid in the identification of the file to its native or parent software.

For common file formats, the file signatures conveniently represent the names of the file types. For example, image files conforming to the widely used GIF87a format in HEX equals 0x474946383761; when converted into ASCII it equates to GIF87a. ASCII is the de facto standard used by computers and communications equipment for character encoding (i.e., associating alphabetic and other characters with numbers).

Likewise, the file signature for image files having the subsequently introduced GIF89a format is 0x347494638396 1. For both types of GIF (Graphic Interchange Format) files, the file signature occupies the first six bytes of the file. They are then followed by additional general information (i.e., metadata) about the file.

Similarly, a commonly used file signature for JPEG (Joint Photographic Experts Group) image files is 0x4A464946, which is the ASCII equivalent of

Remember, "0x - zero$_x$" refers to HEX(adecimal) notational value. Therefore, the value 0x474946383761 is *not* and *should not* be interpreted as a decimal value, but rather as a hexadecimal representation of a decimal equivalent.

JFIF (JPEG File Interchange Format). However, JPEG file signatures are not the first bytes in the file; rather, they begin with the seventh byte. Additional examples include 0x34D546864 for MIDI (Musical Instrument Digital Interface) files and 0x425a6831415925 for bzip2 compressed files.

Notice in the HEX editor of file "systemm32.dll" (Figure 4.12) we see a file signature of "d0 cf 11 e0." This is the known file signature for MS Word. In fact, Microsoft picked the binary code to identify its files with some forethought, as the HEX representation of the binary (which is d0 cf 11 e0) almost spells out (if you look closely and use your imagination) the word "docfile" (d0c f1 1e 0). Perhaps it's an example of tech humor or clever, albeit maybe bored, application designers?

Curious? Why would a file with a .dll file extension contain a "docfile" file signature? If we scroll down through the HEX editor some more, we will also see the actual text contained within the file (Figure 4.13).

Notice the HEX value 58 59 5a and its ASCII equivalent, "XYZ" contained within the ASCII Character Panel. HEX editors, as part of their "tool set," will automatically convert HEX to ASCII, so the rigorous HEX to ASCII

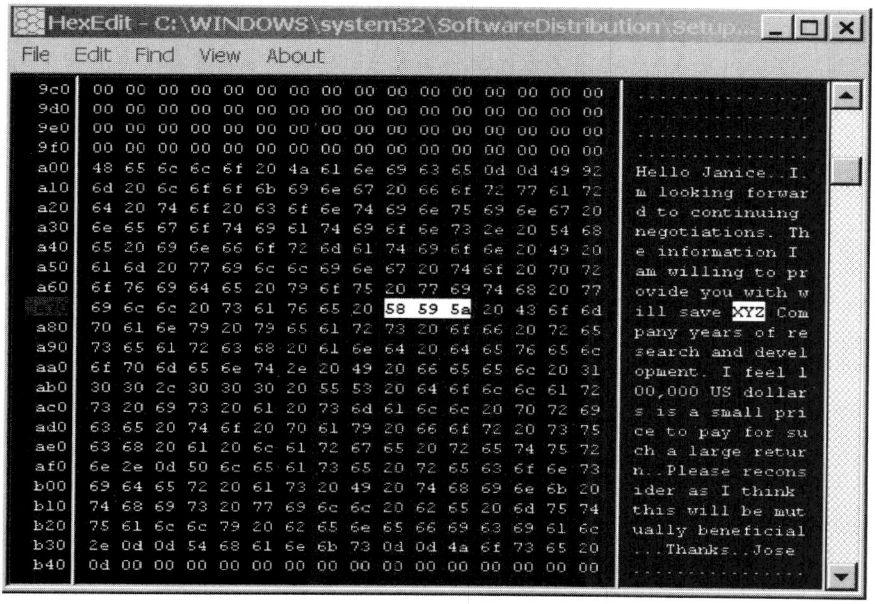

FIGURE 4.13 Text Contained within the .dll File "systemm32.dll"

conversion process we performed in the previous discussion is not necessary here.

The binary values representing the text "XYZ" are contained within the file "systemm32.dll." When we rename "systemm32.dll" to "systemm32.doc" and double click the file we will see that it is not a system file (.dll file) after all but a Word document (.doc).

This example shows us the importance of HEX when viewing files or attempting to view files. Since we already know the file signature for MS Word documents, "d0 cf 11 e0," we can now search the entirety of Jose McCarthy's drive for those specific HEX characters, revealing the existence of an MS Word document.

Notice we couldn't search the drive for the ASCII equivalent. The ASCII equivalent of the binary represented by the HEX is ".....". The "......." will sometimes be displayed when there is no ASCII equivalent to binary code, such as with file signatures. See Appendix 4C for a further review and discussion of file signatures.

ASCII IS *NOT* TEXT OR HEX

Remember, the ASCII equivalent of HEX d0 cf 11 e0, is not the file extension ".doc."

There may not always be an ASCII equivalent to a file type; this is one of the reasons to use HEX, or the importance of HEX. There may not always be an ASCII equivalent of, say, a file header (as in this case), ergo HEX.

Remember, ASCII has limitations and was expanded with Unicode (the Unicode equivalent of the HEX D0 CF 11 E0 is ÐÏ.à¡±.á (seen and pronounced as DIATA). (See Figure 4.14.) However, this isn't something easily searchable either as the characters are not all text based.

Open a .doc file (pre Office 2007) in a HEX editor and you will notice dots "................" for a lot of varying HEX characters. The file signature for this HEX value may not have an ASCII equivalent as well as some of the code and other file header data.

```
00000000  D0 CF 11 E0 A1 B1 1A E1 00 00 00 00 00 00 00 00  ÐÏ.à¡±.á... ....
00000010  00 00 00 00 00 00 00 00 3E 00 03 00 FE FF 09 00  ........>...þÿ..
00000020  06 00 00 00 00 00 00 00 00 00 00 00 01 00 00 00  ................
```

FIGURE 4.14 ASCII Equivalent of HEX D0 CF 11 E0 (MS Word .doc file)

The first eight (8) bytes are contained in the fixed compound document file identifier, so the file identifier would be all eight (8) bytes: D0 CF 11 E0 A1 B1 1A E1.

However, when searching through HEX the first four (4) bytes would certainly suffice, but it is best to be most accurate, so the full file signature for HEX D0 CF 11 E0 (MS Word .doc file) is D0 CF 11 E0 A1 B1 1A E1 (Figure 4.15).

```
00000000 D0 CF 11 E0 A1 B1 1A E1 00 00 00 00 00 00 00 00 ÐÏ.à¡±.á........
00000010 00 00 00 00 00 00 00 00 3E 00 03 00 FE FF 09 00 ........>...þÿ..
00000020 06 00 00 00 00 00 00 00 00 00 00 00 00 01 00 00 00 ...............
```

FIGURE 4.15 ASCII Equivalent of HEX D0 CF 11 E0 (MS Word .doc file)

For a more detailed breakdown of the compound file header, please refer to Appendix 4D.

VALUE OF FILE SIGNATURES

We see that even though a file is renamed we can still view the contents. If we were to search for the binary representation of "XYZ" across the entire drive we would find this value regardless of its modified file extension or file signature. As was discussed previously, many times in the course of normal day-to-day operations and file processing, a deleted file and its associated metadata will be partially overwritten, perhaps missing the entire file signature, or other important formatting information and even some text. However, if the binary values representing a piece of evidence (as in our case, "XYZ") remain within the remnants, then the file can be found.

It is important to note that a forensic examiner cannot always depend on having an intact file or a file with the authorized (correct) file extension (i.e., file type), available in its native format, on which to perform an analysis.

Office 2007 has drastically altered the MS Word file format. The previous example is true for Office 2003 and earlier versions. Microsoft Office 2007 documents are now stored in what is referred to as the Office Open XML File Format.

It is essentially a *ZIP file* of various XML documents describing the entire document.

The point of the previous example is not to discuss the inner workings of an MS Word file format, but to show how file formats and signatures work in general.

All file signatures are different and will continue to evolve. The purpose here is not to cover all file signatures, but to provide the reader with a very practical example of the relevance of a file's signature in locating and identifying potentially incriminating information as part of a cyber forensic investigation.

There are file signature databases and tables available on the Internet. Most forensic tools are able to identify file signatures and header information, and will verify file types in this manner. Forensic tools will convert binary to ASCII, verify file signatures, and search for binary strings (or keywords, such as "XYZ") without much effort on the part of the forensic examiner, and now you know HOW the software accomplishes this. See Appendix 4B for an example of a file signature database.

COMPLEX FILES: COMPOUND, COMPRESSED, AND ENCRYPTED FILES

Before ending this section there are other more complex files worth discussing: compound, compressed, and encrypted files. The full complexities of these files are not covered here, as there are books written about each. We do, however, explain some basics and their importance in forensics.

A *compound file* is a file format that consists of numerous files. The compound file itself is little more than a container for those files. The structure within a compound file is similar to that of a real file system consisting of a hierarchy of storage with one parent directory.

There is a root directory folder, children contained within, and files (data streams) contained therein. Compound files are sometimes associated with Microsoft's Compound File Binary Format (CFBF) file.

All allocations of space within a Compound File are done in "chunks" or units called sectors. The size of a sector is definable at creation time of a Compound File, and those sectors are usually 512 bytes in size. A virtual stream is made up of a sequence of sectors.

At its simplest, the Compound File Binary Format is a container, with little restriction on what can be stored within it.

However, in forensics, the term compound files is sometimes used more loosely, representing any file that may contain a *directory structure*. Again, our goal is not to cover a specific file type or software, but concepts generally.

As with other files, the file header of a compound file will contain a file signature, identifying the file; it will also contain information required to interpret the rest of the file such as the file's size and storage location.

It is this metadata that allows the software to reconstruct the file into the appropriate file format that will display the file's specific information (i.e., size, creation date, change date, etc.). The file therefore needs to be "reconstructed" by its parent software in order for the data to be legible or otherwise accessible.

To further explain, we typically think of data storage as linear. For example, consider the information in the following data stream, "XYZ Corp." The data is displayed in a linear contiguous pattern, X before Y and Y before Z. If that data was displayed in a nonlinear pattern we would see perhaps, "oZ pYCrX."

If that same data now were not contiguous, other data from that same compound file may also be intertwined (e.g., ...?>>o....Z^qL p....77Ymn....C@ qwerbsbdX.........,,.). The original data stream "XYZ Corp" is not as easily discernable now. Even searching for the HEX equivalent wouldn't help us uncover the data in this example.

We would need an instruction set to reconstruct this data.

 ## WHY DO COMPOUND FILES EXIST?

Files have become more complex and need to contain a lot of information. Many files contain *Object Linking and Embedding (OLE)* technology, in which one file may contain many files.

OLE (object linking and embedding) allows users to integrate data from different applications. Object linking allows users to share a single source of data for a particular object. The document contains the name of the file containing the data, along with a picture of the data. When the source is updated, all the documents using the data are updated as well.

With object embedding, one application (referred to as the "source") provides data or an image that will be contained in the document of another application (referred to as the "destination"). The destination application contains the data or graphic image, but does not understand it or have the ability to edit it. It simply displays, prints, and/or plays the embedded item. To edit or update the embedded object, it must be opened in the source application that created it. This occurs automatically when you double-click the item or choose the appropriate edit command while the object is highlighted.

While embedding doesn't allow users to have a single source of data, it does make it easier to integrate applications. An embedded object contains the actual data for the object, the name of the application that created it, and a picture of the data.[3]

For instance, an MS Word document may contain a JPG image; a file within a file. Compound files allow for incremental access, allowing for individual components to be accessed without the need of the entire file. This can save time and resources by not having to load an entire file, only the piece or pieces desired.

 ## COMPRESSED FILES

As we continue on with our discussion, *compressed files* are essentially compound files (and sometimes referred to as such in the forensic community) that are compressed. They work in similar fashion; however, also contained within the compound file are compression instructions.

A common file extension associated with compressed files is .ZIP. This file format has gone mainstream and is supported by many software utilities other than its parent software, PKZIP. The .ZIP file format was publically released, making it an open format which is used by other programs including Microsoft's Open Office XML format. The ZIP file extension name is often used to describe any archival file format. There are other ZIP file formats including WINZIP, 7-Zip, GZip, and RZip.

The file format of a compressed file (or .ZIP file) changes depending upon its compression algorithm. Algorithms are the mathematical operations or instructions for completing a task, in this case compressing data. It is a method of encoding data using fewer bits than used in the original encoding. Algorithms are complex to say the least and books have been written regarding this topic.

To exemplify the difference between a regular file and a more complex file (compound or compressed) it would be best to examine a similar file in both formats.

Let's examine a letter from Jose McCarthy, seized as part of the Ronelle Sawyer investigation. The letter examined was an MS Word file format (i.e., .doc), as was made clear when viewed via the HEX editor, shown here again.

We can easily see the doc file signature, d0 cf 11 e0, displayed in the HEX editor in Figure 4.16.

By knowing the file signature for an MS Word document, we can easily identify and/or search for the text contained within this .doc file, and in doing so, find references to the "XYZ" company, as shown in Figure 4.17.

What happens, however, when an application is upgraded? How might this effect the application's file signature? To see the result of a change in software application file formatting, let us view the same document file from Jose McCarthy

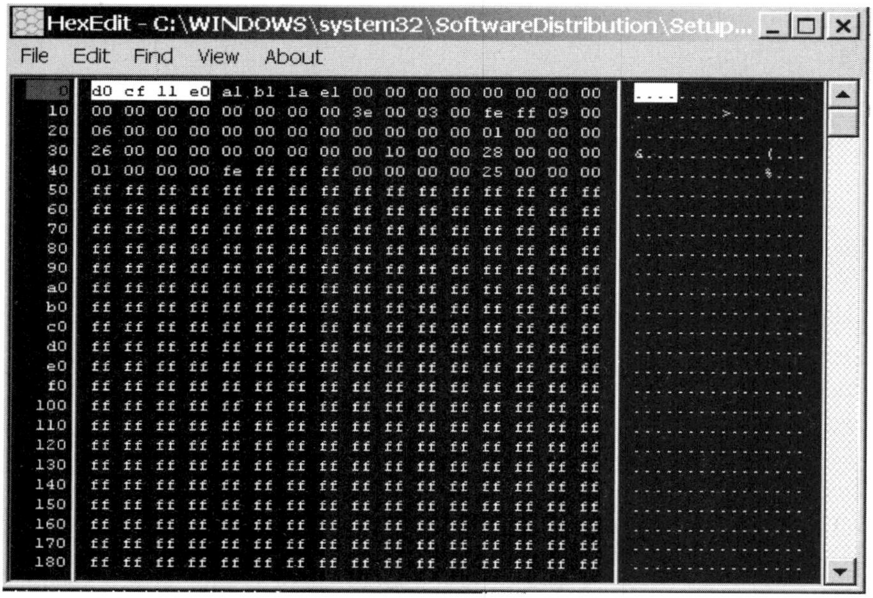

FIGURE 4.16 MS Word Office 2003 Document File Signature

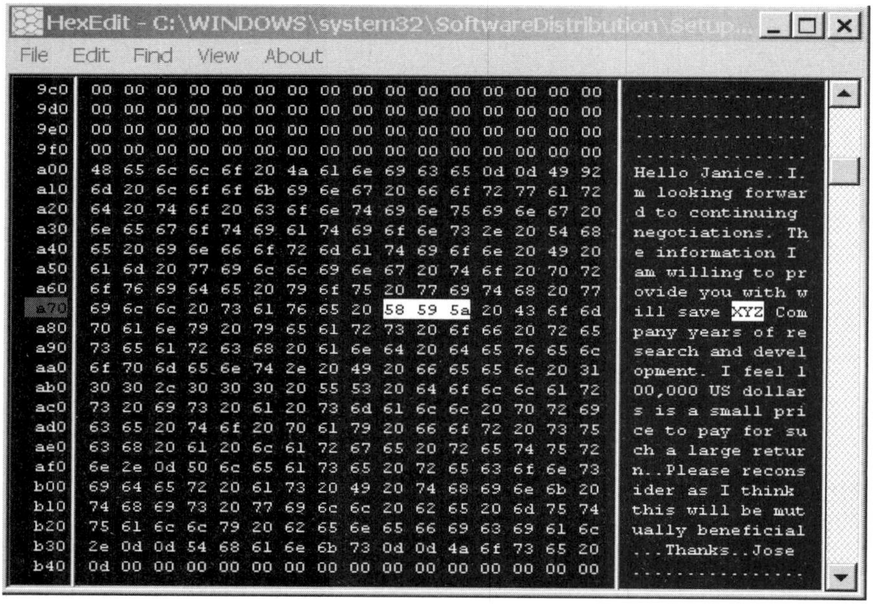

FIGURE 4.17 HEX and ASCII Identification of "XYZ" Company

with a HEX editor, when Microsoft Office 2007 rather than Office 2003 is used to generate the document.

We see in Figure 4.18 that the file signature has changed. If you search for a file signature matching 50 4B 03 04 you will notice it corresponds to a .ZIP file signature (ASCII panel shows PK . . . . format). With the release of Office '07, Microsoft Word documents now use the same file format signature as a .ZIP file.

What is the importance to a cyber forensic investigation and what does this mean? For starters, it means that the file is a compound file consisting of other files. If we were to view the entirety of the file with our HEX editor we would not uncover any legible ASCII characters (see ASCII panel in Figure 4.17).

Why? The file structure and assembly instructions are contained within the file; thus, the file would need to be *mounted* by its native software in order for the contents to be viewed. As can be seen in Figure 4.19, the ASCII representation is not identifiable.

Viewing and, more importantly, searching the contents of these "complex" files are possible once they are mounted. Forensic tools incorporate the software to mount these so that searching is possible. If these complex files are not mounted then no search results will be obtained.

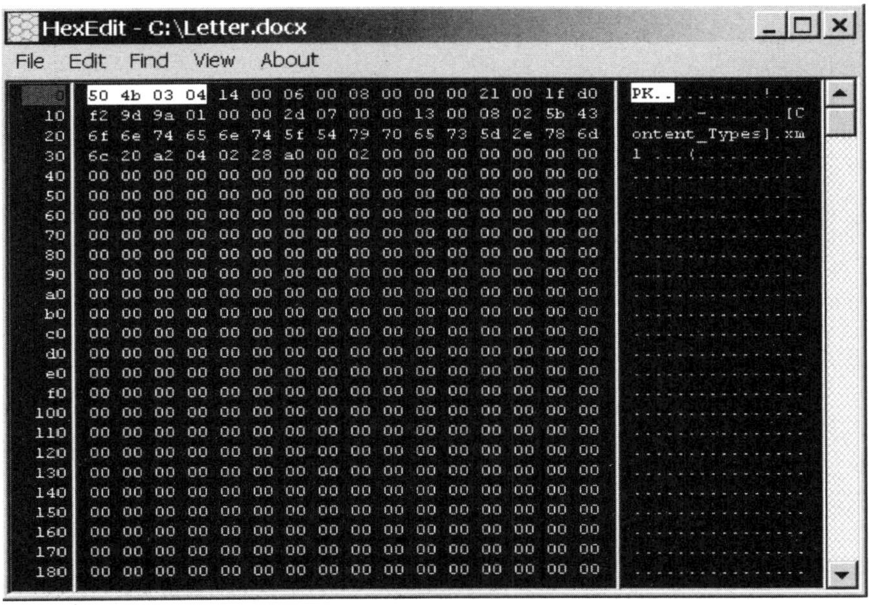

FIGURE 4.18 MS Word Office 2007 Document File Signature

```
HexEdit - C:\Letter.docx                                    _ □ ×
File   Edit   Find   View   About

1e0   00 00 00 00 00 00 00 00 00 00 00 00 00 00 00 00   ................
1f0   00 00 00 00 00 00 00 00 00 00 00 00 00 00 00 00   ................
200   00 00 00 00 00 00 00 00 00 00 00 00 00 00 00 00   ................
210   00 00 00 00 00 00 00 00 00 00 00 00 00 00 00 00   ................
220   00 00 00 00 00 00 00 00 00 00 00 00 00 00 00 00   ................
230   00 00 00 00 00 00 00 00 00 b4 55 cb 4e c3 30 10   .........U.N.0.
240   bc 23 f1 0f 91 af a8 71 cb 01 21 d4 b4 07 1e 47   .#.....q..!...G
250   a8 44 f9 00 d7 de b4 16 89 6d d9 db d7 df b3 49   .D.......m.....I
260   9a 08 41 9b 88 86 5e 22 45 d1 ce cc ce ce 6e c6   ..A..^"E......n.
270   d3 5d 9e 45 1b f0 41 5b 93 b0 51 3c 64 11 18 69   .].E..A[..Q<d..i
280   95 36 cb 84 7d cc 5f 06 f7 2c 0a 28 8c 12 99 35   .6..}._..,.(...5
290   90 b0 3d 04 36 9d 5c 5f 8d e7 7b 07 21 a2 6a 13   ..=.6.\_..{.!.j.
2a0   12 b6 42 74 0f 9c 07 b9 82 5c 84 d8 3a 30 f4 25   ..Bt.....\..:0.%
2b0   b5 3e 17 48 af 7e c9 9d 90 9f 62 09 fc 76 38 bc   .>.H.~...b..v8.
2c0   e3 d2 1a 04 83 03 2c 30 d8 64 fc 46 02 bc 56 10   ......,.0.d.F..V.
2d0   cd 84 c7 57 91 13 0f df 5a af 78 6a 2d 1a 8b 10   ...W....Z.xj-...
2e0   62 82 63 d1 63 55 57 50 27 4c 38 97 69 29 90 84   b.c.cUWP'L8.i)..
2f0   f3 8d 51 3f 48 07 36 4d b5 04 65 e5 3a 27 aa b8   ..Q?H.6M..e.:'..
300   80 73 de 4a 08 81 5a cb b3 b8 81 be 29 a0 f9 64   .s.J.Z....)..d
310   fc 04 a9 58 67 18 3d ef 48 5b 65 87 87 2c fc 8d   ...Xg.=.H[e..,..
320   f5 d0 66 4c 95 a5 b2 b0 d2 2e b4 30 b4 b7 75 50   ..fL.......0..uP
330   76 d2 9e a6 bb 76 98 33 dc 69 90 73 a1 4d ad ff   v....v.3.i.s.M..
340   a4 0e b3 ce 17 e0 c9 d7 ff 1f 53 03 dd 29 22 e0   .........S..)".
350   3e bb 44 50 2a dc 4e 7a 30 ea 42 49 ad 91 db 24   >.DP*.NzO.BI...$
360   d0 bc 66 de ba c0 69 2b 7a 0f 01 8a 0d 50 a0 06   ..f...i+z....P..
```

FIGURE 4.19   Identifiable ASCII Representation for .doc File

FORENSICS AND ENCRYPTED FILES

Encrypted files are also complex but differ in that an *encryption key* is required to *decrypt* an encrypted file.

Encryption uses an algorithm (*cipher*) to alter or transform the data in an attempt to prevent reconstruction by those without the instruction set, a.k.a. Encryption Key. Decryption refers to the reverse process of making the data readable or otherwise accessible.

Encryption is a method by which the confidentiality of data can be protected. For the most part, an encrypted file cannot be decrypted without the encryption key (aka password). The encryption process uses an algorithm or cipher to mathematically transform the plaintext along with the encryption key (password), thereby encoding it in such a manner that it is illegible or indecipherable.

With the correct decryption key (password) the data is then run through its associated cipher text (algorithm) and converted back to clear text, which is, by default, decrypted. Remember, this entire process occurs in binary, as 0s or 1s.

It is the cipher that actually changes the file; the password is just a set of data which are used to "mathematically mix" and set the process in motion, turning the plaintext data into an unreadable end product.

 ## THE STRUCTURE OF CIPHERS

The structure of ciphers depends upon the cipher's type. Types of ciphers vary but generally they can be categorized by the following:

- **Block or stream.** *Block ciphers* generally work on fixed length bits of data called blocks. The cipher may take a 256–bit block of plaintext data and encrypt it, which results in a 256-bit block of encrypted data. In a *stream cipher*, the plaintext bits are encrypted one at a time along with the encryption key.
- **Symmetric or asymmetric.** In symmetric encryption, the same encryption key or password is used for both encryption and decryption, whereas with asymmetric encryption different keys are used. *Symmetric key encryption* is intuitive in that the same password is used to encrypt or decrypt the data. *Asymmetric key encryption*, or public-key cryptography, uses two different encryption keys, a public and a private key. Data is encrypted using a person's public key, one in which everyone may have access to or even be distributed. However, data can only be decrypted using the person's private key, one which is kept secret by the individual.

There are various encryption methods available, such as the Advanced Encryption Standard (AES), which is currently the standard adopted by the United States government and one of the most popular encryption methods available and in use today.

There are other encryption algorithms (or formats) available and many books have been written regarding each. It is not within the scope of this text to cover the various standards of encryption.

A similar attribute shared by all these "complex" file types discussed is that they contain some level or form of instruction needed to reconstruct the file. If that information is overwritten or otherwise missing, the ability to retrieve the data contained within the file will be severely compromised.

If the instructional data needed to reconstruct a compound file is missing, overwritten, destroyed, compromised, etc., the file may not be recoverable, even though the data containing the evidence (e.g., XYZ Corp) may still be contained within the file itself.

However, with that said, it may be possible to reconstruct a complex file which has been *partially* overwritten. Forensic analysts are creative, cutting edge, innovative, and very intelligent; they have developed solutions for some of the most complex problems. However, recovering the data with normal "point and click" methods may not always be possible.

 ## SUMMARY

It is important to understand that not all binary values are convertible into readable ASCII. ASCII is a code, based on the ordering of the English alphabet, and not all data contained within a computer is necessarily text (ASCII) based. There are many programs or software applications which are written in programming code which is not ASCII based.

This programming code is not meant to be viewed in ASCII, it is meant to perform a function. Recall from our earlier discussions, a computer's functions are all based on math, not the English (nor French, Chinese, Slavic, Greek, or Arabic) language; code therefore needs to be based on mathematical principles not grammatical ones.

A file's type or format is based upon its file signature, not a Microsoft Windows extension. The file header, including the file signature is best viewed in HEX as there is no legible or identifiable corresponding ASCII representation. As we discussed, file signature/headers are the pieces of a file which identify the file to its "parent" software, not to the user.

Thus, when we view the HEX editor and see HEX values appearing as "..............." in the ASCII Character Panel, this could mean that there may not be an ASCII representation for those HEX values. The HEX values, when they do exist, are unique and therefore searchable.

It is very easy (and potentially dangerous) to become dependent on the forensic tools and forget the nuts and bolts of the technological process, and forget or even be unaware HOW the answer is obtained.

Reliance on any "tool" without having a solid understanding of how the tool works could spell personal and professional disaster for the cyber forensic investigator.

This is akin to successfully providing the correct answers to all the questions on a mathematics exam, and still receiving a failing grade because you failed to show your work.

If asked to explain how an answer was obtained or on what data analysis a conclusion is reached, if one were to reply, "I used tool 'ABC' and it provided the answer," and if you are unable to explain *how* the tool obtained the answer or *how* you could validate and substantiate that the answer you provided was correct, the validity and reliance of your answer could be called in to question and held suspect.

Use a tool, but be certain you know *how* the tool works and how to replicate the results if you had to do so, without the tool.

 NOTES

1. File format, retrieved January 2010, www.answers.com/topic/file-format.
2. Bellevue Linux Users Group (BLUG), Magic Number Definition," The Linux Information Project, August 21, 2006, retrieved January 2010, www.linfo .org/magic_number.html.
3. "Common Questions: Object Linking and Embedding, Data Exchange," Microsoft Support, retrieved November 2011, http://support.microsoft.com/ kb/122263, © 2007 Microsoft Corporation. All rights reserved. Used with permission from Microsoft.

APPENDIX 4A: COMMON FILE EXTENSIONS*

Common file extensions that are good to know, organized by file format.

Text Files

.doc	Microsoft Word Document
.docx	Microsoft Word Open XML Document
.log	Log File
.msg	Outlook Mail Message
.pages	Pages Document
.rtf	Rich Text Format File
.txt	Plain Text File
.wpd	WordPerfect Document
.wps	Microsoft Works Word Processor Document

Data Files

.123	Lotus 1-2-3 Spreadsheet
.accdb	Access 2007 Database File
.csv	Comma Separated Values File
.dat	Data File
.db	Database File
.dll	Dynamic Link Library
.mdb	Microsoft Access Database
.pps	PowerPoint Slide Show
.ppt	PowerPoint Presentation
.pptx	Microsoft PowerPoint Open XML Document
.sdb	OpenOffice.org Base Database File
.sdf	Standard Data File
.sql	Structured Query Language Data
.vcfv	Card File
.wks	Microsoft Works Spreadsheet
.xls	Microsoft Excel Spreadsheet
.xlsx	Microsoft Excel Open XML Document
.xml	XML File

Image Files

.pct	Picture File

---

* The information in this Appendix came from www.fileinfo.com/common.php.

Raster Image Files

.bmp	Bitmap Image File
.gif	Graphical Interchange Format File
.jpg	JPEG Image File
.png	Portable Network Graphic
.psd	Photoshop Document
.psp	Paint Shop Pro Image File
.thm	Thumbnail Image File
.tif	Tagged Image File

Vector Image Files

.ai	Adobe Illustrator File
.drw	Drawing File
.dxf	Drawing Exchange Format File
.eps	Encapsulated PostScript File
.ps	PostScript File
.svg	Scalable Vector Graphics File

3D Image Files

.3dm	Rhino 3D Model
.dwg	AutoCAD Drawing Database File
.pln	ArchiCAD Project File

Page Layout Files

.indd	Adobe InDesign File
.pdf	Portable Document Format File
.qxd	QuarkXPress Document
.qxp	QuarkXPress Project File

Audio Files

.aac	Advanced Audio Coding File
.aif	Audio Interchange File Format
.iff	Interchange File Format
.m3u	Media Playlist File
.mid	MIDI File
.midi	MIDI File
.mp3	MP3 Audio File
.mpa	MPEG-2 Audio File
.ra	Real Audio File

.wav   WAVE Audio File
.wma   Windows Media Audio File

Video Files

.3g2   3GPP2 Multimedia File
.3gp   3GPP Multimedia File
.asf   Advanced Systems Format File
.asx   Microsoft ASF Redirector File
.avi   Audio Video Interleave File
.flv   Flash Video File
.mov   Apple QuickTime Movie
.mp4   MPEG-4 Video File
.mpg   MPEG Video File
.rm   Real Media File
.swf   Flash Movie
.vob   DVD Video Object File
.wmv   Windows Media Video File

Web Files

.asp   Active Server Page
.css   Cascading Style Sheet
.htm   Hypertext Markup Language File
.html   Hypertext Markup Language File
.js   JavaScript File
.jsp   Java Server Page
.php   Hypertext Preprocessor File
.rss   Rich Site Summary
.xhtml   Extensible Hypertext Markup Language File

Font Files

.fnt   Windows Font File
.fon   Generic Font File
.otf   OpenType Font
.ttf   TrueType Font

Plugin Files

.8bi   Photoshop Plug-in
.plugin   Mac OSX Plug-in
.xll   Excel Add-In File

System Files

.cab	Windows Cabinet File
.cpl	Windows Control Panel
.cur	Windows Cursor
.dmp	Windows Memory Dump
.drv	Device Driver
.key	Security Key
.lnk	File Shortcut
.sys	Windows System File

Settings Files

.cfg	Configuration File
.ini	Windows Initialization File
.prf	Outlook Profile File

Executable Files

.app	Mac OS X Application
.bat	DOS Batch File
.cgi	Common Gateway Interface Script
.com	DOS Command File
.exe	Windows Executable File
.pif	Program Information File
.vb	VBScript File
.ws	Windows Script

Compressed Files

.7z	7-Zip Compressed File
.deb	Debian Software Package
.gz	Gnu Zipped File
.pkg	Mac OS X Installer Package
.rar	WinRAR Compressed Archive
.sit	Stuffit Archive
.sitx	Stuffit X Archive
.zip	Zip File
.zipx	Extended Zip File

Encoded Files

.bin	Macbinary II Encoded File
.hqx	BinHex 4.0 Encoded File

.mim   Multi-Purpose Internet Mail Message
.uue   Uuencoded File

Developer Files

.c   C/C++ Source Code File
.cpp   C++ Source Code File
.java   Java Source Code File
.pl   Perl Script

Backup Files

.bak   Backup File
.bup   Backup File
.gho   Norton Ghost Backup File
.ori   Original File
.tmp   Temporary File

Disk Files

.dmg   Mac OS X Disk Image
.iso   Disc Image File
.toast   Toast Disc Image
.vcd   Virtual CD

Game Files

.gam   Saved Game File
.nes   Nintendo (NES) ROM File
.rom   N64 Game ROM File
.sav   Saved Game

Misc Files

.msi   Windows Installer Package
.part   Partially Downloaded File
.torrent BitTorrent File
.yps   Yahoo! Messenger Data File

APPENDIX 4B: FILE SIGNATURE DATABASE

File Format	File Signature/ Magic Number	ASCII Equivalent	Windows OS File Extension
DeskMate document file	0D 44 4F 43	.DOC	DOC
Perfect Office document	CF 11 E0 A1 B1 1A E1 00	Ï.à¡±.á.	DOC
MS Word document	D0 CF 11 E0 A1 B1 1A E1	ÐÏ.à¡±.á	DOC
Office 2007 documents	50 4B 03 04 14 00 06 00	PK..	DOCX
Rich Text Format file	7B 5C 72 74 66 31	{\rtf1	RTF
Lotus 1-2-3 spreadsheet (v9)	00 00 1A 00 05 10 04	•••••••	123
Dynamic link library	4D 5A	MZ	DLL
PowerPoint slide show	D0 CF 11 E0 A1 B1 1A E1	ÐÏ.à¡±.á	PPS
PowerPoint presentation	D0 CF 11 E0 A1 B1 1A E1	ÐÏ.à¡±.á	PPT
PowerPoint presentation subheader (MS Office)	[512 byte offset] FD FF FF FF nn 00 00 00 (where nn has been seen with values 0x0E, 0x1C, and 0x43)	ýÿÿÿ....	PPT
PowerPoint presentation subheader (MS Office)	[512 byte offset] 00 6E 1E F0	.n.ð	PPT
PowerPoint presentation subheader (MS Office)	[512 byte offset] 0F 00 E8 03	..è.	PPT
Microsoft PowerPoint Office 2007 documents	50 4B 03 04 14 00 06 00	PK......	PPTX

(Continued)

File Format	File Signature/ Magic Number	ASCII Equivalent	Windows OS File Extension
Microsoft Excel spreadsheet	D0 CF 11 E0 A1 B1 1A E1	ÐÏ.à¡±.á	XLS
Microsoft Excel Open XML document	50 4B 03 04 14 00 06 00	PK......	XLSX
XML file	FF FE 3C 00 3F 00 78 00 6D 00 6C 00 20 00 76 00 65 00 72 00 73 00 69 00 6F 00 6E 00 3D 0	? x m l v e r s i o n =	XML
JPEG image file	FF D8 FF E0 xx xx 4A 46	ÿØÿà..JF	JPG/JPEG
	49 46 00		
Digital camera JPG using Exchangeable Image File Format (EXIF)	FF D8 FF E1 xx xx 45 78 69 66 00	ÿØÿá..Ex	JPG
Still Picture Interchange File Format (SPIFF)	FF D8 FF E8 xx xx 53 50 49 46 46 00	ÿØÿè..SP	JPG
	Samsung D807		JPEG
	0xFF-D8-FF-DB		
	Samsung D500		JPEG
	0xFF-D8-FF-E3		
	Canon EOS-1D		JPEG
	0xFF-D8-FF-E2		
Tagged Image File	49 20 49	I I	TIF/TIFF
Tagged Image File Format file (little endian, i.e., LSB first in the byte; Intel)	49 49 2A 00	II*.	TIF/TIFF
Tagged Image File Format file (big endian, i.e., LSB last in the byte; Motorola)	4D 4D 00 2A	MM.*	TIF/TIFF

File Format	File Signature/ Magic Number	ASCII Equivalent	Windows OS File Extension
Big TIFF files; Tagged Image File Format files >4 GB	4D 4D 00 2B	MM.+	TIF/TIFF
Portable Document Format file	25 50 44 46	%PDF	PDF
MP3 audio file	49 44 33	ID3	MP3
WAVE audio file	57 41 56 45 66 6D 74 20	RIFF....	WAV
Audio Video Interleave file	41 56 49 20 4C 49 53 54	AVI LIST	AVI
MPEG-4 video file	33 67 70 35	3gp5	MP4
MPEG video file	00 00 01 Bx	••••	MPG
Windows Media Video file	30 26 B2 75 8E 66 CF 11 A6 D9 00 AA 00 62 CE 6C	0&²u.fî.!Ù.ª.bÎl	WMV/ASF/WMA
Windows Cabinet file	4D 53 43 46	MSCF	CAB
Windows minidump file	4D 44 4D 50 93 A7	MDMP"§	DMP
Windows 64-bit memory dump	50 41 47 45 44 55 36 34	PAGEDU64	DMP
Windows memory dump	50 41 47 45 44 55 4D 50	PAGEDUMP	DMP
File shortcut	4C 00 00 00 01 14 02 00	L.......	LNK
Windows System file	FF FF FF FF	..ÿÿÿÿ	SYS
Windows Executable file	E8 or E9 or EB	è	SYS
Configuration file	19 0D B7 4D 64 CE 0D D1	·MdÎÑ	CFG
DOS Command file	4D 5A	MZ	COM
Windows Executable file	E8 or E9 or EB	è	COM

(Continued)

File Format	File Signature/ Magic Number	ASCII Equivalent	Windows OS File Extension
Windows Executable file	4D 5A	MZ	EXE
7-Zip compressed file	37 7A BC AF 27 1C	7z¼‾'.	7Z
PKZIP archive file	50 4B 03 04	PK..	ZIP
ZLock Pro encrypted ZIP	50 4B 03 04 14 00 01 00 63 00 00 00 00 00	PK...... c.....	ZIP
Mac OS X disk image	78	x	DMG
Disc image file	43 44 30 30 31	CD001	ISO
VideoVCD (GNU VCD Imager) file	45 4E 54 52 59 56 43 44 02 00 00 01 02 00 18 58	ENTRYVCD X	VCD
Virtual CD	45 4E 54 52 59 56 43 44 02 00 00 01 02 00 18 58	ENTRYVCD.......X	VCD
BitTorrent file	64 38 3A 61 6E 6E 6F 75 6E 63 65	d8:announce	TORRENT

APPENDIX 4C: MAGIC NUMBER DEFINITION*

A *magic number* is a number embedded at or near the beginning of a file that indicates its *file format* (i.e., the type of file it is). It is also sometimes referred to as a *file signature*.

Magic numbers are generally not visible to users. However, they can easily be seen with the use of a *HEX editor*, which is a specialized program that shows and allows modification of every byte in a file.

For common file formats, the numbers conveniently represent the names of the file types. Thus, for example, the magic number for image files conforming to the widely used GIF87a format in hexadecimal (i.e., base 16) terms is 0x474946383761, which when converted into ASCII is GIF87a. ASCII is the de facto standard used by computers and communications equipment for *character encoding* (i.e., associating alphabetic and other characters with numbers).

Likewise, the magic number for image files having the subsequently introduced GIF89a format is 0x474946383961. For both types of GIF (Graphic Interchange Format) files, the magic number occupies the first six bytes of the file. They are then followed by additional general information (i.e., *metadata*) about the file.

Similarly, a commonly used magic number for JPEG (Joint Photographic Experts Group) image files is 0x4A464946, which is the ASCII equivalent of JFIF (JPEG File Interchange Format). However, JPEG magic numbers are not the first bytes in the file; rather, they begin with the seventh byte. Additional examples include 0x4D546864 for MIDI (Musical Instrument Digital Interface) files and 0x425a6831415925 for bzip2 compressed files.

Magic numbers are not always the ASCII equivalent of the name of the file format, or even something similar. For example, in some types of files they represent the name or initials of the developer of that file format. Also, in at least one type of file the magic number represents the birthday of that format's developer.

Various programs make use of magic numbers to determine the file type. Among them is the *command line* (i.e., all-text mode) program named *file*, whose sole purpose is determining the file type.

Although they can be useful, magic numbers are not always sufficient to determine the file type. The main reason is that some file types do not have magic numbers, most notably plain text files, which include HTML (hypertext markup

---

* Bellevue Linux Users Group (BLUG), "Magic Number Definition," The Linux Information Project, August 21, 2006, retrieved January 2010, www.linfo.org/magic_number.html.

language), XHTML (extensible HTML), and XML (extensible markup language) files as well as source code.

Fortunately, there are also other means that can be used by programs to determine file types. One is by looking at a file's character set (e.g., ASCII) to see if it is a plain text file. If it is determined that a file is a plain text file, then it is often possible to further categorize it on the basis of the start of the text, such as <*html*> for HTML files and #! (the so-called *shebang*) for *script* (i.e., short program) files.

Another way to determine file type is through the use of filename extensions (e.g., *.exe, .html*, and *.jpg*), which are required on the various Microsoft operating systems but only to a small extent on Linux and other Unix-like operating systems. However, this approach has the disadvantage that it is relatively easy for a user to accidentally change or remove the extensions, in which case it becomes difficult to determine the file type and use the file.

Still another way that is possible in the case of some commonly used filesystems is through the use of file type information that is embedded in each file's metadata. In Unix-like operating systems, such metadata is contained in *inodes*, which are *data structures* (i.e., efficient ways of storing information) that store all the information about files except their names and their actual data.

Magic numbers are referred to as *magic* because the purpose and significance of their values are not apparent without some additional knowledge. The term *magic number* is also used in programming to refer to a constant that is employed for some specific purpose but whose presence or value is inexplicable without additional information.

APPENDIX 4D: COMPOUND DOCUMENT HEADER*

The first 512 bytes of the file may look like Table 4D.1.

TABLE 4D.1 Compound Document Header

00000000ₕ	D0 CF 11 E0 A1 B1 1A E1 00 00 00 00 00 00 00 00
00000010ₕ	00 00 00 00 00 00 00 00 3B 00 03 00 FE FF 09 00
00000020ₕ	06 00 00 00 00 00 00 00 00 00 00 00 01 00 00 00
00000030ₕ	0A 00 00 00 00 00 00 00 00 10 00 00 02 00 00 00
00000040ₕ	01 00 00 00 FE FF FF FF 00 00 00 00 00 00 00 00
00000050ₕ	FF FF FF FF FF FF FF FF FF FF FF FF FF FF FF FF
00000060ₕ	FF FF FF FF FF FF FF FF FF FF FF FF FF FF FF FF
00000070ₕ	FF FF FF FF FF FF FF FF FF FF FF FF FF FF FF FF
00000080ₕ	FF FF FF FF FF FF FF FF FF FF FF FF FF FF FF FF
00000090ₕ	FF FF FF FF FF FF FF FF FF FF FF FF FF FF FF FF
000000A0ₕ	FF FF FF FF FF FF FF FF FF FF FF FF FF FF FF FF
000000B0ₕ	FF FF FF FF FF FF FF FF FF FF FF FF FF FF FF FF
000000C0ₕ	FF FF FF FF FF FF FF FF FF FF FF FF FF FF FF FF
000000D0ₕ	FF FF FF FF FF FF FF FF FF FF FF FF FF FF FF FF
000000E0ₕ	FF FF FF FF FF FF FF FF FF FF FF FF FF FF FF FF
000000F0ₕ	FF FF FF FF FF FF FF FF FF FF FF FF FF FF FF FF
00000100ₕ	FF FF FF FF FF FF FF FF FF FF FF FF FF FF FF FF
00000110ₕ	FF FF FF FF FF FF FF FF FF FF FF FF FF FF FF FF
00000120ₕ	FF FF FF FF FF FF FF FF FF FF FF FF FF FF FF FF
00000130ₕ	FF FF FF FF FF FF FF FF FF FF FF FF FF FF FF FF
00000140ₕ	FF FF FF FF FF FF FF FF FF FF FF FF FF FF FF FF
00000150ₕ	FF FF FF FF FF FF FF FF FF FF FF FF FF FF FF FF
00000160ₕ	FF FF FF FF FF FF FF FF FF FF FF FF FF FF FF FF
00000170ₕ	FF FF FF FF FF FF FF FF FF FF FF FF FF FF FF FF
00000180ₕ	FF FF FF FF FF FF FF FF FF FF FF FF FF FF FF FF
00000190ₕ	FF FF FF FF FF FF FF FF FF FF FF FF FF FF FF FF
000001A0ₕ	FF FF FF FF FF FF FF FF FF FF FF FF FF FF FF FF

---

* D. Rentz, D. "Documentation of the Microsoft Compound Document File Format," OpenOffice .org Source Project, August 7, 2007, retrieved February 2010, http://sc.openoffice.org/comp-docfileformat.pdf.

000001B0$_H$	FF FF FF FF FF FF FF FF FF FF FF FF FF FF FF FF
000001C0$_H$	FF FF FF FF FF FF FF FF FF FF FF FF FF FF FF FF
000001D0$_H$	FF FF FF FF FF FF FF FF FF FF FF FF FF FF FF FF
000001E0$_H$	FF FF FF FF FF FF FF FF FF FF FF FF FF FF FF FF
000001F0$_H$	FF FF FF FF FF FF FF FF FF FF FF FF FF FF FF FF

Examining the details of this Compound Document Header discloses the following: eight (8) bytes containing the fixed compound document file identifier (Table 4D.2).

TABLE 4D.2   Document File Identifier

00000000$_H$	D0 CF 11 E0 A1 B1 1A E1 00 00 00 00 00 00 00 00

Sixteen (16) bytes containing a unique identifier, followed by four (4) bytes containing a revision number and a version number (Table 4D.3).

TABLE 4D.3   Unique Identifier, Revision Number and Version Number

00000000$_H$	D0 CF 11 E0 A1 B1 1A E1 00 00 00 00 00 00 00 00
00000010$_H$	00 00 00 00 00 00 00 00 3B 00 03 00 FE FF 09 00

Two (2) bytes containing the byte order identifier. It should always consist of the byte sequence FEH FFH (Table 4D.4).

TABLE 4D.4   Byte Order Identifier

00000010$_H$	00 00 00 00 00 00 00 00 3B 00 03 00 FE FF 09 00

Two (2) bytes containing the size of sectors, two (2) bytes containing the size of short-sectors. The sector size is 512 bytes, and the short-sector size is 64 bytes here (Table 4D.5).

TABLE 4D.5   Size of Sectors

00000010$_H$	00 00 00 00 00 00 00 00 3B 00 03 00 FE FF 09 00
00000020$_H$	06 00 00 00 00 00 00 00 00 00 00 00 01 00 00 00

Ten (10) bytes without valid data can be ignored (Table 4D.6).

TABLE 4D.6 Bytes without Valid Data

00000020$_H$	06 00 00 00 00 00 00 00 00 00 00 00 01 00 00 00

Four (4) bytes containing the number of sectors used by the sector allocation table (SAT). The SAT uses only one sector here (Table 4D.7).

TABLE 4D.7 Number of Sectors Used by the Sector Allocation Table

00000020$_H$	06 00 00 00 00 00 00 00 00 00 00 00 01 00 00 00

Four (4) bytes containing the SecID of the first sector used by the directory. The directory starts at sector 10 here (Table 4D.8).

TABLE 4D.8 SecID of the First Sector Used by the Directory

00000030$_H$	0A 00 00 00 00 00 00 00 00 10 00 00 02 00 00 00

Four (4) bytes without valid data can be ignored (Table 4D.9).

TABLE 4D.9 Bytes without Valid Data

00000030$_H$	0A 00 00 00 00 00 00 00 00 10 00 00 02 00 00 00

Four (4) bytes containing the minimum size of standard streams. This size is 00001000H = 4096 bytes here (Table 4D.10).

TABLE 4D.10 Minimum Size of Standard Streams

00000030$_H$	0A 00 00 00 00 00 00 00 00 10 00 00 02 00 00 00

Four (4) bytes containing the SecID of the first sector of the short-sector allocation table (Table 4D.11).

TABLE 4D.11 SecID of the First Sector of the Short-Sector Allocation Table

00000030$_H$	0A 00 00 00 00 00 00 00 00 10 00 00 02 00 00 00

Four (4) bytes containing the number of sectors used by the SSAT. In this example, the SSAT starts at sector 2 and uses one sector (Table 4D.12).

TABLE 4D.12 Number of Sectors Used by the SSAT

00000040$_H$	01 00 00 00 FE FF FF FF 00 00 00 00 00 00 00 00

Four (4) bytes containing the SecID of the first sector of the master sector allocation table, followed by four (4) bytes containing the number of sectors used by the MSAT. The SecID here is −2, which states that there is no extended MSAT in this file (Table 4D.13).

TABLE 4D.13 SecID of the First Sector of the Master Sector Allocation Table, Followed by Four (4) Bytes Containing the Number of Sectors Used by the MSAT

00000040$_H$	01 00 00 00 FE FF FF FF 00 00 00 00 00 00 00 00

436 bytes containing the first 109 SecIDs of the MSAT. Only the first SecID is valid, because the SAT uses only one sector (see earlier).

Therefore, all remaining SecIDs are set to the special Free SecID with the value −1.

The only sector used by the SAT is sector 0 (Table 4D.14).

TABLE 4D.14 436 Bytes Containing the First 109 SecIDs of the MSAT

00000040$_H$	01 00 00 00 FE FF FF FF 00 00 00 00 00 00 00 00
00000050$_H$	FF FF FF FF FF FF FF FF FF FF FF FF FF FF FF FF
00000060$_H$	FF FF FF FF FF FF FF FF FF FF FF FF FF FF FF FF

(Continued)

TABLE 4D.14 (*Continued*)

00000070H	FF FF FF FF FF FF FF FF FF FF FF FF FF FF FF FF
00000080H	FF FF FF FF FF FF FF FF FF FF FF FF FF FF FF FF
00000090H	FF FF FF FF FF FF FF FF FF FF FF FF FF FF FF FF
000000A0H	FF FF FF FF FF FF FF FF FF FF FF FF FF FF FF FF
000000B0H	FF FF FF FF FF FF FF FF FF FF FF FF FF FF FF FF
000000C0H	FF FF FF FF FF FF FF FF FF FF FF FF FF FF FF FF
000000D0H	FF FF FF FF FF FF FF FF FF FF FF FF FF FF FF FF
000000E0H	FF FF FF FF FF FF FF FF FF FF FF FF FF FF FF FF
000000F0H	FF FF FF FF FF FF FF FF FF FF FF FF FF FF FF FF
00000100H	FF FF FF FF FF FF FF FF FF FF FF FF FF FF FF FF
00000110H	FF FF FF FF FF FF FF FF FF FF FF FF FF FF FF FF
00000120H	FF FF FF FF FF FF FF FF FF FF FF FF FF FF FF FF
00000130H	FF FF FF FF FF FF FF FF FF FF FF FF FF FF FF FF
00000140H	FF FF FF FF FF FF FF FF FF FF FF FF FF FF FF FF
00000150H	FF FF FF FF FF FF FF FF FF FF FF FF FF FF FF FF
00000160H	FF FF FF FF FF FF FF FF FF FF FF FF FF FF FF FF
00000170H	FF FF FF FF FF FF FF FF FF FF FF FF FF FF FF FF
00000180H	FF FF FF FF FF FF FF FF FF FF FF FF FF FF FF FF
00000190H	FF FF FF FF FF FF FF FF FF FF FF FF FF FF FF FF
000001A0H	FF FF FF FF FF FF FF FF FF FF FF FF FF FF FF FF
000001B0H	FF FF FF FF FF FF FF FF FF FF FF FF FF FF FF FF
000001C0H	FF FF FF FF FF FF FF FF FF FF FF FF FF FF FF FF
000001D0H	FF FF FF FF FF FF FF FF FF FF FF FF FF FF FF FF
000001E0H	FF FF FF FF FF FF FF FF FF FF FF FF FF FF FF FF
000001F0H	FF FF FF FF FF FF FF FF FF FF FF FF FF FF FF FF

CHAPTER FIVE

The Boot Process and the Master Boot Record (MBR)

I N CHAPTER 4, OUR DISCUSSIONS further examined HEX. Also discussed was the relevance of HEX when examining file signature metadata. We noted that some data contained within a file cannot be viewed in a legible or searchable text format such as ASCII or Unicode, specifically data contained within file headers, such as the file signature, thus the necessity of a working knowledge of HEX.

This was made even more apparent as we explored complex files including compound and compressed files, files that contain even more data which is not legible in a text based code, specifically the instructions on how to assemble the complex file. In explaining these file structures we noted that these files needed to be "mounted" in order for the data to be "extracted" or "assembled."

As we discussed previously, mounting a file is the process of making a file ready to be used by compatible software. The process described by the word "mount" may very well derive its name from a similar process that occurs on a larger, overarching scale with a computer's operating system. This "system-wide" file-mounting process must occur in order for any data contained within a hard drive to be made accessible, and to be acted upon.

Mounting is the process of taking the raw data contained on a hard drive or other storage media and making it accessible, legible, and useable information. In essence, it is the process of taking the magnetically stored 0s and 1s that are understandable by the machine and converting those to folders and files that are understandable by the machine's human operator. It is this mounting process, which identifies or defines the boundaries of the computer's data or *file system*.

A computer needs to be operational (powered on and running) in order for it to mount a file system. Regardless of whether it's the file system of the primary hard drive, the file system contained on a CD, or the file system of an external USB hard drive, a computer must be on and running for it to mount the file system.

A computer when first turned on needs to mount a "primary" file system first, a file system containing an operating system by which the computer can be operated. This being the case, and in order to better understand a file system and its structure, it's best to start from the beginning.

Before a computer can mount its own file system, it must be powered on. The process of turning a computer "on" is oftentimes referred to as "booting up."

This "booting-up" process and the associated Master Boot Record (MBR), and their importance in understanding the essentials of the cyber forensic process, are the subjects of this chapter.

At times in this chapter we venture specifically into the *Basic Input Output System (BIOS)* as it pertains to a Windows/IBM PC-based system. In fact, the term BIOS was originally used to describe the startup program of IBM PC-based systems. It has since adopted a broader, nonvendor-specific connotation. All computer models, from IBM compatibles to Unix to MACs, have a BIOS or BIOS type function.

All systems must boot up and all systems have file systems. The boot process as we describe in this chapter may at times target an IBM compatible Windows machine, but the boot process concepts are the same across most operating systems.

The objective in Chapter 5 is to explore the boot process, the BIOS as an element in that boot process, and the overall relationship and relevance of these to cyber forensics.

The reader, aware that there are many operating systems and thus various boot processes, is encouraged to seek out specific vendor documents or specialty, single-focused texts that address the operating system associated with the computer under examination, and to use the material presented in this chapter to establish a basis for an overall understanding of the boot process, BIOS, and the interrelationship to the cyber forensic process.

BOOTING UP

The process of turning on a system, irrespective of flipping the power switch to "on" and sending electric power to the machine, is often referred to as "booting up." "Booting up the computer" is a common phrase used to describe the process by which the code necessary to bring the computer to life is initiated.

Being that a computer is logically in the "off" mode prior to being turned on, the start-up process was originally compared to pulling oneself up by one's own bootstraps, ergo the term "boot"—starting the machine up from an off state.

Thus, the code that allows a computer to pull itself "up" (i.e., to start itself), has since retained the iconic name "bootstrap code." Bootstrap code is essentially a catalyst, a small program used to initiate or start a larger program.

The concept and details of file systems and their relationship to the cyber forensic process are addressed in a later chapter. For now, let us go back to the beginning and our examination of the boot process.

PRIMARY FUNCTIONS OF THE BOOT PROCESS

Power On Self Test or *POST*, for short, is a self-diagnostic program used to perform a single test of the CPU, RAM, and various input/output (I/O) devices.

The reader should be aware that the boot process does not necessarily need to directly precede the mounting of a file system.

A file system can be mounted independently of the boot process and the file system can reside elsewhere other than the bootable hard drive. File systems can exist on external USB drives, other areas of the hard drive, and CDs. File systems can be mounted well after a system has been "booted up." This can be accomplished via various software, including but not limited to specific forensic software.

If file systems are independent of the boot process, why cover the boot process here? To best explain file systems it is best to explain where file systems reside: in partitions and volumes. To explain partitions and volumes we need to first explain how partitions and volumes are "mounted" or "booted."

The computer hardware is tested to ensure the hardware is functioning properly before the process of loading the operating system is initialized. The POST is performed at startup when the computer is first turned on and is stored in *ROM* BIOS.

BIOS

The BIOS prepares the system for a "known state," so that software stored on compatible media can be loaded, executed, and given control of the PC.

As explained earlier, the term BIOS was originally coined to describe the boot loading firmware on IBM PC compatible computers. However, the acronym has taken on a more encompassing meaning, and is now used to describe the boot loading firmware of other non-IBM-compatible Operating Systems. Its major functions include:

- Enumerating, testing, and initializing peripheral devices (keyboard, mouse, disk drives, printers, video cards, etc.).
- Loading the operating system (primary file system) into main memory.

After start-up, BIOS programs may manage data flow between the operating system (OS) and the peripherals, so neither the OS nor the application programs need to know the details of the peripherals (such as hardware addresses).

Loading of this firmware is, in part, necessary to prepare the machine into a known state, a state of operational readiness, so that software stored on compatible media can be loaded, executed, and given control of the PC. Once the operating system is loaded into memory there is the potential for data to be saved, stored, altered, or otherwise changed.

At this point in the boot process, if a disk is not *write protected* then the files being accessed on that file system can and will be altered. It is extremely important to understand that when files are accessed changes occur; *metadata* such as accessed times and modified times are altered.

BIOS/CMOS Setup Menu

BIOS setup is a program used to display and edit user configurable settings in the BIOS of a PC. On earlier PCs, users had to change a setting when a new drive was added, but auto-detect features were later added. Although many settings are quite arcane and only changed by experienced technicians, users might want to change the boot order of their PCs.

The BIOS setup has also been called the "CMOS setup" or the "CMOS RAM," because user settings were initially held in a tiny, battery-backed *CMOS memory* bank that is part of the PC's real-time clock circuit. Subsequently, more user configuration settings were stored in the BIOS flash memory.

A computer can be made to boot from almost any applicable media such as a floppy, zip disk, CD, DVD, USB device, external hard drive, or the machine's own internal hard drive. The BIOS enumerates these drives, and their respective boot sequence/order. In other words, the BIOS determines which boot device will load; this is referred to as "first boot sequence."

The "first boot sequence" is the peripheral order the computer uses to look for the operating system. If it does not find a bootable OS in the first device, it looks to the second and so on. Although computers typically boot from the primary hard disk, the first boot sequence enables it to load a different operating system when necessary by placing a bootable disk into the drive. The first boot sequence is configured in the BIOS and can be changed as needed.

In the early days of personal computers, the floppy disk was chosen as the first device and the hard disk second. Subsequently, the CD-ROM is typically chosen to be the first in line, followed by the floppy and hard disk. Only one device will be accessed and loaded under this boot-up process.

The BIOS, however, can be accessed and changes to the BIOS can be made. These changes take place on a ROM chip and as a result, do not cause anything to be written to the hard drive, where our evidence may be residing.

An understanding of the BIOS is important in the forensic world, as there may be a need to enter the BIOS as part of a cyber forensic investigation. Some reasons include:

▪ Verify and validate the system clock. The system clock in most machines is not 100 percent accurate; the system clock can potentially loose a number of minutes each day, or stop incrementing the time when the system is turned off. (Refer to Chapter 11 where we discuss the critical role and importance of time in the cyber forensic process.)

  The most common cause of this problem is the *CMOS battery*, which also backs up the date and time so it isn't lost when the machine is turned off. A weak CMOS battery can lead to problems with the real-time clock, even if the battery isn't weak enough to cause the loss of BIOS settings. Some motherboards apparently disable the clock as a power-saving measure when the battery voltage gets low. Of course, sometimes the problem with the clock is simply that it is inaccurate.[1]

▪ As explained in the BIOS setup menu section, a computer may need to be booted to a stand-alone boot disk. A technical problem with the integrity of the computer's hard drive may require an alternative boot device, such as an emergency repair disk. Perhaps the most important reason for changing the boot sequence is to prevent the computer from booting up the evidence drive. Why not boot to the evidence drive? Read on!

FORENSIC IMAGING AND EVIDENCE COLLECTION

A digital forensic investigator, as with any investigator, will at times be responsible for collecting and capturing evidence.

Understanding that data can be written to a hard drive (evidence) during the boot process is critical as this process alters the evidence. Knowing when and how data is altered on a piece of evidence (hard drive or otherwise) is not only important when investigating evidence, but also important when acquiring evidence.

As we have discussed, during the boot process of the primary file system (or *partition*) data is, in most cases, written to the hard drive, such that dates are changed and files are written and altered. It is critical to a sound investigation not to alter evidence for which you have been entrusted to image in a forensically sound manner.

Booting up a computer could very well contaminate the integrity of the data contained within the evidence (hard drive). It would be analogous to a homicide detective stomping through blood splatter at a crime scene. Even if the detective could explain away his/her foot prints, at the very least, the quality of his/her work and competency would be called into question.

A good defense lawyer could quickly and easily discredit an investigation. Questions may arise, such as, "what else did you alter at the crime scene?" and "with such sloppy work, do you even know what other evidence you may have altered?" As you can imagine, even if such mistakes can be explained by an investigator, they can have drastic negative effects and not only prevent critical evidence from being admitted as evidence, but also have the potential to ruin an investigator's career.

So in an effort to avoid writing data to a piece of evidence an investigator will usually connect a *write blocker* directly to the evidence hard drive. A write blocker will allow the drive to be powered on and copied, but will block any writing attempts (accidently or intentionally) directly to the evidence drive. (Refer to Chapter 10, Figure 10.15 for an example of a write blocker used to protect original evidence during this process.)

Examples of some write-blocking techniques, although perhaps a bit dated for today's status of technology include:

- Cassette tapes had a plastic tab that could be broken off to block the write or taping feature on that cassette (See Chapter 10, Figure 10.12.)

- 3½-inch floppy disks with a little plastic tab which could be positioned to write block. (See Chapter 10, Figure 10.13.)
- A CD player without burning abilities is a write blocker, as it cannot write or burn.
- An LP and record player.

A cyber forensic investigator essentially does the same thing when confronted with a hard drive. The only difference is the write blocking equipment is not found at the corner electronic store and can be costly. The investigator essentially connects one end of the write blocker to the Source (evidence hard drive assuming removal from system) and the other end to a Target (storage area—e.g., hard drive, CD, DVD, USB device, etc.).

The write blocker then allows for the hard drive to be powered up and read, but not written to. Data, usually at the bit level as binary, is then "copied" from an evidence drive to the storage area.

In a theoretically perfect environment a hard drive is simply removed from the computer and its potential latent data evidence acquired independently, as described.

However, sometimes this is not possible or practical, as in the case where the hard drive may be so imbedded in a laptop that removing it would require dismantling the laptop, as with some MACs or Sony VAIOs. Other cases that would make removal of the hard drive a less than viable alternative include:

1. A "state-of-the-art" computer containing new hard drive technology with a cutting edge bus adapter (a port which receives data cable) for which there are no write blocker adapters.
2. An older computer with a hard drive for which an adapter may not exist.
3. A server may have multiple hard disk drives (HDD) configured as a single logical hard drive (as in a *RAID array*). It would be less complicated to acquire this as a single drive (logically) versus removing and acquiring each drive within the array individually, especially if an adapter for a peculiar HDD is not at hand.

Whatever the reason, removing the hard drive and connecting it to a write blocker for imaging may not be an option. When this is the case the computer needs to be powered on, without booting to the hard drive's operating system thereby avoiding the destruction or tainting of potential evidence. Understanding the BIOS may be extremely beneficial if not imperative when collecting this evidence.

The boot sequence is altered so that the BIOS hands control over to the investigator's operating system, found on the floppy disk, USB, or compact disc, and not to the operating system found on the hard disk, that is, the evidence. In other words, this allows the system to continue booting via the operating system or utility contained within the boot disk, not relying on use of the internal operating system that is stored on the machine's internal hard drive. This also allows the cyber forensic investigator access to the data contained on the system without altering the evidence contained within the hard drive.

 ## SUMMARIZING THE BIOS

Some of the BIOS functions or components found in many systems include:

- **POST.** Test computer hardware, ensuring hardware is properly functioning before starting the process of loading the operating system.
- **Bootstrap Loader.** The process of locating the operating system. If a capable operating system is located, BIOS will pass the control to it.
- **BIOS.** Software/Drivers that interface between the operating system and your hardware. When running DOS or Windows you are using complete BIOS support.
- **BIOS/CMOS Setup.** A configuration program that allows you to configure hardware settings including system settings such as computer passwords, time, and date.[2]

 ## BIOS SETUP UTILITY: STEP BY STEP

The BIOS is accessed at startup. Soon after a PC is turned on, a short text message typically passes by very quickly on screen indicating which key to press (usually the DEL, F1, or F2 key). A prompt will appear on the screen stating something similar to that shown in Figure 5.1.

Starting

Press F2 to enter SETUP, F12 for Network Boot, ESC for Boot Menu

FIGURE 5.1 Setting Up Phoenix BIOS

At this point, hitting F2 for this particular IBM compatible system will interrupt the boot process and enter "BIOS." Different systems will have different keys or key strokes to enter their respective "BIOS."

After hitting F2 (or the appropriate function key (e.g., F12, F8, F10, ESC, or DEL), you will be shown the main screen of the BIOS setup utility, which will enable you to access each of the other sections of the BIOS. Figure 5.2 shows a typical BIOS setup screen—Main Tab, for a popular BIOS product, PhoenixBIOS. As we can see, the system time and date can be verified and/or altered.

In Figure 5.3, we see the Boot tab. This is where the boot device sequence can be changed. In this example, we see "removable devices" as the first boot device; the hard drive is the second and the CD-ROM is the third.

The instructions for changing the sequence are usually found on the tab. Here we can see that the positive or plus sign (+) will move the device up in sequence and the negative or minus sign (−) will move the device down in sequence. So, in order to boot this system from a boot disk (CD) the CD-ROM will need to be moved to the top of the boot order.

Figures 5.4 and 5.5 are other examples of BIOS setup menus that you may encounter.

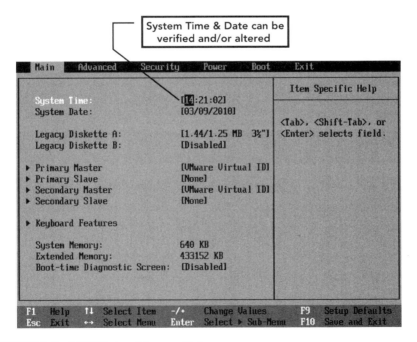

FIGURE 5.2   BIOS Setup Menu—Main

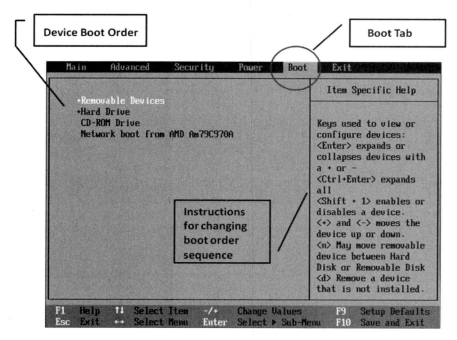

FIGURE 5.3 BIOS Setup Menu—Boot

There are many BIOS versions and varieties, thus the BIOS screen shots shown here may not look similar to the BIOS screens on your system. Also, there are many ways to enter the BIOS—usually F2, but not always! *Do your research! Be very careful!*

You do not want to skip the BIOS and let the Operating System boot up, resulting in files being accessed and being written to and ultimately changed!

Phase Two of the Boot Process

Once all of the tests ensure that the hardware is properly functioning and before starting the process of loading the operating system, the physical drives are enumerated and the boot code attempts to find and load an operating system or software utility. Once this has transpired the boot process terminates and the primary drive is active.

Writing and changes to the primary drive begin to occur!

Remember, intercepting and accessing the BIOS halts the boot process and prevents the boot code from accessing the active (or primary) drive.

If the boot processes' "second phase" were allowed to continue with the HDD as the primary boot device, changes would be made to that hard drive, and the

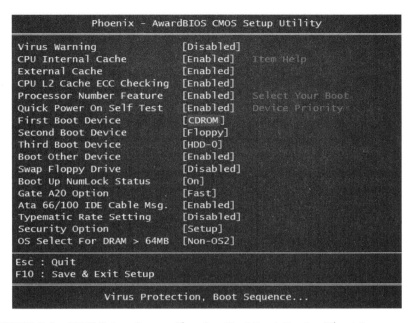

FIGURE 5.4 BIOS Setup Screen Showing First Boot Device (Phoenix Software)

```
                    Dell - Dimension 8100
              Intel Pentium 4 Processor: 1.30 Ghz
                LEVEL 2 Cache: 256 KB Integrated

   System Time ...................
   System Date ...................

   Primary Drive 0 ...............
   Primary Drive 1 ...............
   Secondary Drive 0 ............
   Secondary Drive 1 ............

   Boot Sequence .................

      * 1. IDE CD-ROM Device
      * 2. Hard-Disk Drive C:

          SPACE to enable/disable | +,- to move down/up

   System Memory ................
   AGP Aperture .................
   CPU Information ..............

        Up/Down to Select | SPACE +,- to Change | ESC to Exit
```

FIGURE 5.5 Dell Dimension BIOS Setup Screen

result would be an unintended manipulation of data on that hard drive, thus the potential for the destruction or alteration of data, leading to the loss of data integrity in relation to the evidentiary value of data contained on that hard drive.

If the HDD is first in the boot sequence, then the boot code looks there first. Knowing how the BIOS is configured, and the identification of the first boot device, is an essential piece of information for the cyber forensic investigator, in the investigator's efforts to access the hard drive to be examined while always ensuring the integrity of the data collected.

THE MASTER BOOT RECORD (MBR)

It is in this second phase of booting that the BIOS contained within these Intel-based computers (or IBM compatible computers) will load the first sector of the hard drive into memory.

This first sector is called the *Master Boot Record (MBR)*. The boot code looks to the very first sector of the default drive (the first drive on the list in the boot sequence in BIOS; see Figure 5.3). This first sector contains the MBR or Master Boot Record.

The MBR contains three components, which we discuss in detail:

1. A small amount of executable code called the master boot code.
2. The disk signature.
3. The partition table for the disk.

The boot loader works by looking for the active partition in the partition table and loading the first sector in that partition. That sector is known as the Partition Boot Record. The Partition Boot Record will then start the process of loading the operating system's kernel.[2]

The boot process (code) searches the available drives (already identified in the BIOS) for an operating system. Once found, the operating system tests for the disk signature (a unique number at offset 0x01B8, which identifies the disk to the operating system).

The last two sectors of the MBR contain a two-byte structure called a *signature word* or end of sector marker, which is always set to 0x55AA (HEX 55AA). A signature word also marks the end of an extended boot record (EBR) and the boot sector. For a validly configured/bootable drive, HEX 55AA must be found in the last two bytes of this sector. The boot code searches for a bootable drive, which is identified by the value 0x55AA.

The master boot code performs the following activities:

1. Scans the partition table for the active partition.
2. Finds the starting sector of the active partition.
3. Loads a copy of the boot sector from the active partition into memory.
4. Transfers control to the executable code in the boot sector.

If the master boot code cannot complete these functions, the system may display one of the following error messages:

- Invalid partition table
- Error loading operating system
- Missing operating system[3]

Figure 5.6 shows a visual/graphical representation of the *First Sectors* of a physical hard drive as depicted by the forensic software Encase. Be advised this is *only* a visual representation of the physical construct of the hard drive.

Each square represents a single sector. How many bytes per sector? Remember from our discussion in Chapter 4, a sector contains 512 bytes.

Figure 5.7 shows further detail of the first sectors of a physical hard drive, indicating the positioning of the MBR, the *Volume Boot Record* (VBR), and the remaining allocated space on the hard drive.

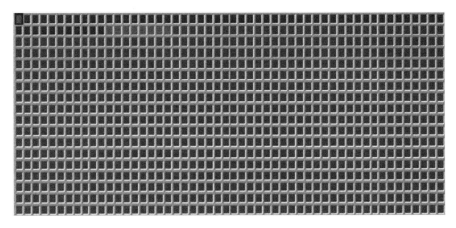

FIGURE 5.6 Graphical Representation of the First Sectors of a Physical Hard Drive

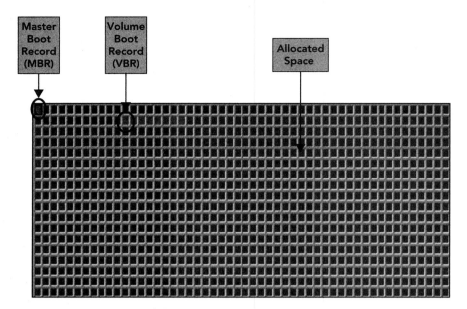

FIGURE 5.7 Location of the MBR and VBR in the First Sectors of a Physical Hard Drive

It is important to note that each square shown here represents a single sector (512 bytes).

Remember, that the MBR's signature bytes are the two final bytes of the first sector, and they are used as a simple validation of the MBR's contents.[4]

What's a HEX Editor? Let's Review

Certain concepts need to be understood when reading a HEX editor:

1. ACSII (discussed in Chapter 2)
2. HEX (discussed in Chapter 3)
3. Offset (discussed next)

What Is an Offset?

In computer science, an offset within an array or other data structure object is an integer indicating the distance (displacement) from the beginning of the object up (a *base address*) until a given element or point, presumably within the same object. The concept of distance is valid only if all elements of the object are the same size (typically given in bytes or words).

In this (original) meaning of offset, only the basic address unit, usually the 8-bit byte, is used to specify the offset's size. In this context an offset is sometimes called a *relative address*. The *absolute address* is derived by adding it (the relative address) to the base address.

For example, in Figure 5.8, given an array of characters A containing the contents abcdef, one can say that the element containing the letter "c" has an *offset* of 2 from the element containing "a."

A HEX editor is a computer program used to view and edit binary files. A binary file is a file that contains data in machine-readable form (as opposed to a text file that can be read by a human; see Figure 5.9).[5]

HEX editors allow editing the raw data contents of a file, instead of other programs which attempt to interpret the data for you. Since a HEX editor is used to edit binary files, they are sometimes called a binary editor or a binary file editor. If you edit a file with a HEX editor, you are said to HEX edit the file, and the process of using a HEX editor is called HEX editing.

A typical HEX editor has three areas: an address area on the left, a hexa-decimal area in the center, and a character area on the right (see Figure 5.10).[6]

a	b	c	d	e	f
0	1	2	3	4	5

FIGURE 5.8 Array of Characters A Containing "abcdef"

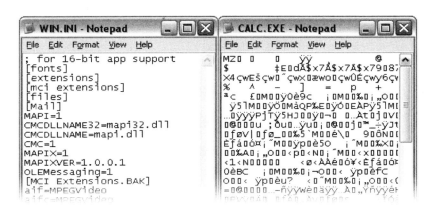

FIGURE 5.9 A Text File Loaded in Notepad on the Left (Human Readable) versus a Binary (Machine Readable) File on the Right

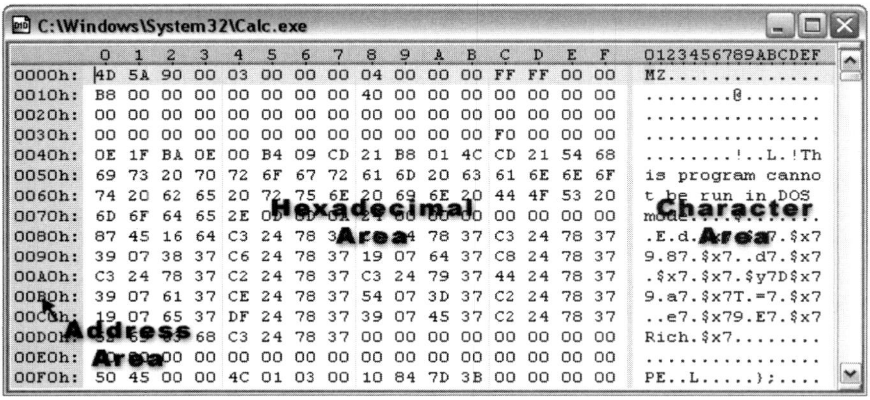

FIGURE 5.10 A HEX Editor with Addresses on the Left, a Hexadecimal Area in the Middle, and a Character Area on the Right

The left pane (address area) displays the byte offset (16 bytes/row), the middle pane (hexadecimal area) displays the two-digit value comprising each byte, and the right pane (character area) shows the ASCII equivalent of each byte of data.

A HEX editor is used mainly for two specific reasons:

1. Analyzing file structure. You can't see the bytes stored in a file using a regular application to open it. You may need this knowledge to write an application that will interpret the contents of the file. (Cyber forensic investigator's objective)
2. Editing file contents. This also requires knowledge of the exact file structure. If you don't know how watermarks are stored in an MPEG file, for example, you could not do anything about them. (Programmer's objective)

In Figure 5.11, our example shows that there are 16 bytes in each line, the first line contains bytes 0 through 15; the second line's offset is 16.

Recall we were discussing the MBR before we took a short deviation to look closer at the HEX editor and the concept of "offsets." Let us continue on now with further discussion of the MBR. Recapping, the MBR contains three main components:

1. The boot loader
2. The partition table
3. The signature bytes

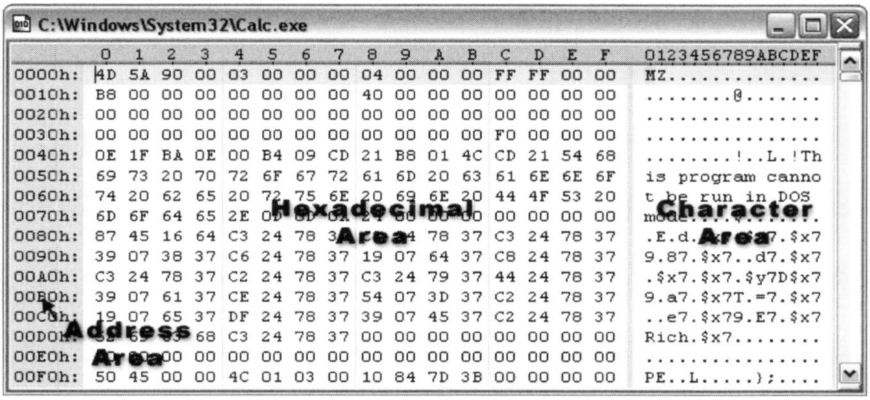

FIGURE 5.11 Common HEX Editor Layout

The *boot loader* (i.e., bootstrapping) typically loads the main operating system for the computer.

The MBR's boot loader consists of code that the BIOS loads to boot an operating system. The boot loader works by looking for the active partition in the *partition table* and loading the first sector in that partition.

That sector is known as the *Partition Boot Record* and usually (but not always) is an OS's boot record. The Partition Boot Record will then start the process of loading the operating system's kernel.

Figure 5.12 displays a graphical representation of the MBR, with the boot loader code highlighted in gray.

While the boot loader area is always 446 bytes (Byte Offset 0–445), the number of bytes that are actually used for the boot loader code varies with the program that is installed in this area. An MBR created with DOS's FDISK uses a smaller program in the boot loader area so you will see more 00h bytes.

The partition table, which begins immediately after the boot loader area (shown highlighted in gray in Figure 5.13) starts with a value of 0x80 that represents the active (bootable) partition. It contains four descriptors that are 16 bytes long each. The descriptors represent the logical information needed to access a partition on the drive.

The signature bytes should always be 0x55AA in a valid MBR (shown highlighted in gray in Figure 5.19). It is unlikely that the signature bytes alone will change without other parts of the MBR changing as well. If the signature bytes are not 0x55AA, your hard drive will not boot until they are changed to this hexadecimal number.[8]

BOOT LOADER CODE   MASTER BOOT RECORD

																	ASCII
000	FA	EB	01	00	8C	C8	8E	D8	8E	C0	8E	D0	BC	00	7C	FB	:	Ú.ë.. ▨È▨Ø▨À▨Đ¼|û
016	BE	00	7C	BF	00	06	B9	00	01	F3	A5	E9	00	8A	BE	B2	:	¾¿ ¹....ó¥é ▨¾²
032	07	38	0C	74	3C	BB	00	08	51	0F	B6	0C	BA	80	00	E8	:	8 t<» Q ¶ ° ▨è
048	A5	00	59	72	21	46	FE	C5	81	C3	00	02	38	0C	75	E8	:	¥Yr!FþÅ ▨Ã 8 uè
064	33	C0	BE	00	08	03	04	46	46	E2	FA	3B	06	B0	07	0F	:	3À¾
080	85	0E	00	E9	4C	02	BE	10	07	E8	6E	00	BE	6A	07	E8	:	ßEä¾; ën¾j ë
096	03	BE	42	07	E8	63	00	33	C0	CD	16	33	C0	BF	00	08	:	
112	B9	00	7C	F3	AB	BE	AE	07	B9	04	00	83	C6	10	80	3C	:	¾¡.▨¡¾Å¡ 3À¿▨Æ ▨<
128	80	74	0B	38	2C	75	02	E2	F2	BE	F6	06	EB	37	8B	D6	:	t 8,u âò¾ö ë7 ▨Ö
144	49	74	09	83	C6	10	38	2C	75	EF	E2	F7	BB	00	7C	8B	:	It ▨Æ 8,uïâ÷»▨
160	F2	8B	14	8B	4C	02	E8	2E	00	72	12	8B	FB	81	BD	FE	:	ò▨ ▨L.è.r ▨û▨½þ
176	01	55	AA	75	0D	B8	50	00	8B	EE	06	53	CB	BE	10	07	:	..UªuᵖP ▨ SË¾...
192	EB	03	BE	27	07	E8	02	00	EB	FE	B4	0E	BB	07	00	AC	:	ë
208	CD	10	38	3C	75	F9	C3	60	BF	05	00	B8	01	02	CD	13	:	▨ëëΆ`¿ y ¬í
224	73	0A	4F	74	06	33	C0	CD	13	EB	F0	F9	61	C3	00	00	:	s.Ot 3Àì ëðùaÃ
240	00	00	00	00	00	00	00	0A	0D	50	61	72	74	69	69	6F	:	.... Partitio
256	6E	20	74	61	62	6C	65	20	69	6E	76	61	6C	69	64	00	:	n table invalid.
272	0A	0D	45	72	72	6F	72	20	72	65	61	64	69	6E	67	20	:	..Error reading
288	73	65	63	74	6F	72	00	0A	0D	4F	70	65	72	61	74	69	:	sector...Operati
304	6E	67	20	73	79	73	74	65	6D	20	6D	69	73	73	69	6E	:	ng system missin
320	67	00	4D	42	52	20	63	6F	72	72	75	70	74	21	20	52	:	gMBR corrupt! R
336	75	6E	20	42	6F	6F	74	4D	61	67	69	63	20	63	6F	6E	:	un BootMagic con
352	66	69	67	75	72	61	74	69	6F	6E	0A	0D	50	72	65	73	:	figuration..Pres
368	73	20	61	6E	79	20	6B	65	79	20	74	6F	20	62	6F	6F	:	s any key to boo
384	74	20	61	63	74	69	76	65	20	70	61	72	74	69	74	69	:	t active partiti
400	6F	6E	0A	0D	00	00	00	00	00	00	00	00	00	00	00	00	:	on..............
416	00	00	00	00	00	00	00	00	00	00	00	00	00	00	00	00	:	....
432	50	51	02	03	04	05	00	03	0D	21	0D	21	00	00	80	01	:	PQ......▨▨▨▨▨!
448	01	00	0B	FE	7F	09	3F	00	00	00	4B	34	41	00	00	00	:	... þ▨?..K4A...
464	C1	FF	0F	FE	FF	FF	EE	3D	D2	01	6B	D1	C1	01	00	00	:	Áÿ ÿÿï=Ò.kÑÁ
480	41	0A	17	FE	FF	91	8A	34	41	00	88	D8	9E	00	00	00	:	A.. þý ▨4A.▨Ø▨...
496	C1	92	83	FE	FF	FF	12	0D	E0	00	DC	30	F2	00	55	AA	:	Á ▨ÿÿ.. àÜòò.Uª

FIGURE 5.12 Contents of an MBR with PowerQuest's BootMagic Code in Its Boot Loader Section (in gray, 000–432)

Source: Adapted from R. Zamora, "Saving and Restoring the Partition Table," July 24, 2001, retrieved March 2010, www.articles.techrepublic.com, http://articles.techrepublic.com.com/5100-10878_11-1055302.html, used with permission.

PARTITION TABLE

The partition table shown in Figure 5.13 starts with a value of 0x80 that represents the active (bootable) partition. The Partition Table or P-Table contains four descriptors that are each 16 bytes long for a total length of 64 bytes (offsets 446–509). The descriptors represent the logical information needed to access a partition on the drive.[7]

The Partition Table is a part of the master boot record that describes how the disk is partitioned. The MBR reads the partition table to determine which partition is active (contains the operating system) and where its boot sector is located.

PARTITION TABLE MASTER BOOT RECORD

000	FA	EB	01	00	8C	C8	8E	D8	8E	C0	8E	D0	BC	00	7C	FB	:	Ú.ë.. ▮È▮Ø▮À▮Ð¼|û
016	BE	00	7C	BF	00	06	B9	00	01	F3	A5	E9	00	8A	BE	B2	:	¾|¿ ¹...ó¥é ▮¾²
032	07	38	0C	74	3C	BB	00	08	51	0F	B6	0C	BA	80	0D	E8	:	8 t<» Q ¶ ° ▮è
048	A5	00	59	72	21	46	FE	C5	81	C3	00	02	38	0C	75	E8	:	¥Yr!FþÅ ▮Ã 8 uè
064	33	C0	BE	00	08	03	04	46	46	E2	FA	3B	06	B0	07	0F	:	3À¾
080	85	0E	00	E9	4C	02	BE	10	07	E8	6E	00	BE	6A	07	EB	:	▮Ê▮; ên¾j ë
096	03	BE	42	07	E8	63	00	33	C0	CD	16	33	C0	BF	00	08	:	
112	B9	00	7C	F3	AB	BE	AE	07	B9	04	00	83	C6	10	80	3C	:	▮▮▮▮▮Á▮3Á¿▮Æ ▮<
128	80	74	0B	38	2C	75	02	E2	F2	BE	F6	06	EB	37	8B	D6	:	t 8,u âò¾ö ë7 ▮Ö
144	49	74	09	83	C6	10	38	2C	75	EF	E2	F7	BB	00	7C	8B	:	It ▮Æ 8,uïâ+»▮
160	F2	8B	14	8B	4C	02	E8	2E	00	72	12	8B	FB	81	BD	FE	:	ò▮▮ è.r ▮▮▮½þ
176	01	55	AA	75	0D	B8	50	00	8B	EE	06	53	CB	BE	10	07	:	..Uªu.P ▮ SË¾...
192	EB	03	BE	27	07	E8	02	00	EB	FE	B4	0E	BB	07	00	AC	:	ë
208	CD	10	38	3C	75	F9	C3	60	BF	05	00	B8	01	02	CD	13	:	▮è.ëÃ`▮ ¬Í
224	73	0A	4F	74	06	33	C0	CD	13	EB	F0	F9	61	C3	00	00	:	s.Ot 3Àí ëðuaÃ
240	00	00	00	00	00	00	0A	00	0D	50	61	72	74	69	74	69	:	.... Partitio
256	6E	20	74	61	62	6C	65	20	69	6E	76	61	6C	69	64	00	:	n table invalid.
272	0A	0D	45	72	72	6F	72	20	72	65	61	64	69	6E	67	20	:	..Error reading
288	73	65	63	74	6F	72	00	0A	0D	4F	70	65	72	61	74	69	:	sector...Operati
304	6E	67	20	73	79	73	74	65	6D	20	6D	69	73	73	69	6E	:	ng system missin
320	67	00	4D	42	52	20	63	6F	72	72	75	70	74	21	20	52	:	gMBR corrupt! R
336	75	6E	20	42	6F	6F	74	4D	61	67	69	63	20	63	6F	6E	:	un BootMagic con
352	66	69	67	75	72	61	74	69	6F	6E	0A	0D	50	72	65	73	:	figuration..Pres
368	73	20	61	6E	79	20	6B	65	79	20	74	6F	20	62	6F	6F	:	s any key to boo
384	74	20	61	63	74	69	76	65	20	70	61	72	74	69	74	69	:	t active partiti
400	6F	6E	0A	0D	00	00	00	00	00	00	00	00	00	00	00	00	:	on............
416	00	00	00	00	00	00	00	00	00	00	00	00	00	00	00	00	:	....
432	50	51	02	03	04	05	00	03	0D	21	0D	21	00	00	80	01	:	PQ......▮▮▮▮▮▮!
448	01	00	0B	FE	7F	09	3F	00	00	00	4B	34	41	00	00	00	:	... þ▮?...K4A...
464	C1	FF	0F	FE	FF	FF	EE	3D	D2	01	6B	D1	C1	01	00	00	:	Áÿ þÿÿ=Ò.kÑÁ
480	41	0A	17	FE	FF	91	8A	34	41	00	88	D8	9E	00	00	00	:	A.. þ ▮4A.▮▮...
496	C1	92	83	FE	FF	FF	12	0D	E0	00	DC	30	F2	00	55	AA	:	Á ▮þÿÿ.. àÛ0ò.U▮

FIGURE 5.13 Partition Table of the MBR (in gray 432–496)

Source: Adapted from R. Zamora, "Saving and Restoring the Partition Table," July 24, 2001, retrieved March 2010, www.articles.techrepublic.com, http://articles.techrepublic.com.com/5100-10878_11-1055302.html, used with permission.

Refer to Figure 5.14 to view the boot flag. The boot flag is set to 0x80 (HEX 80), which is located at offset 446. This is a normal partition record, in a single partitioned hard drive.

Figure 5.15 shows the MBR for a *multi-partitioned drive.*

 ## HARD DISK PARTITION

A hard disk partition is a defined storage space on a hard drive.

Hard drives start with a single "partition" that holds the operating system, your applications, games, music, photos, videos, and all of your important data. Over time, your hard drive becomes very cluttered and messy; you can

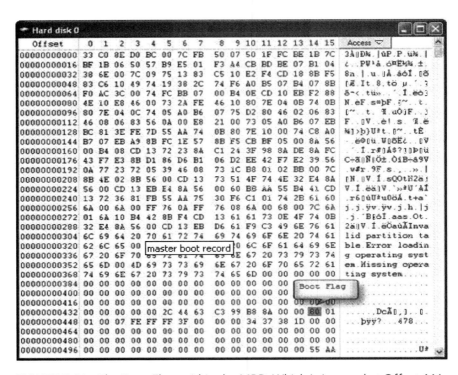

FIGURE 5.14 The Boot Flag, within the MBR, Which Is Located at Offset 446
Source: D. Correa, "The Black Art of Data Recovery: BIOS, MBR, VIRUS," June 13, 2007, DTIDATA, www.DTIDATA.com, retrieved March 2010, www.dtidata.com/resourcecenter/ 2007/06/22/black-art-data-recovery-mbr-bios-virus-part-2/, used with permission.

significantly improve your hard drive's speed and organization by separating your operating system, applications, and important data into separate partitions on the same drive. This enables your hard drive to find files faster and easier.[8]

A partition is created when you format the hard disk. Typically, a one-partition hard disk is labeled the "C:" drive ("A:" and "B:" are typically reserved for diskette drives), see Figure 5.16.

A two-partition hard drive would typically contain "C:" and "D:" drives. (CD-ROM drives typically are assigned the last letter in whatever sequence of letters have been used as a result of hard disk formatting, or typically with a two-partition, the "E:" drive.)

A user may decide to split a hard disk into multiple partitions because smaller partitions often have smaller *cluster* sizes.

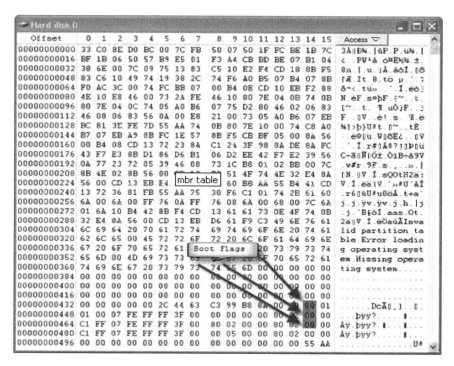

FIGURE 5.15 View of a Multi-Partitioned Drive

Source: D. Correa, "The Black Art of Data Recovery: BIOS, MBR, VIRUS," DTIDATA, www .DTIDATA.com, June 13, 2007, retrieved March 2010, www.dtidata.com/resourcecenter/ 2007/06/22/black-art-data-recovery-mbr-bios-virus-part-2/, used with permission.

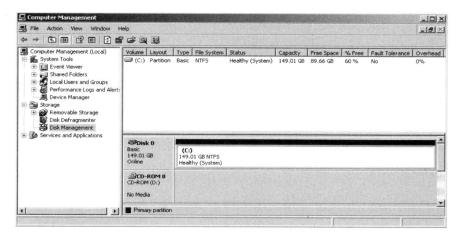

FIGURE 5.16 A Single Partitioned Hard Drive

A cluster is the unit of disk space allocation for files and directories. To reduce the overhead of managing on-disk data structures, the *filesystem* does not allocate individual disk sectors, but contiguous groups of sectors, called clusters.

On a disk that uses 512-byte sectors, a 512-byte cluster contains one sector, whereas a 4-kibibyte (KB) cluster contains eight sectors. (See Figure 5.17.)

A cluster is the smallest logical amount of disk space that can be allocated to hold a file.

If you have many small files, cluster size is an issue, since regardless of size each file is stored in at least one cluster. This means that a file with one character (five bytes in size) could occupy 16KB of space on the disk.

In a smaller partition, a cluster may only be allocated 4KB. This is an efficient strategy if you are storing a large number of small files.[9]

Most operating system use the "fdisk" command to create hard disk partitions. (See Figure 5.18.)

Many operating systems also have graphical tools which accomplish the same task.

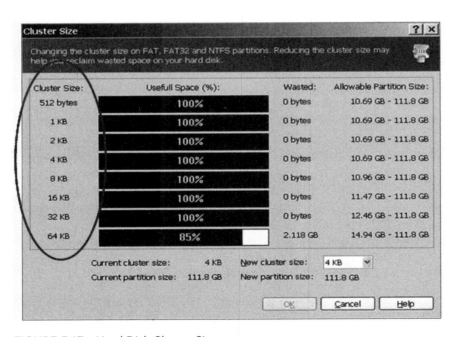

FIGURE 5.17 Hard Disk Cluster Size

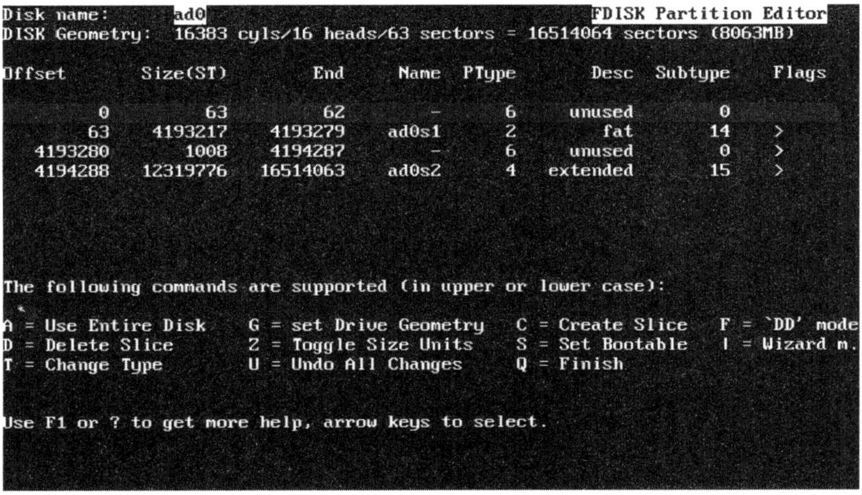

```
Disk name:        ad0                              FDISK Partition Editor
DISK Geometry:   16383 cyls/16 heads/63 sectors = 16514064 sectors (8063MB)

Offset        Size(ST)         End    Name  PType       Desc  Subtype     Flags

       0            63          62       -      6     unused        0
      63       4193217     4193279   ad0s1      2        fat       14        >
 4193280          1008     4194287       -      6     unused        0        >
 4194288      12319776    16514063   ad0s2      4   extended       15        >




The following commands are supported (in upper or lower case):

A = Use Entire Disk    G = set Drive Geometry   C = Create Slice    F = `DD' mode
D = Delete Slice       Z = Toggle Size Units    S = Set Bootable    I = Wizard m.
T = Change Type        U = Undo All Changes      Q = Finish

Use F1 or ? to get more help, arrow keys to select.
```

FIGURE 5.18 FDISK Partition Editor

What's a Logical Partition (aka Volume)?

1. A volume is how the operating system (you, me, us, we, etc.) "sees" your free disk space.
2. Volumes (also called logical drives) are represented in Windows by drive letters such as C:, K:, X:, Y:, Z:, and so on.
3. Volumes must be formatted with a file system before data can be stored on them.[10]

The Signature Word

The signature bytes should always be 0x55AA in a valid MBR (shown highlighted in gray in Figure 5.19).

If the signature bytes are not 0x55AA, your hard drive will not boot until they are changed to this hexadecimal number.[11]

Summarizing the Boot Process

After turning on your computer, the first thing that happens is that the BIOS (Basic Input Output System) takes control, initializes the screen and keyboard, and tests the main memory. At this point, no storage media or external devices are known to the system.

After that, the system reads the current date and time as well as information about the most important peripheral devices from the CMOS setup. After

END OF THE MBR   MASTER BOOT RECORD

000	FA	EB	01	00	8C	C8	8E	D8	8E	C0	8E	D0	BC	00	7C	FB	:	Ú.ë.. ▨È▨Ø▨Ä▨Ð¼|û
016	BE	00	7C	BF	00	06	B9	00	01	F3	A5	E9	00	8A	BE	B2	:	¾|¿ ¹....ó¥é ▨¾²
032	07	38	0C	74	3C	BB	00	08	51	0F	B6	0C	BA	80	00	E8	:	8 t<» Q ¶ ° ▨è
048	A5	00	59	72	21	46	FE	C5	81	C3	00	02	38	0C	75	E8	:	¥Yr!FþÅ ▨Å 8 uè
064	33	C0	BE	00	08	03	04	46	46	E2	FA	3B	06	B0	07	0F	:	3À¾
080	85	0E	00	E9	4C	02	BE	10	07	E8	6E	00	BE	6A	07	EB	:	▨E▨; ên¾j ë
096	03	BE	42	07	E8	63	00	33	C0	CD	16	33	C0	BF	00	08	:	
112	B9	00	7C	F3	AB	BE	AE	07	B9	04	00	83	C6	10	80	3C	:	¹|ó«¾®Á 3À¿▨Æ ▨<
128	80	74	0B	38	2C	75	02	E2	F2	BE	F6	06	EB	37	8B	D6	:	t 8,u âò¾ö ë7 ▨Ö
144	49	74	09	83	C6	10	38	2C	75	EF	E2	F7	BB	00	7C	8B	:	It ▨Æ 8,uïã÷»▨
160	F2	8B	14	8B	4C	02	E8	2E	00	72	12	8B	FB	81	BD	FE	:	ò▨ ▨L è.r ▨▨½þ
176	01	55	AA	75	0D	B8	50	00	8B	EE	06	53	CB	BE	10	07	:	..UªuP ▨ SË¾...
192	EB	03	BE	27	07	E8	02	00	EB	FE	B4	0E	BB	07	00	AC	:	ë
208	CD	10	38	3C	75	F9	C3	60	BF	05	00	B8	01	02	CD	13	:	▨<ù▨`▨` ▨ ¬
224	73	0A	4F	74	06	33	C0	CD	13	EB	F0	F9	61	C3	00	00	:	s.Ot 3ÀÍ ëðùaÃ
240	00	00	00	00	00	00	0A	0D	50	61	72	74	69	74	69	6F	:	........Partitio
256	6E	20	74	61	62	6C	65	20	69	6E	76	61	6C	69	64	00	:	n table invalid.
272	0A	0D	45	72	72	6F	72	20	72	65	61	64	69	6E	67	20	:	..Error reading
288	73	65	63	74	6F	72	00	0A	0D	4F	70	65	72	61	74	69	:	sector...Operati
304	6E	67	20	73	79	73	74	65	6D	20	6D	69	73	73	69	6E	:	ng system missin
320	67	00	4D	42	52	20	63	6F	72	72	75	70	74	21	20	52	:	gMBR corrupt! R
336	75	6E	20	42	6F	6F	74	4D	61	67	69	63	20	63	6F	6E	:	un BootMagic con
352	66	69	67	75	72	61	74	69	6F	6E	0A	0D	50	72	65	73	:	figuration..Pres
368	73	20	61	6E	79	20	6B	65	79	20	74	6F	20	62	6F	6F	:	s any key to boo
384	74	20	61	63	74	69	76	65	20	70	61	72	74	69	74	69	:	t active partiti
400	6F	6E	0A	0D	00	00	00	00	00	00	00	00	00	00	00	00	:	on............
416	00	00	00	00	00	00	00	00	00	00	00	00	00	00	00	00	:	....
432	50	51	02	03	04	05	00	03	0D	21	0D	21	00	00	80	01	:	PQ.......▨▨▨▨▨!
448	01	00	0B	FE	7F	09	3F	00	00	00	4B	34	41	00	00	00	:	... þ8?...K4A...
464	C1	FF	0F	FE	FF	FF	EE	3D	D2	01	6B	D1	C1	01	00	00	:	Áÿ þÿÿî=Ò.kÑÁ
480	41	0A	17	FE	FF	91	8A	34	41	00	88	D8	9E	00	00	00	:	A..þ ▨▨4A.▨▨...
496	C1	92	83	FE	FF	FF	12	0D	E0	00	DC	30	F2	00	55	AA	:	Á▨▨þÿÿ.. .àÜ0ò.Uª

FIGURE 5.19 The End of the MBR—Two-Byte Signature Word (in gray)

Source: Adapted from R. Zamora, "Saving and Restoring the Partition Table," www.articles
.techrepublic.com, July 24, 2001, retrieved March 2010, http://articles.techrepublic.com
.com/5100-10878_11-1055302.html, used with permission.

reading the CMOS, the BIOS should recognize the first hard disk, including
details such as its geometry. It can then start to load the operating system (OS)
from there.

To load the OS, the system loads a 512-byte data segment from the first
hard disk into main memory and executes the code stored at the beginning of
this segment. The instructions contained in it determine the rest of the boot
process. This is why the first 512 bytes of the hard disk are often called the
Master Boot Record (MBR).

Up to this point (loading the MBR), the boot sequence is independent
of the installed operating system and is identical on all PCs. Also, all the

PC has to access peripheral hardware are those routines (drivers) stored in the BIOS.[12]

Summarizing the MBR

The MBR contains three main components (see Table 5.1):

1. Boot loader (Byte Offset 0–445)
2. Partition table (Byte Offset 446–509)
3. Signature bytes (Byte Offset 510–511)

   Figure 5.20 shows a graphical representation of the MBR.

1. **Boot loader** (Byte offset 0–445). The MBR's boot loader consists of code that the BIOS loads to boot an operating system. The boot loader works by looking for the active partition in the partition table and loading the first sector in that partition. That sector is known as the Partition Boot Record. The Partition Boot Record will then start the process of loading the operating system's kernel.[13]
2. **Partition table** (Byte offset 446–509). 64 bytes in length, consists of four 16 byte entries ($4 \times 16 = 64$). The partition table contains four descriptors that are 16 bytes long each. The table defines or describes the storage space or partition. The descriptors represent the logical information needed to access a partition on the drive.[14] The partition table starts with a value of 80 (HEX), which represents the active (bootable) partition.
3. **Signature bytes** (Byte offset 510–511). The MBR's signature bytes are the two final bytes of the first sector, and they are used as a simple validation of the MBR's contents.[15] When the MBR is loaded the BIOS checks the last two bytes of the sector. The last two sectors must contain the HEX values 55AA. If this boot record signature is not present, error messages such as "insert boot disk" or "nonsystem boot" will appear.

TABLE 5.1   Master Boot Record (MBR) Structure of Intel-based Computers

Byte Offset	Description	Size
0–445	Boot Loader	446 Bytes
446–509	Partition Table	64 Bytes
510–511	MBR Signature	2 Bytes
MBR Size		512

MASTER BOOT RECORD

000	FA	EB	01	00	8C	C8	8E	D8	8E	C0	8E	D0	BC	00	7C	FB	:	Ú.ë.. ▨È▨Ø▨À▨Ð¼|û
016	BE	00	7C	BF	00	06	B9	00	01	F3	A5	E9	00	8A	BE	B2	:	¾|¿ ¹....ó¥é ▨¾²
032	07	38	0C	74	3C	BB	00	08	51	0F	B6	0C	BA	80	00	E8	:	8 t<» Q ¶ ° ▨è
048	A5	00	59	72	21	46	FE	C5	81	C3	00	02	38	0C	75	E8	:	¥Yr!FþÅ ▨Ã 8 uè
064	33	C0	BE	00	08	03	04	46	46	E2	FA	3B	06	B0	07	0F	:	3À¾
080	85	0E	00	E9	4C	02	BE	10	07	E8	6E	00	BE	6A	07	EB	:	▨Eⁿ¾; ën¾j ë
096	03	BE	42	07	E8	63	00	33	C0	CD	16	33	C0	BF	00	08	:	
112	B9	00	7C	F3	AB	BE	AE	07	B9	04	00	83	C6	10	80	3C	:	▨¹;▨▨¹Áⁱ 3Á¿▨Æ ▨<
128	80	74	0B	38	2C	75	02	E2	F2	BE	F6	06	EB	37	8B	D6	:	t 8,u âò¾ö ë7 ▨Ö
144	49	74	09	83	C6	10	38	2C	75	EF	E2	F7	BB	00	7C	8B	:	It ▨Æ 8,uïâ÷»▨
160	F2	8B	14	8B	4C	02	E8	2E	00	72	12	8B	FB	81	BD	FE	:	ò▨ ▨L è.r ▨û▨½þ
176	01	55	AA	75	0D	B8	50	00	8B	EE	06	53	CB	BE	10	07	:	..Uªu ▨ SË¾...
192	EB	03	BE	27	07	E8	02	00	EB	FE	B4	0E	BB	07	00	AC	:	ë
208	CD	10	38	3C	75	F9	C3	60	BF	05	00	B8	01	02	CD	13	:	▨å.é▨ïÁ`¿ ¬ⁱ
224	73	0A	4F	74	06	33	C0	CD	13	EB	F0	F9	61	C3	00	00	:	s.Ot 3ÀÍ ëðùaÃ
240	00	00	00	00	00	00	0A	0D	50	61	72	74	69	74	69	6F	:	.... Partitio
256	6E	20	74	61	62	6C	65	20	69	6E	76	61	6C	69	64	00	:	n table invalid.
272	0A	0D	45	72	72	6F	72	20	72	65	61	64	69	6E	67	20	:	..Error reading
288	73	65	63	74	6F	72	20	0A	0D	4F	70	65	72	61	74	69	:	sector...Operati
304	6E	67	20	73	79	73	74	65	6D	20	6D	69	73	73	69	6E	:	ng system missin
320	67	00	4D	42	52	20	63	6F	72	72	75	70	74	21	20	52	:	gMBR corrupt! R
336	75	6E	20	42	6F	6F	74	4D	61	67	69	63	20	63	6F	6E	:	un BootMagic con
352	66	69	67	75	72	61	74	69	6F	6E	0A	0D	50	72	65	73	:	figuration..Pres
368	73	20	61	6E	79	20	6B	65	79	20	74	6F	20	62	6F	6F	:	s any key to boo
384	74	20	61	63	74	69	76	65	20	70	61	72	74	69	74	69	:	t active partiti
400	6F	6E	0A	0D	00	00	00	00	00	00	00	00	00	00	00	00	:	on..............
416	00	00	00	00	00	00	00	00	00	00	00	00	00	00	00	00	:	....
432	50	51	02	03	04	05	00	03	0D	21	0D	21	00	00	80	01	:	PQ......▨▨▨▨▨▨!
448	01	00	0B	FE	7F	09	3F	00	00	00	4B	34	41	00	00	00	:	... þ▨?...K4A...
464	C1	FF	0F	FE	FF	FF	EE	3D	D2	01	6B	D1	C1	01	00	00	:	Áÿ þÿì=Ò.kÑÁ
480	41	0A	17	FE	FF	91	8A	34	41	00	88	D8	9E	00	00	00	:	A.. þý ▨▨4A.▨▨...
496	C1	92	83	FE	FF	FF	12	0D	E0	00	DC	30	F2	00	55	AA	:	Á▨▨þÿ.. .àÜ0ò.U▨

FIGURE 5.20 Graphical Representation of the MBR

Source: Adapted from R. Zamora, "Saving and Restoring the Partition Table," www
.articles.techrepublic.com, July 24, 2001, retrieved March 2010, http://articles.techrepublic
.com.com/5100-10878_11-1055302.html, used with permission.

SUMMARY

Understanding that the HEX value 55AA is the boot record signature may not
make or break a case. In reality, a cyber forensic investigator may never even
find a need to seek out or verify such data.

Why then should we study such meticulous detail?

It is a piece of the puzzle that needs to be understood in order to get
a complete understanding of the boot process. As discussed throughout this
chapter, a firm understanding of the boot process is necessary if, for one thing,
knowing when evidence can, may, or is altered and thereby avoiding contaminating evidence through the imaging process is important.

Understanding the boot process is also important as it will lead us into the next logical step toward gaining a better understanding of cyber forensics: file systems. Chapter 7 will address the next step in the natural progression of accessing information on a system, mounting of the file system.

Chapter 6 focuses on endianness, the attribute of a system that indicates whether integers are represented from left to right or right to left. Knowing how information is written to a disk is very important to the cyber forensic investigator.

 NOTES

1. C. Kozierok, "The System Clock Is Losing Time or Not Keeping Time Accurately," retrieved March 2010, www.pcguide.com/ts/x/comp/mbsys/cmosLosingTime-c.html.
2. R. Zamora, "Saving and Restoring the Partition Table," www.articles.techrepublic .com, July 24, 2001, retrieved March 2010, http://articles.techrepublic.com .com/5100-10878_11-1055302.html, used with permission.
3. "Master Boot Record," Microsoft Technet, retrieved March 2010, http:// technet.microsoft.com/en-us/library/cc976786.aspx, used with permission from Microsoft.
4. R. Zamora, "Saving and Restoring the Partition Table."
5. G. Sweet, "What Is a Hex Editor?" SweetScape Software, 148 Pownal Rd. RR#1, Pownal, PEI, C0A 1Z0, Canada, info@sweetscape.com, retrieved March 2010, www.sweetscape.com/articles/hex_editor.html, used with permission.
6. Ibid.
7. Ibid.
8. "How Do I Add or Remove a Hard Disk Partition?" retrieved February 2009, www.rickysays.com/add-remove-hard-disk-partitions.
9. "What Is a Hard Disk Partition?" retrieved February 2009, www.tech-faq.com/ hard-disk-partition.shtml.
10. Beginners Guides: Formatting and Partitioning a Hard Drive, retrieved February 2009, www.pcstats.com/articleview.cfm?articleID=1778.
11. R. Zamora, "Saving and Restoring the Partition Table."
12. "Booting and Boot Managers," chapter 7 in SUSE LINUX—Administration Guide, Novell Corporation, www.novell.com/documentation/suse91/suselinux-adminguide/html/ch07.html, retrieved March 2010.
13. R. Zamora, "Saving and Restoring the Partition table."
14. Ibid.
15. Ibid.

Endianness and the Partition Table

When 900 years you reach, look as good, you will not.

—Yoda

Speak in Big Endian, most of us do.

—Authors

S OME HUMAN LANGUAGES are read and written from left to right; others from right to left; some from bottom to top and others from top to bottom. The order in which data is assembled can vary dramatically from culture to culture, region to region, and country to country.

In the United States and many North American countries, for example, the following date 12/09/12 would represent December 9th, 2012; in the United Kingdom (UK), and many European countries, however, this would represent the date September 12th, 2012. What happened? Why do we have this confusion? This is because the order and interpretation of the numeric values are viewed differently by different society groups.

In the United States the date has been and continues to be traditionally written as MM/DD/YYYY, whereas in many other societies/countries around the globe, representation of the current date is written and viewed as DD/MM/YYYY. That said, even in the United States, the recording and displaying of the date is sometimes shown as DD/MM/YYYY (e.g., U.S. customs immigrations entry forms for all persons arriving into the United States from a foreign country use the DD/MM/YYYY date format). Thus, data representation is not consistent, even within the same country.

In order to correctly interpret these data in the given date format used, the order in which the information is stored and interpreted would need to be known, otherwise the result would be grossly inaccurate. A similar issue arises in the field of computers involving the representation of numbers and their interpretation.

As we have discussed, electronic data is stored at the lowest level in bits, bits are assembled to form bytes, bytes into words, words into *dwords*, and so on. *Endianness* of electronic data involves the ordering of these fundamental units. Endianness is the attribute of a system that indicates whether integers are represented from left to right or right to left.

Why then in today's world of virtual machines and gigahertz processors, would a programmer or a cyber forensic investigator care about such a base-level technical specification? The reason is that endianness must be chosen every time either a hardware or software architecture is designed, and there isn't much in the way of natural law to help decide or to dictate. So, implementations of endianness vary among hardware manufacturers and software developers.

 ## THE FLAVOR OF ENDIANNESS

Generally, in computing, endianness comes in two flavors: big endian and little endian.

In big endian the most significant unit (or byte) of a data field is ordered first, or left justified. With little endian, however, the least significant unit (or byte) of a data field is ordered first with the most significant byte on the right, that is, right justified.

The question may arise, what determines the most significant byte? With bytes, integers, and numbers, in general the first byte is usually the most significant. *The first digit will usually have the greatest value. For example, in the* U.S. dollar value of $123,456,789.00, which digit in that rather large number is the most important? The one (1) of course, as it represents 100 million. Independently, the nine (9) may be bigger than the 1, but the 9 only represents nine dollars.

In the previous date example, if we were to put the date in a big endian format it would be written as YYYY-MM-DD or 2012-12-09. In this case, a year is a more significant period of time than a day, so being that it is big endian we order the data from most significant to least. The same date written in little endian would therefore be written as DD-MM-YYYY, or 09-12-2012. The date format typically used in the United States (i.e., MM-DD-YY), however, is normally neither; this ordering is sometimes called mixed endian or middle endian.

The following definitions are more precise:

- Big endian exist when the most significant byte of any multibyte data field is stored at the lowest memory address, which is also the address of the larger field.
- Little endian means that the least significant byte of any multibyte data field is stored at the lowest memory address, which is also the address of the larger field.[1]

Big Endian Example

In big endian, you store the *most* significant byte in the smallest address. Table 6.1 shows how it would look.

TABLE 6.1 Example of Number Storage Using Big Endianness

Address	Value
1000	90
1001	AB
1002	12
1003	CD

Little Endian Example

In little endian, you store the *least* significant byte in the smallest address. Table 6.2 shows how it would look.

TABLE 6.2 Example of Number Storage Using Little Endianness

Address	Value
1000	CD
1001	12
1002	AB
1003	90

Notice that this is in the reverse order compared to big endian. To remember which is which, recall whether the least significant byte is stored first (thus, little endian) or the most significant byte is stored first (thus, big endian).[2]

All processors must be designated as either big endian or little endian. Intel's 80 × 86 processors and their clones are little endian. Sun's SPARC, Motorola's 68K, and the PowerPC families are all big endian. The Java Virtual Machine is big endian as well. Some processors even have a bit in a register that allows the programmer to select the desired endianness.

An endianness difference can cause problems if a computer unknowingly tries to read binary data written in the opposite format from a shared memory location or file.

ENDIANNESS

Endianness describes how multibyte data is represented by a computer system and is dictated by the CPU architecture of the system. Unfortunately, not all computer systems are designed with the same Endian-architecture. The difference in endian-architecture is an issue when software or data is shared between computer systems. An analysis of the computer system and its interfaces will determine the requirements of the endian implementation of the software.

Endianness only makes sense when you want to split a large value (such as a word) into several small ones. You must decide on an order to place it in memory.

However, if you have a *32-bit register* storing a 32-bit value, it makes no sense to talk about endianness. The register is neither big endian nor little endian. It's just a register holding a 32-bit value. The rightmost bit is the least significant bit, and the leftmost bit is the most significant bit.

There's no reason to rearrange the bytes in a register in some other way.

Endianness only makes sense when you are splitting up a multibyte data field, and attempting to store the bytes at consecutive memory locations. In a register, it doesn't make sense. A register is simply a 32-bit quantity, b31 . . . b0, and endianness does not apply to it.

With regard to endianness, you may argue there is a very natural way to store four bytes in four consecutive addresses, and that the other way looks strange. In particular, it looks "backwards." However, what's natural to you may not be natural to someone else. The fact of the matter is that the word is split in four bytes, and most people would agree that you need some order to place it in memory.[3]

Most Intel-based computers (x86, AMD, etc.) use little endian. Non–Intel based Apple computers and other RISC-based processors for example, use big endian. It is also important to note that network traffic uses big endian ordering.

THE ORIGINS OF ENDIAN

The origin of the odd terms *big endian* and *little endian* can be traced to the 1726 book *Gulliver's Travels*, by Jonathan Swift. In one part of the story, resistance to an imperial edict to break soft-boiled eggs on the "little end" escalates to civil war. (The plot is a satire of England's King Henry VIII's break with the Catholic Church.)[4]

In 1981, Danny Cohen, in his paper "On Holy Wars and a Plea for Peace," using Jonathan Swift's *Gulliver's Travels* as a backdrop for the controversy raging in Lilliput, applied the terms and the satire to the question "What is the proper byte order in messages?" More specifically, the question debated was, "Which bit should travel first—the bit from the little end of the word or the bit from the big end of the word? Cohen concluded that "Agreement upon an order is more important than the order agreed upon."[5]

PARTITION TABLE WITHIN THE MASTER BOOT RECORD

In Chapter 5 we discussed the Master Boot Record (MBR) and the data contained within. In cyber forensics, how data is stored on a drive is crucial information, as often, the cyber forensic analyst will have to look at raw data in a HEX editor for possible evidence; thus, knowing how the information is written to disk, big endian or little endian, is *very* important.

Let's take a look at the MBR in a HEX editor once again (see Figure 6.1).

To recap, let's look at the partition table (highlighted in gray) at byte offsets 446–509. It starts with a value of 80 (HEX) that represents the active (bootable) partition. It contains four descriptors that are 16 bytes long each. The descriptors represent the logical information needed to access a *partition* on the drive.[6]

The partition table is divided into four sections or four primary partitions. A primary partition is a partition on a hard drive that can contain only one logical drive (or section). Each section can hold the information necessary to define a single partition, meaning that the partition table can define no more than four partitions.

MASTER BOOT RECORD

000	FA	EB	01	00	8C	C8	8E	D8	8E	C0	8E	D0	BC	00	7C	FB	:	Ú.ë.. ▨▧▨▨Å▨Ð¼	û
016	BE	00	7C	BF	00	06	B9	00	01	F3	A5	E9	00	8A	BE	B2	:	¾	¿ ¹....ó¥é ▨¾²
032	07	38	0C	74	3C	BB	00	08	51	0F	B6	0C	BA	80	00	E8	:	8 t<» Q ¶ ° ▨è
048	A5	00	59	72	21	46	FE	C5	81	C3	00	02	38	0C	75	E8	:	¥Yr!FþÅ ▨Ã 8 uè
064	33	C0	BE	00	08	03	04	46	46	E2	FA	3B	06	B0	07	0F	:	3À¾
080	85	0E	00	E9	4C	02	BE	10	07	E8	6E	00	BE	6A	07	EB	:	ÉÊ▨; ên¾j ë
096	03	BE	42	07	E8	63	00	33	C0	CD	16	33	C0	BF	00	08	:	
112	B9	00	7C	F3	AB	BE	AE	07	B9	04	00	83	C6	10	80	3C	:	▨▨▨▨▨Ã¯ 3À¿▨Æ ▨<
128	80	74	0B	38	2C	75	02	E2	F2	BE	F6	06	EB	37	8B	D6	:	t 8,u âòö ë7 ▨Ö
144	49	74	09	83	C6	10	38	2C	75	EF	E2	F7	BB	00	7C	8B	:	It ▨Æ,uïâ÷»▨
160	F2	8B	14	8B	4C	02	E8	2E	00	72	12	8B	FB	81	BD	FE	:	ò▨ ▨L è.r ▨▨½þ
176	01	55	AA	75	0D	B8	50	00	8B	EE	06	53	CB	BE	10	07	:	..U▪u P ▨ SË¾...
192	EB	03	BE	27	07	E8	02	00	EB	FE	B4	0E	BB	07	00	AC	:	ë
208	CD	10	38	3C	75	F9	C3	60	BF	05	00	B8	01	02	CD	13	:	▨▨ ▪▪▪Ã¯ ▪ ¬	
224	73	0A	4F	74	06	33	C0	CD	13	EB	F0	F9	61	C3	00	00	:	s.Ot 3Àí ëðuaÃ
240	00	00	00	00	00	00	0A	0D	50	61	72	74	69	74	69	6F	:	.... Partitio
256	6E	20	74	61	62	6C	65	20	69	6E	76	61	6C	69	64	00	:	n table invalid.
272	0A	0D	45	72	72	6F	72	20	72	65	61	64	69	6E	67	20	:	..Error reading
288	73	65	63	74	6F	72	00	0A	0D	4F	70	65	72	61	74	69	:	sector...Operati
304	6E	67	20	73	79	73	74	65	6D	20	6D	69	73	73	69	6E	:	ng system missin
320	67	00	4D	42	52	20	63	6F	72	72	75	70	74	21	20	52	:	gMBR corrupt! R
336	75	6E	20	42	6F	6F	74	4D	61	67	69	63	20	63	6F	6E	:	un BootMagic con
352	66	69	67	75	72	61	74	4D	6F	6E	00	0A	50	72	65	73	:	figuration..Pres
368	73	20	61	6E	79	20	6B	65	79	20	74	6F	20	62	6F	6F	:	s any key to boo
384	74	20	61	63	74	69	76	65	20	70	61	72	74	69	74	69	:	t active partiti
400	6F	6E	0A	0D	00	00	00	00	00	00	00	00	00	00	00	00	:	on............
416	00	00	00	00	00	00	00	00	00	00	00	00	00	00	00	00	:	....
432	50	51	02	03	04	05	00	03	0D	21	0D	21	00	00	80	01	:	PQ...........▨▨▨▨▨
448	01	00	07	FE	FF	FF	3F	00	00	00	89	7E	9B	1D	00	00	:	... þ▨?...K4A...
464	C1	FF	0F	FE	FF	FF	EE	3D	D2	01	6B	D1	C1	01	00	00	:	Áÿ þÿï=Ò.kÑÁ
480	41	0A	17	FE	FF	FF	91	8A	34	41	00	88	D8	9E	00	00	:	A.. þ▨ ▨▨4A.▨▨▨...
496	C1	92	83	FE	FF	FF	12	0D	E0	00	DC	30	F2	00	55	AA	:	Á ▨▨ÿÿ.. àÜ0ò.U▪

FIGURE 6.1 Master Boot Record Displayed in a HEX Editor

Source: Adapted from R. Zamora, "Saving and Restoring the Partition Table," www.articles .techrepublic.com, July 24, 2001, retrieved March 2010, http://articles.techrepublic.com .com/5100-10878_11-1055302.html, used with permission.

In the DOS/Windows world, partitions are named using the following method:

- Each partition's type is checked to determine if it can be read by DOS/Windows.
- If the partition's type is compatible, it is assigned a "drive letter." The drive letters start with a "C" and move on to the following letters, depending on the number of partitions to be labeled.
- The drive letter can then be used to refer to that partition as well as the file system contained on that partition.

Each *partition table* entry contains several important characteristics of the partition:

1. Whether the partition is "active." (See Figure 6.2.)
2. The location on the disk where the partition starts. (See Figure 6.3.)

3. Total number of sectors contained within the partition. (See Figure 6.4.)
4. The partition's type. (See Figure 6.5.)

The "Active" Partition

The partition table contains entries (descriptors) that act as pointers to each of the drive's partitions (*volumes*) and contain critical information such as the type of partition, whether or not the partition is active (bootable), where the partition starts and ends, and the size of the partition. Remember, the partition table can point to a maximum of four partitions. (*A technique called "extended" partitioning is used to allow more than four, and often times it is used when there are more than two partitions.*)

HEX 80 denotes the *active partition*, at the beginning of the Partition Table, shown in (Figure 6.2). The "active" flag is used by some operating systems' boot loaders. In other words, the operating system in the partition that is marked "active" is booted.

Take a look at byte offset 08–11 of the first partition (Figure 6.2). In the MBR of a Windows based operating system, this is where we would find the location for the starting sector of this partition.

The Start of the Partition

HEX 3F 00 00 00, as shown in Figure 6.3, depicts the start of the first partition, and is displayed as (or in) BIG ENDIAN format. Reversing this value into LITTLE EDIAN format results in a value of 00 00 00 3F, or after dropping the leading zeros simply HEX 3F.

We are reversing this value (HEX 3F 00 00 00) so we can get to the true value of HEX 3F, which is 63, the value for the starting partition.

One knows when or why this value needs to be reversed just as one knows where to obtain this value in the first place. So one may ask, "How do we

HEX 80-
Beginning of
Partition Table

416	00	00	00	00	00	00	00	00	00	00	00	00	00	00	00	00	:	....
432	50	51	02	03	04	05	00	03	0D	21	0D	21	00	00	80	01	:	PQ.......ᵡᵡᵡᵡᵡᵡ!
448	01	00	07	FE	FF	FF	3F	00	00	00	89	7E	9B	1D	00	00	:	... þᵡ?...K4A...
464	C1	FF	0F	FE	FF	FF	EE	3D	D2	01	6B	D1	C1	01	00	00	:	Aÿ bÿÿï=Ò.kÑÁ
480	41	0A	17	FE	FF	91	8A	34	41	00	88	D8	9E	00	00	00	:	A.. þÿ ᵡᵡ4A.ᵡᵡᵡ...
496	C1	92	83	FE	FF	FF	12	0D	E0	00	DC	30	F2	00	55	AA	:	Áᵡᵡþÿÿ.. .àÛ0ò.Uᵖ

FIGURE 6.2 Active Partition and the Beginning of the Partition Table

know that the HEX 0x80 in the first sector of the partition table identifies the active partition?"

"How do we know where the partition table starts in the first place? How do we know those values identify the starting spot of the partition, much less the order?"

The very nontechnical answer to these very logical and important questions is that we do research and learn. We learn which operating systems store data in which endianness format and commit this to memory. In the end, some things just have to be learned.

So, as we have previously discussed endianness and how the order of numerical values can be reversed, this HEX value needs to be reversed in order to get the correct value. If we don't reverse the endianness we won't get the correct data.

Deciphering the Partition's Hex Starting Value

The HEX value 3F is converted to the decimal value 63, because that is how the system is converting it. It's just how the system handles this data reference. As the system boots up, it looks to the bytes in this sector and pulls those data that it needs. The system knows what to do with these data because the system is specifically looking for a value of HEX 80.

The system looks to the MBR, in those predefined offsets (bytes 08–11) for HEX 80. When it finds the value it is looking for, HEX 80, it knows it has found the active partition (see Figure 6.2). The same is true for the starting sector (see Figure 6.3); the system looks to those byte offsets to extract data, reverse endian, and convert to decimal. This "process" is included in the instruction set of the boot process itself.

HEX 3F has a decimal equivalent of 63. This decimal value provides us with the relative sector address for the start of the partition.

FIGURE 6.3 HEX 3F 00 00 00—Starting Sector of the Partition

The Partition's Size

The multi-byte data field contained within byte offset 12–15 of the partition table defines the number of sectors contained within the partition, in other words, its size (see Figure 6.4).

This HEX value (89 7E 9B 1D in our example) is also "measured" in little endian and converted to a decimal value. This value also defines the last sector of the partition. As we obtained the starting sector from partition table byte offset 8–11, we can simply add the number of sectors to the starting sector and obtain the last sector.

So in this example, 89 7E 9B 1D is the multi-byte data field. We first reverse the order of bytes within this data field (little endian) to 1D 9B 7E 89. Being that this is a multi-byte data field, all the bytes are examined as one. So the data is converted to a decimal value.

1D 9B 7E 89 HEX, converted to its decimal equivalent, equals 496,729,737. This defines the number of sectors, 496,729,737. Since we know that there are 512 bytes per sector, we take the value 496,729,737 and multiply it by 512, and obtain the value 254,325,625,344 bytes.

So we can now conclude that we have a 236 GB (250GB drive).

The Partition's Type

The partition's type can be a bit confusing. The type is a number that identifies the partition's anticipated usage. If that statement sounds a bit vague, that is because the meaning of the partition type is a bit vague.

Some operating systems use the partition type to denote a specific file system type, to flag the partition as being associated with a particular operating

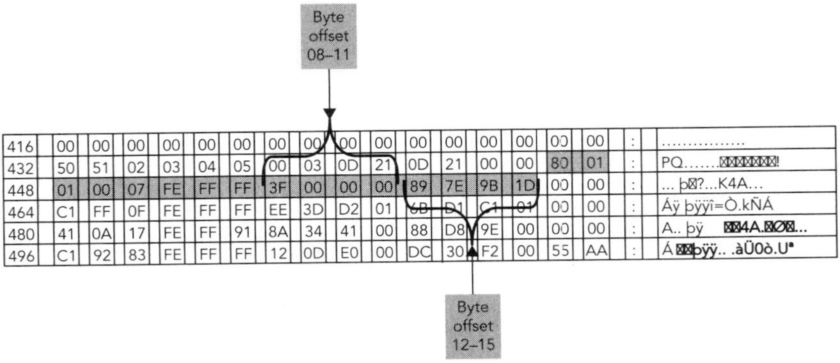

FIGURE 6.4 Total Number of Sectors Contained within the Partition

system, to indicate that the partition contains a bootable operating system, or some combination of the three.[3]

The partition type refers to the partition's relationship with the other partitions on the disk drive. There are three different partition types:

1. Primary partitions (partitions that take up one of the four primary partition slots in the disk drive's partition table).
2. Extended partitions (developed in response to the need for more than four partitions per disk drive. An extended partition can itself contain multiple partitions, greatly extending the number of partitions possible).
3. Logical partitions (those partitions contained within an extended partition).

Each partition has a type field that contains a code indicating the partition's anticipated usage. In other words, if the partition is going to be used as Windows NT, the partition's type should be set to 07 (which is the code representing Windows NTFS).

Table 6.3 shows several partition types associated with specific operating systems and their assigned values.

TABLE 6.3 Partition Types

Partition Type	Value
Empty	00
DOS 12-bit FAT	01
DOS 16-bit <=32M	04
DOS 3.3+ Extended Partition	05
DOS 3.31+ 16-bit FAT > 32M	06
Windows NT NTFS	07
OS/2 Boot Manager	0a
Win95 FAT32	0b
Win95 FAT32 (LBA)	0c
Win95 FAT16 (LBA)	0e
Win95 Extended (LBA)	0f
Novell	51
Novell Netware 286	64
Novell Netware 386	65
Linux native	83
Linux extended	85
Partition Magic recovery partition	3c
Xenix Bad Block Table	ff

To determine the type of partition in use, we look to the System ID field (byte offset 04) within the partition (see Figure 6.5).

For primary partitions and logical drives, the System ID field describes the *file system* used to format the volume.

Chapter 7 discusses file systems in much greater depth; for now it is important to only know that a file system (sometimes written *filesystem*) is the way in which files are named and where they are placed logically for storage and retrieval.

The operating system uses the System ID field (see Table 6.4) to determine what file system device drivers to load during startup.

From Table 6.5, we can determine the exact file system used to format the volume.

A review of the Partition Table shown in Figure 6.6 tells us that the volume type is an *NTFS partition*.

When a hard disk is formatted (initialized), it is divided into partitions or major divisions of the total physical hard disk space. Within each partition, the operating system keeps track of all the files that are stored by that operating system.

Volume Type
Byte offset 04

416	00	00	00	00	00	00	00	00	00	00	00	00	00	00	00	00	:	....
432	50	51	02	03	04	05	00	03	0D	21	0D	21	00	00	80	01	:	PQ......▨▨▨▨▨!
448	01	00	07	FE	FF	FF	3F	00	00	00	89	7E	9B	1D	00	00	:	... þ▨?...K4A...
464	C1	FF	0F	FE	FF	FF	EE	3D	D2	01	6B	D1	C1	01	00	00	:	Áÿ þÿÿ=Ò.kÑÁ
480	41	0A	17	FE	FF	91	8A	34	41	00	88	D8	9E	00	00	00	:	A.. þÿ ▨▨4A.▨Ø▨...
496	C1	92	83	FE	FF	FF	12	0D	E0	00	DC	30	F2	00	55	AA	:	Á ▨▨þÿÿ.. .àÜoò.Uª

FIGURE 6.5 System ID Field

Volume Type
Byte offset 04

416	00	00	00	00	00	00	00	00	00	00	00	00	00	00	00	00	:	....
432	50	51	02	03	04	05	00	03	0D	21	0D	21	00	00	80	01	:	PQ......▨▨▨▨▨!
448	01	00	07	FE	FF	FF	3F	00	00	00	89	7E	9B	1D	00	00	:	... þ▨?...K4A...
464	C1	FF	0F	FE	FF	FF	EE	3D	D2	01	6B	D1	C1	01	00	00	:	Áÿ þÿÿ=Ò.kÑÁ
480	41	0A	17	FE	FF	91	8A	34	41	00	88	D8	9E	00	00	00	:	A.. þÿ ▨▨4A.▨Ø▨...
496	C1	92	83	FE	FF	FF	12	0D	E0	00	DC	30	F2	00	55	AA	:	Á ▨▨þÿÿ.. .àÜoò.Uª

FIGURE 6.6 Byte Offset 04 Value HEX 7 (NTFS partition)

TABLE 6.4 Partition Table Fields

Byte Offset	Field Length	Value	Meaning
00	BYTE	0 × 80	Boot Indicator. Indicates whether the partition is the system partition. Legal values are: 00 = Do not use for booting. 80 = System partition.
01	BYTE	0 × 01	Starting Head.
02	6 bits	0 × 01	Starting Sector. Only bits 0–5 are used. Bits 6–7 are the upper two bits for the starting cylinder field.
03	10 bits	0 × 00	Starting Cylinder. This field contains the lower 8 bits of the cylinder value. Starting cylinder is thus a 10-bit number, with a maximum value of 1023.
04	BYTE	0 × 07	System ID. This byte defines the volume type.
05	BYTE	0 × 0F	Ending Head.
06	6 bits	0 × 3F	Ending Sector. Only bits 0–5 are used. Bits 6–7 are the upper two bits for the ending cylinder field.
07	10 bits	0 × 196	Ending Cylinder. This field contains the lower 8 bits of the cylinder value. Ending cylinder is thus a 10-bit number, with a maximum value of 1,023.
08	DWORD	3F 00 00 00	Relative Sector.
12	DWORD	51 42 06 00	Total Sectors.

TABLE 6.5 Values for the System ID Field (byte offset 04)

Value	Meaning
0 × 01	12-bit FAT partition or logical drive. The number of sectors in the volume is fewer than 32,680.
0 × 04	16-bit FAT partition or logical drive. The number of sectors is between 32,680 and 65,535.
0 × 05	Extended partition.
0 × 06	BIGDOS FAT partition or logical drive.
0 × 07	NTFS partition or logical drive.

Each file is actually stored on the hard disk in one or more clusters or disk spaces of a predefined uniform size. Using NTFS, the sizes of *clusters* range from 512 bytes to 64 kilobytes.

Read more about file systems and their importance to the cyber forensic investigator in Chapter 7.

In the Windows properties view of the partition (see Figure 6.7), all the characteristics of a partition which have been explained are displayed by the Windows Operating System. Our calculations are now verified, in that:

1. Status = 80—active partition
2. Relative = 63—starting location
3. Size = 496,729,737—in sectors
4. Type = 07—NTFS

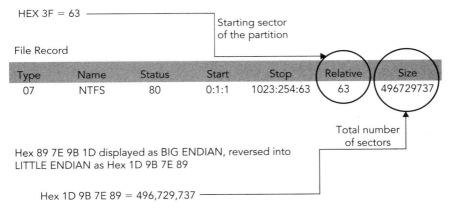

Hex 3f 00 00 00 displayed as BIG ENDIAN, reversed into LITTLE ENDIAN as 00 00 00 37 or simply HEX 3F

HEX 3F = 63 ——————

Starting sector of the partition

File Record

Type	Name	Status	Start	Stop	Relative	Size
07	NTFS	80	0:1:1	1023:254:63	63	496729737

Total number of sectors

Hex 89 7E 9B 1D displayed as BIG ENDIAN, reversed into LITTLE ENDIAN as Hex 1D 9B 7E 89

Hex 1D 9B 7E 89 = 496,729,737 ——————

FIGURE 6.7   Windows Properties View of the Partition

 SUMMARY

In cyber forensics, how data is stored on a drive is crucial information, as often, the cyber forensic investigator will have to look at raw data (via a HEX editor) for possible evidence. Thus, knowing how the information is written to disk, and how data are represented and presented physically and logically, is very important.

After touching upon important key concepts in the earlier chapters, such as HEX and binary, it was logical to start at the beginning, with the initial booting of a system. We discussed the importance of the Master Boot Record (MBR) and its contents such as the partition table, and how the system identifies the active partition (HEX 80), its starting sector, and its size.

We deviated from the boot process and delved into endianness in order to understand how a system handles or interprets this data. Being that the endianness or order of data contained within the MBR is subject to such measure, it was imperative to expand upon this essential concept, as we have in this section. Bear in mind endianness is not exclusive to data contained within the MBR. Other data contained within the hard drive is also subject to such measure.

A question may arise, how does the computer know to look at a specific range of bytes in a specific sector? And, how does it know to switch the order? Why wouldn't it just handle all binary as it comes across it, just like how many humans read, from left to right?

It is important to understand that not all binary data are treated equally. The way in which binary (HEX, in our view) is handled all depends upon the system architecture, or the code. As a system boots it will encounter code that will tell it to go here and do this or that or something else.

The logic loosely interpreted may make better sense to view in this way:

Step 1—go to byte offset 8–11 in the partition table.
Step 2—view these four bytes of data as one value (data field)—Dword.
Step 3—before applying math reverse the order of the bytes—that is, little endian.
Step 4—convert the Dword to a decimal value.
Answer = starting sector of the partition.

How a system knows where to look or how it knows how to compute values is what is known as system architecture. A cyber forensic investigator doesn't necessarily need to understand all the logic behind the design and architecture of each and every system. What is important is that we can obtain this information through whatever source possible.

The important factor is to confirm, test, and verify those data retrieved. A source may state that the size of a partition can be determined by obtaining a decimal value byte offset 12–15 of the partition table in little endian. It is wise to confirm this with another source, test it, and verify the test. Even if you are 100 percent sure, it is worth testing so that you can fully understand the complexities involved.

Chapter 7 introduces and discusses further the concepts of logical block addresses and file systems, and further investigates the storage and representation of data and its importance to the cyber forensic investigation process and to the cyber forensic investigator.

 ## NOTES

1. C. Brown and M. Barr, "Introduction to Endianness," Embedded Systems Programming, 55–56, Netrino, 6030 Marshalee Dr, #355, Elkridge, MD 21075, (866) 783-6233, retrieved April 2010, www.netrino.com/Embedded - Systems/How-To/Big-Endian-Little-Endian, used with permission.
2. C. Lin (2003), University of Maryland, Department of Computer Science, www .cs.umd.edu/class/sum2003/cmsc311/Notes/Data/endian.html, retrieved April 2010.
3. Endianness White Paper, (November 15, 2004), Intel Corporation. www.intel .com/design/intarch/papers/endian.pdf, retrieved April 2010.
4. Brown and Barr, "Introduction to Endianness," 55–56.
5. D. Cohen (October 1981), "On Holy Wars and a Plea for Peace," *Computer* 14, no. 10 (October 1981): 48–54, retrieved April 2010.
6. Brown and Barr, "Introduction to Endianness," 55–56.
7. "Partitions: Turning One Drive Into Many," www.centos.org/docs/5/html/5.1/ Installation_Guide/s2-partitions-partitioning-x86.html, Red Hat®, Inc., and The CentOS project, released via the Open Publication License, retrieved May 2010.

7

Volume versus Partition

N CHAPTER 5 WE DISCUSSED the boot-up process after touching upon important key concepts, files in Chapter 4, and in Chapters 2 and 3, HEX and binary.

We have also discussed the importance of the Master Boot Record (MBR) and its contents such as the partition table, and how the system identifies the active partition (HEX 80) and its starting sector and its size.

In order to explain how some of the data contained within the partition table is interpreted we deviated and delved into endianness. Being that the order of some of the data contained within the MBR is subjected to this endianness, it was imperative to expound upon how data is ordered and the importance of endianness, as it affects data within the MBR.

To continue on to the next step in our sequence, the process of data being assembled into human interpretable information, it is necessary for those data to be located and identified by the system.

We know already how the active partition's starting sector and its size are derived from the partition table; however, there are several additional byte offsets within the partition table which we have not yet discussed.

These offsets, called Cylinder, Head, and Sector (CHS) or, more currently, Logical Block Address (LBA), help to quantify partition location and size.

This chapter explains how partitions are located and identified and the significant role of volumes in making these data "mountable" or accessible and readable by your system at startup.

 ## TECH REVIEW

Prior to launching directly into our examination of volumes and partitions, it may be best to pause for a moment for a brief review of the technology that drives the hardware, where the data resides.

Hard or fixed disks store information on a revolving platter of metal or glass coated with a magnetic material. The disk typically consists of several physical platters on a common spindle.

Each disk consists of platters, rings on each side of each platter called *tracks,* and sections within each track called *sectors.* A sector is the smallest physical storage unit on a disk, almost always 512 bytes in size.

Tracks and Cylinders

On hard disks, the data are stored on the disk in thin, concentric bands called tracks. There can be more than 1,000 tracks on a 3½ inch hard disk. Tracks are a logical rather than physical structure, and are established when the disk is low-level formatted. Track numbers start at 0, and track 0 is the outermost track of the disk. The highest numbered track is next to the spindle. If the disk geometry is being translated, the highest numbered track would typically be 1,023.

See Figure 7.1 for an illustrative example of tracks on a typical hard disk.

A *cylinder* consists of the set of tracks that are at the same head position on the disk.[1] (See Figure 7.2.)

Sectors and Clusters

Each track is divided into sections called sectors. A sector is the smallest physical storage unit on the disk. The data size of a sector is always a power of two, and is almost always 512 bytes. (See Figure 7.3.)

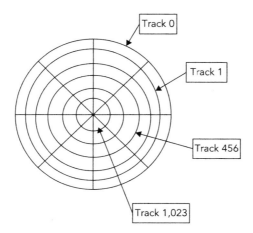

FIGURE 7.1 Tracks on a Typical Hard Disk

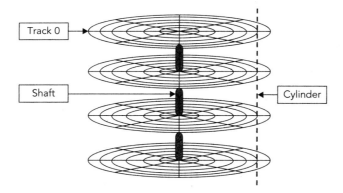

FIGURE 7.2 Cylinder

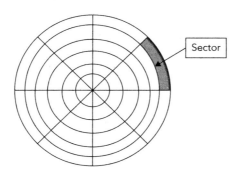

FIGURE 7.3 Sector

Each track has the same number of sectors, which means that the sectors are packed much closer together on tracks near the center of the disk. The disk controller uses the sector identification information stored in the area immediately before the data in the sector to determine where the sector itself begins.

As a file is written to the disk, the *file system* allocates the appropriate number of clusters to store the file's data. For example, if each cluster is 512 bytes and the file is 800 bytes, two clusters are allocated for the file. Later, if you update the file to, for example, twice its size (1,600 bytes), another two clusters are allocated.

If contiguous clusters (clusters that are next to each other on the disk) are not available, the data are written elsewhere on the disk and the file is considered to be fragmented. Fragmentation is a problem when the file system must search several different locations to find all the pieces of the file you want to read. The search causes a delay before the file is retrieved. A larger cluster size reduces the potential for fragmentation, but increases the likelihood that clusters will have unused space.[2]

CYLINDER, HEAD, SECTOR, AND LOGICAL BLOCK ADDRESSING

On older x86-based systems, back when hard drives did not exceed 8 *gigabytes*, the starting and ending *Cylinder, Head, and Sector (CHS)* fields of the active partition (HEX 80) were very important during the system boot. These values, contained within the Partition Table of the MBR were used to find and load this partition. *Logical Block Addressing (LBA)* virtually did away with this and involves a newer way of addressing sectors using exact sector locations.

Instead of referring to a cylinder, a head, and a sector number, each sector is instead assigned a unique "sector number." So instead of using a sort of triangulation in identifying a location on the disk, LBA simply numbers each sector with a unique number. In essence, the sectors are numbered 0, 1, 2, etc. up to (N−1), where N is the number of sectors on the disk.[3]

An analogy would be as follows.

Your address (assuming you live in the United States and have a typical address) is composed of a street number, street name, city name, and state name. This is similar to how conventional CHS addressing works. Instead however, let's say that every house in the United States was given a unique identifying number. This would be more how LBA works.[4]

Cylinder, Head, and Sector

Table 7.1 shows the corresponding CHS *tuple* for a select group of LBA values, and how one would sequentially count through a number of sectors which these values represent.

The data listed in Table 7.1 will only be valid for hard disks having *63 sectors per track* and *255 heads per cylinder.*

TABLE 7.1 512-Byte Blocks Identified Using LBA and CHS

LBA Value	CHS Tuple
0	0, 0, 1
1	0, 0, 2
2	0, 0, 3
62	0, 0, 63
63	0, 1, 1
64	0, 1, 2
65	0, 1, 3
125	0, 1, 63
126	0, 2, 1
127	0, 2, 2
188	0, 2, 63
189	0, 3, 1
190	0, 3, 2
16,063	0, 254, 62
16,064	0, 254, 63
16,065	1, 0, 1
16,606	1, 0, 2
16,127	1, 0, 63
16,128	1, 1, 1
16,450,497	1,023, 254, 1
16,450,558	1,023, 254, 62
16,450,559	1,023, 254, 63

Entries of the First Partition Table Entry

Let's again examine the partition table contained within the MBR (see Figure 7.4) and review those values, which we have already covered (see Table 7.2).

1. The value, HEX 80, indicates that the partition is an active, bootable partition.
2. HEX 07 indicates the file system, *NTFS*.
3. HEX 3F 00 00 00 indicates the relative or starting sector, 63.
4. HEX 89 7E 9B 1D indicates the total sectors or length (496, 729, 737).

Remaining Byte Entries of the First Partition Table Entry

The remaining HEX values are those for starting and ending CHS values. We did not cover these previously because the concepts of CHS and LBA had not yet been introduced. Let's review these now!

Starting CHS Value

Byte offset 01 through 03 of the partition table—01 01 00 (see Figure 7.5). First byte is reserved for the Head value—01, the remaining HEX values are

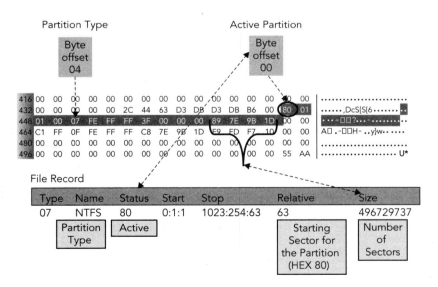

FIGURE 7.4 The Partition Table Contained within the MBR

TABLE 7.2 Byte Entries of the First Partition Table Entry

First 16-Byte Entry of Partition Table			
HEX Value	**Byte Offset**	**Description**	**Result**
80	0	Bootable/Active— 80 = Yes; 00 = No	YES
01 01 00	1, 2, 3	Starting Sector in CHS	0:01:01
07	4	Partition Type	NTFS
FE FF FF	5, 6, 7	Last Sector in CHS	1023:254:63
3F 00 00 00	8, 9, 10, 11	Relative Sectors— Starting Sector—LBA	63
89 7E 9B 1D	12, 13, 14, 15	Total Sectors/Length	496729737

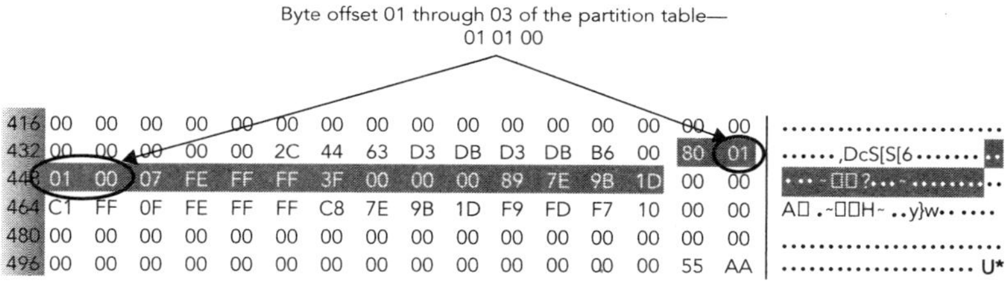

Byte offset 01 through 03 of the partition table—
01 01 00

```
416 00 00 00 00 00 00 00 00 00 00 00 00 00 00 00 00   .................
432 00 00 00 00 00 2C 44 63 D3 DB D3 DB B6 00 80 01   ......,DcS[S[6.......
448 01 00 07 FE FF FF 3F 00 00 00 89 7E 9B 1D 00 00   .....□□?...~........
464 C1 FF 0F FE FF FF C8 7E 9B 1D F9 FD F7 10 00 00   A□.-□□H-..y}w.....
480 00 00 00 00 00 00 00 00 00 00 00 00 00 00 00 00   .................
496 00 00 00 00 00 00 00 00 00 00 00 00 00 00 55 AA   ................U*
```

FIGURE 7.5 Starting CHS Value

01 00. The next byte is assigned the Sector value and the third byte is assigned the Cylinder Value.

Thus the CHS value 00:01:01 (0, 1, 1) (see Table 7.1):

- Head Value = 01
- Sector Value = 01
- Cylinder Value = 00

This may seem backwards, but remember, so is little endian. Why does the Sector value byte come before the Cylinder value byte? It's all in the code. Why assign the value of HEX 80 to the active partition? This all has to do with coding. You can view this as a little endian reordering of the last two bytes.

Ending CHS Value

Byte offset 05 through 07 of the partition table—FE FF FF (see Figure 7.6).

First value is reserved for the Head value (H = FE); when HEX FE is converted to decimal, the resulting value is equal to 254.

The remaining calculation gets a little tricky. The values are not reversed (little endian), but they are regrouped. Remember, HEX is our representation of binary. Also, remember that code can be written to perform any mathematical function on any binary values.

As stated, the first byte, in this case FE, is reserved for the HEAD value, so we remove that value. We are left with HEX FF FF.

This next step is where we regroup, but in order to do so we must convert our HEX values to their binary equivalents, which results in:

FF = 11111111
FF = 11111111

We put these binary values together—11111111 11111111, and we regroup those values, the first 6 bits, and the next 10 bits.

Why this regrouping?

It all has to do with how the code handles the binary. It is important to remember that binary is, at its base, simply 0s and 1s. It is code that combines them into bytes just as it is code that regroups and splits them. Ultimately, if we were to look at the numerical data representation embedded within the disk's surface (i.e., platter) all we would see would be a long string of consecutively joined 0s and 1s.

What defines the partition table? What defines sectors? What defines bytes? Why words and Dwords? Why endianness? Why this regrouping of byte offset 05 through 07 of the partition table?

It's all in the code (e.g., firmware, ROM, boot code, OS code, programmers and developers, etc.—it depends on "how" the code has been written). The code

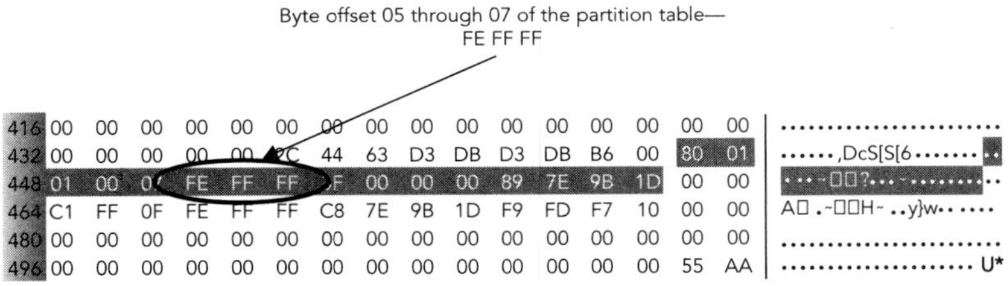

FIGURE 7.6 Byte Offset 05 through 07 of the Partition Table

is telling the system "how" to handle "which" binary bits and how to arrange these bits within the grouping for interpretation.

This gives us a binary number grouping as such:

(11 1111) (11 1111 1111)

Now converting 111111 binary into its decimal equivalent, gives us a value of 63 (the sector address). Converting 1111111111 binary into its decimal equivalent gives us a value of 1,023 (the cylinder address).

The sector is assigned the first grouping and the cylinder is assigned the second grouping:

63 = Sector
1,023 = Cylinder

The final CHS tuple is 1023:254:63.

Using the legacy CHS system, the starting point for the partition is 0:1:1, and the end point is 1023:254:63.

This is a long explanation for extracting CHS values from a partition table, but for what reason is this information valuable or even necessary?

The more meaningful information follows the CHS addressing, which is the starting sector (in the relative column) and the size in sectors. The size of the partition is 496,729,737 sectors, *relative* to sector 63.

Thus, this implies that the starting point if utilizing CHS reference is 0:1:1, whereas if using LBA reference, it would be 63. Therefore, the location of the starting sector for the partition in CHS is 0:1:1 and in LBA, 63.

Why Is This Important?

As a cyber forensic investigator it is important to understand *where* data and *how* data are located on the hard drive. Nowadays forensic tools do this behind the scenes. Cyber forensic investigators may not necessarily need to concern themselves with this information in order to perform a forensic examination. But, *it is imperative to understand how and why this occurs*. If called to the witness stand and the defense attorney asks, "Can you please tell the court exactly where on the hard drive did you find the evidence and how you made that determination?" you will need to understand these basic concepts.

CHS Summary

This is a legacy system, CHS, that in its day was helpful in identifying size in smaller drives. It is constrained by the amount of bits available in the partition table, which are used to represent these values.

Recall from Chapter 1 we discussed the possible outcomes or combinations around a Base two encoding scheme; with one (1) bit we only had two outcomes—on or off, and with two (2) bits we had four (4) outcomes or combinations. As we just discussed, one full byte is used to compute the Head value. If one byte contains eight (8) bits, how many possible outcomes can we have in a Base two encoding scheme with eight (8) bits? 256! So, we can only have 256 values for the Head variable.

Note: there are really only 255 possible values for Head due to a Microsoft bug. For details see http://thestarman.pcministry.com/asm/mbr/DiskTerms. htm#HDcnt.

Since Head value starts count at zero (0), then the greatest possible value for Head is 254. Also recall that in order to compute the sector value, we removed the leading two bits of the second (or middle) byte and slid them over to the Cylinder value, thus leaving six bits for the sector value.

Therefore, the largest value you can have for a Sector is [11 1111] (six bits), or 63, and likewise the largest value that can be obtained for a Cylinder is [11 1111 1111] or 1,023.

So the largest size for a drive using the constraining CHS labeling method is determined by multiplying the cylinder, head, and sector values (C * H * S) thus, 1,023 * 254 * 63, which equals 16,370,046 sectors. Multiplying the number of sectors by the number of bytes per sector (512), (16,370,046 * 512), results in a total number of bytes for the drive of 8,381,463,552 bytes, or roughly an 8 GB drive. The CHS parameter ceases to be much of an ending sector identifier once a drive exceeds 8 GB.

 VOLUMES AND PARTITIONS

In the greater world of information technology, *volumes* and *partitions* are often times used by practitioners as referring to the same thing; however, there are subtle differences between the two and sometimes the lines between the two can get fuzzy. In short, volumes exist at the logical OS level, and partitions exist at the physical, media specific level. Sometimes there is a one-to-one correspondence, but it is not guaranteed to be true.

A partition is a collection of (physically) consecutive sectors (see Figure 7.7), where a volume is a collection of (logically) addressable sectors (see Figure 7.8). Herein lies the difference; the data contained within a volume may appear consecutive, but only logically.

A partition, as explained in previous chapters, is an area of the hard disk drive that is defined by an entry in the partition table of the MBR, and is

FIGURE 7.7 A Partition Is a Collection of (PHYSICALLY) Consecutive Sectors

FIGURE 7.8 A Volume Is a Collection of (LOGICALLY CONSECUTIVE) Addressable Sectors

recognized system wide. The partition is interpreted by code contained within that same sector, the MBR, and a partition is usually a subdivision. As the name implies, it is the process of splitting something larger into smaller pieces.

A volume is an area defined or interpreted by an operating system. A volume is recognized by the operating system and will have a drive letter associated with it. It is often used synonymously with the term *drive* or *disk*. (See Table 7.3.)

In this example:

1. "C:," "D:," and "E:" are volumes.
2. Hard Disk 1 and Hard Disk 2 are physical disks.
3. Any of these can be called a "drive."

Perhaps most importantly, a volume contains the *file system*, which is unique to the operating system and only understood by the specific operating system. File systems will be addressed in depth in Chapter 8.

The physical verses logical nature of the partition and volume however are not necessarily always mutually exclusive. The difference or similarities

TABLE 7.3   Volumes and Partitions

Physical Disk	Partition	Filesystem	Drive Letter
Hard Disk 1	Partition 1	NTFS	C:
	Partition 2	FAT32	D:
Hard Disk 2	Partition 1	FAT32	E:

sometimes get fuzzy as they were not created with the idea of the other in mind. In fact, many times they are the same thing.

For example, if a system contains one hard disk drive then it will contain one volume, such that if a hard disk were to be divided into partitions (as set forth by the partition table in the MBR), then each partition would become a volume. In this case, the partition is also a volume and they are essentially the same, although their definitions remain unique.

So a volume can be a whole hard disk or a partition. A volume can be a partition, a flash drive like an iPod, a floppy disk, mounted from a network server, or even a RAID array.

Reasons Why We Have Partitions and Volumes

Partitioning a drive may help to increase *HDD* efficiency by making cluster size smaller. Volumes, on the other hand, create logically intuitive storage areas (e.g., "Save it to the K drive").

Volumes are identified by file systems, and file Systems are the way in which files are accessed and stored by an operating system. So, one may have two separate volumes in order to have two separate operating systems running on the same machine. Volumes provide enhanced recovery, data availability, performance, and storage configuration options. (See Figure 7.9.)

Extended Partitions

We already know that a single hard drive can have up to four partitions. The reason being is that there are only enough bytes available in the partition table of the MBR to accommodate four entries. We are also aware that typically when a partition is created on a single hard drive, it automatically becomes a volume and is assigned a drive letter (e.g., C:, D:, etc.). A volume and a partition are the same at this point, albeit with varying definitions.

As with everything else there are always exceptions. One of the four partitions defined by the partition table of a hard drive may be subdivided

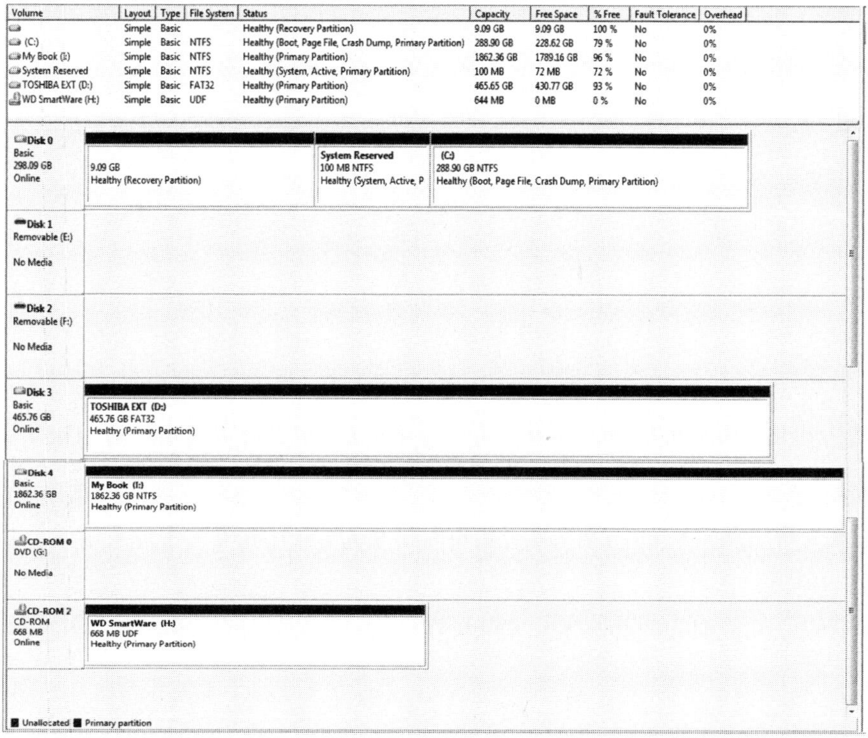

Volume	Layout	Type	File System	Status	Capacity	Free Space	% Free	Fault Tolerance	Overhead
	Simple	Basic		Healthy (Recovery Partition)	9.09 GB	9.09 GB	100 %	No	0%
(C:)	Simple	Basic	NTFS	Healthy (Boot, Page File, Crash Dump, Primary Partition)	288.90 GB	228.62 GB	79 %	No	0%
My Book (I:)	Simple	Basic	NTFS	Healthy (Primary Partition)	1862.36 GB	1789.16 GB	96 %	No	0%
System Reserved	Simple	Basic	NTFS	Healthy (System, Active, Primary Partition)	100 MB	72 MB	72 %	No	0%
TOSHIBA EXT (D:)	Simple	Basic	FAT32	Healthy (Primary Partition)	465.65 GB	430.77 GB	93 %	No	0%
WD SmartWare (H:)	Simple	Basic	UDF	Healthy (Primary Partition)	644 MB	0 MB	0 %	No	0%

Disk 0
Basic
298.09 GB
Online

9.09 GB	System Reserved	(C:)
Healthy (Recovery Partition)	100 MB NTFS	288.90 GB NTFS
	Healthy (System, Active, P	Healthy (Boot, Page File, Crash Dump, Primary Partition)

Disk 1
Removable (E:)

No Media

Disk 2
Removable (F:)

No Media

Disk 3
Basic
465.76 GB
Online

TOSHIBA EXT (D:)
465.76 GB FAT32
Healthy (Primary Partition)

Disk 4
Basic
1862.36 GB
Online

My Book (I:)
1862.36 GB NTFS
Healthy (Primary Partition)

CD-ROM 0
DVD (G:)

No Media

CD-ROM 2
CD-ROM
668 MB
Online

WD SmartWare (H:)
668 MB UDF
Healthy (Primary Partition)

■ Unallocated ■ Primary partition

FIGURE 7.9 Disk Manager View—Partitions

into multiple logical partitions (volumes), therefore allowing two or more volumes to exist within one partition. This subdivided partition is referred to as an *extended partition.* (See Figure 7.10.)

The extended partition was created to allow for additional logical partitions or volumes. Since a partition essentially becomes a volume upon creation, then a hard disk was limited to four volumes. In order to overcome this shortcoming the extended partition is created. It allows for itself to be further subdivided into logical volumes. Mind you, the partition table contained within the MBR still only defines four partitions and as far as it is concerned only four partitions exists.

When an extended partition is created, an extended partition table is also created. In essence, the extended partition is akin to a disk drive in its own right—it has its own partition table that points to one or more partitions (now called logical partitions, as opposed to the four primary partitions) contained entirely within the extended partition itself.[5]

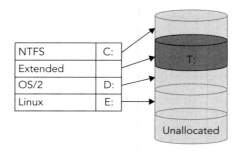

NTFS	C:
Extended	
OS/2	D:
Linux	E:

FIGURE 7.10 Disk Drive with Extended Partition

There is no limit on the number of logical volumes other than the fact that there are only 26 letters in the alphabet and A, B, and C have been taken.

Figure 7.10 shows the existence of five volumes. In order for there to be five volumes on a single disk an extended partition would need to be created. As we can see, these exist as logical partitions and are all part of an extended partition.

 ## SUMMARY

We conclude this chapter with a discussion of extended partitions to demonstrate the existence of partition defining data contained within an area of the hard drive other than the partition table, contained within the MBR.

The extended partition contains its own "sub" or extended partition boot record to identify its subdivisions. This concept of further identifying and defining parameters continues within volumes as well. Volumes also contain boot sectors that identify the file system contained within and its parameters, just as the MBR contains data that identifies itself so to do volumes.

Why are the review and discussion of volumes and partitions so important to the cyber forensic examiner? Partitions in some form or another were covered in the past three chapters; why spend so much time covering, reviewing, and discussing partitions?

Partitions are extremely important as they identify the layout of the hard drive. As a cyber forensic examiner it is extremely important to understand where data resides and how it resides there.

The forensic tools available to investigators today automatically perform much of the function of identifying partitions, and examiners don't have to go through the painstaking steps of identifying where partitions start and end. Investigators have grown to develop a certain level of dependency on these tools.

However, remove those tools and how are you able to identify the partition type and size? How would you make sense of all the 0s and 1s without the knowledge of knowing where data starts and where it stops? Before you can properly investigate you must properly "enumerate." What if you are called to the witness stand and then asked to explain such concepts? Stating, "the tool did it for me" won't be enough, especially not enough to prove your expertise or knowledge of "how" the data were identified, found, and examined.

The importance of identifying or enumerating data can be seen in the ongoing case of Ronelle Sawyer, who is investigating whether Jose McCarthy has potentially engaged in the unlawful distribution of his organization's intellectual property to a competitor, Janice Witcome, managing director of the XYZ Company.

Jose McCarthy, in an effort to conceal his actions, created two partitions on his 80 GB hard drive; one in which he used for day-to-day activity and a second he used to store his malicious activity. When confronted with the possibility of criminal prosecution he quickly deleted the second partition, therefore making it "invisible" to the operating system.

Ronelle would be able to clearly see that the hard drive is 80 GB, but how would she be able to identify the size of the partition? How would she be able to account for all 80 GB of data?

If the second partition is not identified she may miss a lot of evidence; in this case, all the "essential criminal evidence."

As a cyber forensic investigator, Ronelle would, by protocol, examine the partition table and see only one partition of 60 GB, and the starting and ending points of that single partition could quickly be determined. Without the use of forensic tools, if Ronelle did not have working knowledge of the specifics and functioning of the partition table, how would our investigator be able to explain the missing 20 GB?

Sure, there are other ways to identify the missing space but the validity of understanding the functioning and role of the partition table remains.

Keep in mind that when deleting a partition only the partition table entry is deleted. All the data contained within the partition remains until they are overwritten. Being that the partition is no longer used and inactive the data contained within will not be overwritten. So it is likely that these data will remain intact and retrievable as part of an investigation.

Identifying the end of the first partition will be helpful to Ronelle in locating the starting point of the deleted partition. Finally, the deleted partition can be recovered and all those data associated with the second partition retrieved, accessed, and analyzed. Recovering a partition, and its critical data information, may be difficult without a firm grasp of the functioning of partitions.

Chapter 8 continues with the natural progression of how the computer "mounts" data and goes into greater detail on the important topics of volumes and file systems, and their relationship to the overall cyber forensic investigation.

NOTES

1. "Chapter 17—Disk and File System Basics," TechNet, 2010 Microsoft Corporation, retrieved June 2010, http://technet.microsoft.com/en-us/library/cc750198.aspx.
2. Ibid.
3. C. Kozierok, C., "Logical Block Addressing (LBA)," *The PC Guide*, Site Version: 2.2.0—Version Date: April 17, 2001, retrieved June 2010, www.pcguide.com/ref/hdd/bios/modesLBA-c.html.
4. Ibid.
5. "Appendix C. An Introduction to Disk Partitions," *Red Hat Enterprise Linux 4: Installation Guide for the IBM® POWER Architecture*, retrieved June 2010, http://web.mit.edu/rhel-doc/4/RH-DOCS/rhel-ig-ppc-multi-en-4/ap-partitions.html.

CHAPTER EIGHT

File Systems—FAT 12/16

W E ARE CONTINUING with the natural sequence of events of how data is stored electronically. We discussed the boot process and partition table to exemplify concepts of how data is stored on the hard drive. We follow the computer boot sequence, as it is the primary way in which data are "assembled" into information which we can use, or for which we may be searching as part of an investigation.

The next piece of "data assembly" is more logical in nature and actually brings data to a state in which we can actually access and use it. This chapter covers file systems and concepts related to the "mounting" of data into identifiable information.

 TECH REVIEW

In the previous chapter we have started to cross the line between the physical storage of data and the logical storage of data. The definition of physical being the actual on/off state of the bit and its location on the hard drive platter, as defined by Cylinder, Head, and Sector (CHS) and Logical Block Address (LBA), with the partition defining the more physical boundary of data as they reside in the disk itself.

We discussed how contiguous physical bits are assembled together into physical constructs called sectors. Consecutive sectors are then logically assembled into what is called a cluster. As discussed, a cluster is a logical unit of storage which is made up of at least one sector.

When a file is saved it automatically receives a full cluster as a "container" for its storage. If the file is smaller than the container, it only occupies that one cluster. If the file is larger than a cluster then it will occupy as many clusters as needed until its contents are allocated.

Here is a brief example to reinforce this important concept.

Let's assume a cluster contains eight sectors; at 512 bytes per sector the total cluster size would therefore equal 4,096 bytes (8 × 512). Let's take a basic file, File A, whose size is a total of 1,040 bytes.

Our "File A" occupies one full cluster. Determining how many sectors File A occupies within this single cluster simply involves dividing File A's size (1,040 bytes) by 512 bytes per sector. We see that File A uses two full sectors and 16 bytes of the third sector in the cluster (see Figure 8.1).

Clusters do not necessarily need to be used contiguously, meaning a large file needing multiple clusters may save a piece of the file to one cluster and another piece to another cluster somewhere else on the hard drive. Large files will often need to be fragmented in such a manner in order to find a resting place. Logically it appears as one file but physically it is fragmented throughout the drive.

We often hear the phrase "defrag a hard drive." Defragmentation of the hard drive means to actually move the data so that the clusters are physically

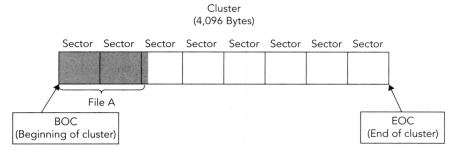

FIGURE 8.1   Sector Utilization of a File Stored within a Cluster

next to one another, therefore not fragmented. When files are heavily fragmented the system will need to reassemble those clusters before presenting data. The hard drive must spin around and pull components together. This takes time and, when multiplied, may impede overall performance and operational efficiency.

FILE SYSTEMS

A file system is a tool used for storing and retrieving data on a computer. It is the tool that tracks the allocation of the clusters, and it allows for a hierarchy of directories, folders, and files. A file system addresses and manages all the clusters contained within a volume.

A file system is usually defined during the creation of a partition; it is at this point that the partition "becomes" a volume. File systems determine how and where files are placed on a hard drive, with the goal of trying to optimize data retrieval speeds. As discussed, saving files to contiguous clusters is optimally more efficient for data access and retrieval.

When looking for a file, the operating system needs a system or method to determine where on the hard drive the file has been placed. Imagine if you will a Microsoft Word document saved on a hard drive being analogous to a book in a library. It is nice and convenient for us to click on an icon and access our document. As users, we have no care as to where that document resides physically on the hard drive.

We may know where that document resides logically within a folder structure, but we are oblivious (and justifiably so), as to which specific bits on the hard drive are allocated to this individual document. This is not something the end user needs to be concerned with; however, it is imperative that the file system knows otherwise when we click on the Word document icon nothing would happen.

To find a book within a library one simply looks up the name of the book (or title, author, and/or other pertinent information) in a card catalog (see Figure 8.2).

This directs a potential reader to a certain aisle (see Figure 8.3).

And then points to the book's exact location within the library (see Figure 8.4).

Ah, the good ol' days . . . now we search for the same book electronically!

Imagine, for instance, if libraries did not have a cataloging system (such as the Dewey Decimal System) for all its books. A library contains thousands

FIGURE 8.2 Library Card Catalog System (circa mid-twentieth century)

and thousands of books. Anyone who has ever stepped foot in a library can imagine how daunting a task it would be to locate a specific book with no idea of its exact location. Finding a single book could literally take hours, days, or even weeks, depending on the number of books residing within the library. The cataloging system used within a library makes finding the exact location of a book relatively painless (see Figure 8.5).

The catalog entry will contain information about the book such as author, title, dates, and location within the library. File systems in computers must use a similar method, otherwise locating files would be impossible. The computer's file system will contain information about the file such as the file's name, size, and starting location (address on the disk).

The information contained within this filing system is often referred to as Metadata. Metadata in its simplest definition is data about data. It is essentially those data that would exist on the physical card residing within the manual card catalog itself. The card would not contain the entire contents of the book (the story), but rather would contain the title, author, publishing date, and the exact location of the book within the library.

FIGURE 8.3 Physical Storage Location of Book within a Library
Source: © GlobalTrekk Photos, used with permission.

 METADATA

We have discussed metadata and will again as it is relevant here in our discussion of file systems. Metadata consists of information that characterizes data. In essence, metadata answers the who, what, when, where, why, and how about the data/document. Whenever an electronic document is created, opened, or saved, metadata is altered. Operating systems require file systems in order for them to function, and information about these file systems is contained in part in metadata.

Metadata are used for a variety of reasons, such as to enhance publishing, editing, viewing, filing, and retrieval. Some metadata are accessible through

FIGURE 8.4 Exact Location of Desired Book within a Library (specific floor, aisle, shelf, and position on the shelf)
Source: © GlobalTrekk Photos, used with permission.

operating software or parent software interfaces. For example, open a folder on a Windows operating system and select the "Details" view. Information made available and visible includes name, size, type, and document modified date of its contents. Open the "properties" tab on an MS Word document and more information about the document is revealed. This is metadata. Other metadata is only accessible through HEX editors or other, more specialized tools.

Here are some examples of metadata that may be stored along with a document:

- Your name
- Your initials
- Your company or organization name
- The name of your computer
- The name of the network server or hard disk where you saved the document
- Other file properties and summary information
- Non-visible portions of embedded OLE objects
- The names of previous document authors
- Document revisions
- Document versions

FIGURE 8.5 A Library's "File System"
Source: © David Fulmer, used with permission.

- Template information
- Hidden text
- Comments

The concept of metadata can be seen in many day-to-day areas other than electronic evidence. As we discussed earlier, the data contained within a card catalog is metadata.

Take a look, for example, at the very simple graphic of planet Earth as shown in Figure 8.6.

Longitude and latitude (maps in general) contain metadata about our planet, Earth. They are artificial; after all, our planet does not have grid lines going through it, or superimposed upon it. This metadata was necessary to allow an individual to identify a unique location on the planet, and it was principally designed by those who needed to navigate the oceans, which are notably lacking in visible features. If it weren't for these metadata, we might never have mapped the Earth correctly in its entirety.

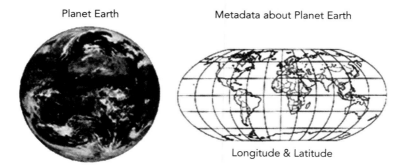

Planet Earth   Metadata about Planet Earth

Longitude & Latitude

FIGURE 8.6 Planet Earth and Metadata

Metadata is often imperative to accessing and identifying the object it defines. Just as a map aids us in locating an unfamiliar geographic location or a card catalog aids in locating one book out of thousands, so too does a file system aid us in locating the few bits out of billions that make up a file.

There are different library filing systems such as the Dewey Decimal System or the Library of Congress' classification system. The same is true for computing file systems. Microsoft Windows operating systems have unique file systems, as do Apple-, Linux-, and Unix-based operating systems.

TABLE 8.1 Computer Operating Systems with Corresponding File Systems

Operating System	File System Used
PC floppy disks	FAT 12 only
DOS	FAT 16 only
Windows 3.x	FAT 16 only
Windows 95	FAT 16 or FAT32
Windows 98	FAT 16 or FAT32
Windows ME	FAT 32
Windows 2000	FAT 16, FAT 32 or NTFS
Windows XP	NTFS
Windows Server 2003	NTFS
Windows Vista	NTFS
Windows 7	NTFS
HFS	MAC
Ext2, Ext3	Linux
UFS	Unix

Some varieties of computer operating systems with corresponding file systems are shown in Table 8.1.

FILE ALLOCATION TABLE (FAT) FILE SYSTEM

The FAT filing system is a bit dated and used in earlier Microsoft operating systems. It is discussed here to best explain and exemplify the concepts involved within file systems. Any one specific file system will likely become obsolete, but the general concepts are worth examination. The important thing here is to understand the concept of how file systems work.

FAT is used to place files in free *clusters* of space on the hard drive. This is not like a videocassette tape, phonographic record, or even a CD, where files are placed in a physical order from beginning to end. Each entry in the File Allocation Table corresponds directly to one cluster, at which point the cluster becomes *allocated* to that data referenced in the FAT.

As discussed, there are different versions of the FAT filing system: FAT 12, 16, and 32. File Allocation Table entries can be 12, 16, or 32 bits long corresponding to FAT 12, FAT 16, or FAT 32 respectively. It is these table entries which are used to identify or demarcate a cluster. A single file is allocated (or saved) to a cluster, even if the file does not completely fill up the entire cluster. A large file of course may need to be allocated across multiple clusters.

The FAT filing system consists of three main components:

1. Volume Boot Record
2. Directory Entries
3. File Allocation Table

Volume Boot Record (VBR)

The *volume boot record* is also known as volume boot sector or volume boot. This is typically the first sector of a partition. As the Master Boot Record (MBR) defines the partitions of a physical disk, the VBR performs a similar function for an individual volume/partition. It defines the partition type (file system) and holds the parameter information such as bytes per sector and sector per cluster within the volume.

We do not cover all the byte offsets within the VBR, but do discuss those that bring key concepts to light. For additional information on specific byte offset values within the VBR and further discussions on the VBR, it is suggested that the reader review the following appendices:

We see in Figure 8.7 that byte offset 54–58 identifies the file system, in this example, FAT 16. If you "convert" the HEX values 46:41:54:31:36 (as bytes) to ASCII as shown in Table 8.2, the individual HEX value FAT 16 is returned. See the individual HEX values marked in Figure 8.8.

located at byte offset 54–58

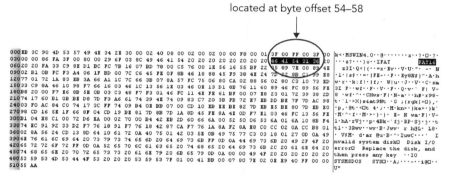

FIGURE 8.7 File System Type Identified at Byte Offset 54–58

TABLE 8.2 VBR Byte Offset 54–58 HEX Value and ASCII Equivalent

Byte Offset	HEX Value	ASCII Character Equivalent
54	46	F
55	41	A
56	54	T
57	31	1
58	36	6

Bytes per Sector

In Chapters 4 and 5 we discussed the fact that typically there are usually 512 bytes per sector. This is pretty standard knowledge; however, just the same, this fact but must be defined somewhere in order for the OS to know that this is the bytes per sector size that the system is using.

Dec	Hex	Name	Char	Ctrl-char	Dec	Hex	Char	Dec	Hex	Char	Dec	Hex	Char
0	0	Null	NUL	CTRL-@	32	20	Space	64	40	@	96	60	`
1	1	Start of heading	SOH	CTRL-A	33	21	!	65	41	A	97	61	a
2	2	Start of text	STX	CTRL-B	34	22	"	66	42	B	98	62	b
3	3	End of text	ETX	CTRL-C	35	23	#	67	43	C	99	63	c
4	4	End of xmit	EOT	CTRL-D	36	24	$	68	44	D	100	64	d
5	5	Enquiry	ENQ	CTRL-E	37	25	%	69	45	E	101	65	e
6	6	Acknowledge	ACK	CTRL-F	38	26	&	70	46	F	102	66	f
7	7	Bell	BEL	CTRL-G	39	27	'	71	47	G	103	67	g
8	8	Backspace	BS	CTRL-H	40	28	(	72	48	H	104	68	h
9	9	Horizontal tab	HT	CTRL-I	41	29	)	73	49	I	105	69	i
10	0A	Line feed	LF	CTRL-J	42	2A	*	74	4A	J	106	6A	j
11	0B	Vertical tab	VT	CTRL-K	43	2B	+	75	4B	K	107	6B	k
12	0C	Form feed	FF	CTRL-L	44	2C	,	76	4C	L	108	6C	l
13	0D	Carriage feed	CR	CTRL-M	45	2D	-	77	4D	M	109	6D	m
14	0E	Shift out	SO	CTRL-N	46	2E	.	78	4E	N	110	6E	n
15	0F	Shift in	SI	CTRL-O	47	2F	/	79	4F	O	111	6F	o
16	10	Data line escape	DLE	CTRL-P	48	30	0	80	50	P	112	70	p
17	11	Device control 1	DC1	CTRL-Q	49	31	1	81	51	Q	113	71	q
18	12	Device control 2	DC2	CTRL-R	50	32	2	82	52	R	114	72	r
19	13	Device control 3	DC3	CTRL-S	51	33	3	83	53	S	115	73	s
20	14	Device control 4	DC4	CTRL-T	52	34	4	84	54	T	116	74	t
21	15	Neg acknowledge	NAK	CTRL-U	53	35	5	85	55	U	117	75	u
22	16	Synchronous idle	SYN	CTRL-V	54	36	6	86	56	V	118	76	v
23	17	End of xmit block	ETB	CTRL-W	55	37	7	87	57	W	119	77	w
24	18	Cancel	CAN	CTRL-X	56	38	8	88	58	X	120	78	x
25	19	End of medium	EM	CTRL-Y	57	39	9	89	59	Y	121	79	y
26	1A	Substitute	SUB	CTRL-Z	58	3A	:	90	5A	Z	122	7A	z
27	1B	Escape	ESC	CTRL-[	59	3B	;	91	5B	[	123	7B	{
28	1C	File separator	FS	CTRL-\	60	3C	<	92	5C	\	124	7C		
29	1D	Group separator	GS	CTRL-]	61	3D	=	93	5D	]	125	7D	}
30	1E	Record separator	RS	CTRL-^	62	3E	>	94	5E	^	126	7E	~
31	1F	Unit separator	US	CTRL-_	63	3F	?	95	5F	_	127	7F	DEL

FIGURE 8.8 Standard ASCII Chart/ASCII Table—HEX to Decimal Code Conversion

In FAT that somewhere is in the Volume Boot Record, at byte offset 11–12. In our example, the HEX editor shown in Figure 8.9, we see the HEX values 00 02.

If we pull out the old scientific calculator to determine the decimal equivalent to HEX 00 02 (or simply 2) we find the answer to be 2.

But, wait a minute! Two bytes per sector? Wasn't it pretty standard to have 512 bytes per sector?

The HEX value is correct. Remember, it all has to do with how the operating system instructs the code to process and handle data, and in this case the endianness is important as it is reversed, from the perception of reading the value from left-to-right (big endian) to reading the data's value from right-to-left or in this case, little endian.

Therefore, the HEX value is 02 00, or simply 200. Again, back to our calculators, and we see that the decimal equivalent of HEX 200 is indeed 512. Thus there are 512 bytes per sector!

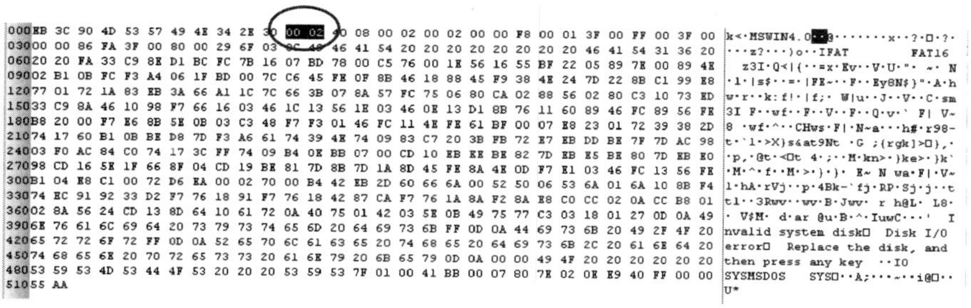

```
000 EB 3C 90 4D 53 57 49 4E 34 2E 3(00 02)0 08 00 02 00 02 00 00 F8 00 01 3F 00 FF 00 3F 00   k<•MSWIN4.0••••••••x••?•0•?•
030 00 00 86 FA 3F 00 80 00 29 6F 03 9C 48 46 41 54 20 20 20 20 20 20 20 46 41 54 31 36 20   •••z?••)o•IFAT      FAT16
060 20 20 FA 33 C9 8E D1 BC FC 7B 16 07 BD 78 00 C5 76 00 1E 56 16 55 BF 22 05 89 7E 00 89 4E   z3I•Q•{••=x•Ev•V•U•~• •• N
090 02 B1 0B FC F3 A4 06 1F BD 00 7C C6 45 FE 0F 8B 46 18 88 45 F9 38 4E 24 7D 22 8B C1 99 E8   •l•|sf•••=•|FE••F••Ey8Nf}"•A•h
120 77 01 72 1A 83 EB 3A 66 A1 1C 7C 66 3B 07 8A 57 FC 75 06 80 CA 02 88 56 02 80 C3 10 73 ED   w•r••k:f••|f;• W|u••J••V••C•sm
150 33 C9 8A 46 10 98 F7 66 16 03 46 1C 13 56 1E 03 46 0E 13 D1 8B 76 11 60 89 46 FC 89 56 FE   3I F••wf••F••V••F••Q•v•' F| V•
180 B8 20 00 F7 E6 8B 5E 0B 03 C3 48 F7 F3 01 46 FC 11 4E FE 61 BF 00 07 E8 23 01 72 39 38 2D   8 •wf•^••CHws•F|•N•a••h$•r98-
210 74 17 60 B1 0B BE D8 7D F3 A6 61 74 39 4E 74 09 83 C7 20 3B FB 72 E7 EB DD BE 7F 7D AC 98   t•`l•>X)s&at9Nt••G ;(rgk]>O},•
240 03 F0 AC 84 C0 74 17 3C FF 74 09 B4 0E BB 07 00 CD 10 EB EE BE 82 7D EB E5 BE 80 7D BE E0   •p,•@t•<Ot 4;••M•kn>•)ke>•)k•
270 98 CD 16 5E 1F 66 8F 04 CD 19 BE 81 7D 8B 7D 1A 8D 45 FE 8A 4E 0D F7 E1 03 46 FC 13 56 FE   •M•^•f••M•>•)•)• E~ N wa•F|•V•
300 B1 04 E8 C1 00 72 D6 EA 00 02 70 00 B4 42 EB 2D 60 66 6A 00 52 50 06 53 6A 01 6A 10 8B F4   l•hA•rVj••p•4Bk-`fj•RP•Sj•j••t
330 74 EC 91 92 33 D2 F7 76 18 91 F7 76 18 42 87 CA F7 76 1A 8A F2 8A E8 C0 CC 02 0A CC B8 01   tl••3Rwv••wv•B•Jwv•  r h@L• L8•
360 02 8A 56 24 CD 13 8D 64 10 61 72 0A 40 75 01 42 03 5E 0B 49 75 77 C3 03 18 01 27 0D 0A 49   • VfM• d•ar @u•B•^•IuwC•••' I
390 6E 76 61 6C 69 64 20 73 79 73 74 65 6D 20 64 69 73 6B FF 0D 0A 44 69 73 6B 20 49 2F 4F 20   nvalid system diskO  Disk I/O
420 65 72 72 6F 72 FF 0D 0A 52 65 70 6C 61 63 65 20 74 68 65 20 64 69 73 6B 2C 20 61 6E 64 20   errorO  Replace the disk, and
450 74 68 65 6E 20 70 72 65 73 73 20 61 6E 79 20 6B 65 79 20 0D 0A 00 00 49 4F 20 20 20 20 20   then press any key  ••IO
480 53 59 53 4D 53 44 4F 53 20 20 20 53 59 53 7F 01 00 41 BB 00 07 80 7E 02 0E E9 40 FF 00 00   SYSMSDOS    SYSO••A;••••••i@O••
510 55 AA                                                                                        U•
```

FIGURE 8.9   Determining Bytes per Sector from the VBR at Byte Offset 11–12

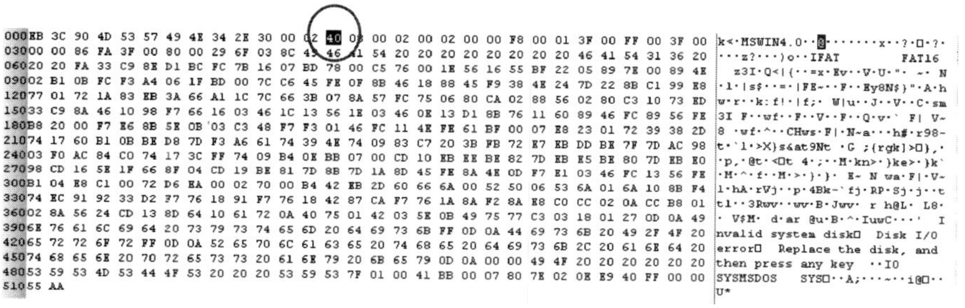

```
000 EB 3C 90 4D 53 57 49 4E 34 2E 30 00(02 40 0)0 00 02 00 02 00 00 F8 00 01 3F 00 FF 00 3F 00   k<•MSWIN4.0•••••••••x••?•0•?•
030 00 00 86 FA 3F 00 80 00 29 6F 03 8C 46 41 54 20 20 20 20 20 20 20 46 41 54 31 36 20   •••z?••)o•IFAT      FAT16
060 20 20 FA 33 C9 8E D1 BC FC 7B 16 07 BD 78 00 C5 76 00 1E 56 16 55 BF 22 05 89 7E 00 89 4E   z3I•Q•{••=x•Ev•V•U•~• •• N
090 02 B1 0B FC F3 A4 06 1F BD 00 7C C6 45 FE 0F 8B 46 18 88 45 F9 38 4E 24 7D 22 8B C1 99 E8   •l•|sf•••=•|FE••F••Ey8Nf}"•A•h
120 77 01 72 1A 83 EB 3A 66 A1 1C 7C 66 3B 07 8A 57 FC 75 06 80 CA 02 88 56 02 80 C3 10 73 ED   w•r••k:f••|f;• W|u••J••V••C•sm
150 33 C9 8A 46 10 98 F7 66 16 03 46 1C 13 56 1E 03 46 0E 13 D1 8B 76 11 60 89 46 FC 89 56 FE   3I F••wf••F••V••F••Q•v•' F| V•
180 B8 20 00 F7 E6 8B 5E 0B 03 C3 48 F7 F3 01 46 FC 11 4E FE 61 BF 00 07 E8 23 01 72 39 38 2D   8 •wf•^••CHws•F|•N•a••h$•r98-
210 74 17 60 B1 0B BE D8 7D F3 A6 61 74 39 4E 74 09 83 C7 20 3B FB 72 E7 EB DD BE 7F 7D AC 98   t•`l•>X)s&at9Nt••G ;(rgk]>O},•
240 03 F0 AC 84 C0 74 17 3C FF 74 09 B4 0E BB 07 00 CD 10 EB EE BE 82 7D EB E5 BE 80 7D BE E0   •p,•@t•<Ot 4;••M•kn>•)ke>•)k•
270 98 CD 16 5E 1F 66 8F 04 CD 19 BE 81 7D 8B 7D 1A 8D 45 FE 8A 4E 0D F7 E1 03 46 FC 13 56 FE   •M•^•f••M•>•)•)• E~ N wa•F|•V•
300 B1 04 E8 C1 00 72 D6 EA 00 02 70 00 B4 42 EB 2D 60 66 6A 00 52 50 06 53 6A 01 6A 10 8B F4   l•hA•rVj••p•4Bk-`fj•RP•Sj•j••t
330 74 EC 91 92 33 D2 F7 76 18 91 F7 76 18 42 87 CA F7 76 1A 8A F2 8A E8 C0 CC 02 0A CC B8 01   tl••3Rwv••wv•B•Jwv•  r h@L• L8•
360 02 8A 56 24 CD 13 8D 64 10 61 72 0A 40 75 01 42 03 5E 0B 49 75 77 C3 03 18 01 27 0D 0A 49   • VfM• d•ar @u•B•^•IuwC•••' I
390 6E 76 61 6C 69 64 20 73 79 73 74 65 6D 20 64 69 73 6B FF 0D 0A 44 69 73 6B 20 49 2F 4F 20   nvalid system diskO  Disk I/O
420 65 72 72 6F 72 FF 0D 0A 52 65 70 6C 61 63 65 20 74 68 65 20 64 69 73 6B 2C 20 61 6E 64 20   errorO  Replace the disk, and
450 74 68 65 6E 20 70 72 65 73 73 20 61 6E 79 20 6B 65 79 20 0D 0A 00 00 49 4F 20 20 20 20 20   then press any key  ••IO
480 53 59 53 4D 53 44 4F 53 20 20 20 53 59 53 7F 01 00 41 BB 00 07 80 7E 02 0E E9 40 FF 00 00   SYSMSDOS    SYSO••A;••••••i@O••
510 55 AA                                                                                        U•
```

FIGURE 8.10   Determining Clusters per Sector from the VBR at Byte Offset 13

Sectors per Cluster

The sectors per cluster are also defined here in the VBR. This value is defined in sector offset 13. (See Figure 8.10.)

The HEX value of sector offset 13 is 40 (see Figure 8.10). However, if we convert HEX 40 first to its decimal equivalent we get 64, then decimal 64 to its ASCII equivalent; we get "@." However, this value (HEX 40) is actually used to perform a mathematical function. So, we convert the HEX value 40 to a decimal value (again back to our scientific calculator).

After performing the calculation with the scientific calculator, we see that the HEX value 40 returns a decimal equivalent of 64.

As we have already touched upon, typically there are 512 bytes per sector. This is fairly common and as with the sector size of our example VBR in Figure 8.9, we have determined it to be 512 bytes. We now have identified how many sectors exist per cluster, again in our example (Figure 8.10), to be 64.

If we multiply the number of bytes per sector by number of sectors per cluster we arrive at the total size of the cluster, in bytes. Thus:

(Bytes per sector) × (Sectors per cluster) or 512 × 64, which yields a value
  of 32,768 bytes per cluster.
A full cluster then, in our example, is 32K bytes.

To verify this, all we need to do is view a document's properties, a document
that has been saved to a FAT 16 file system.

See Figure 8.11, where we have created a document named "hello.txt." If we
view the document's properties we see that the document's size is 5 bytes, and
that the size on disk (or cluster allocation) is 32,768 bytes.

 ## SLACK

The document in Figure 8.11 is allocated to at least one cluster and in this case
only one; however, we see a very inefficient use of space. As we discussed in the
tech review at the beginning of this chapter, when a file is written to a drive it
automatically receives at a minimum, one cluster.

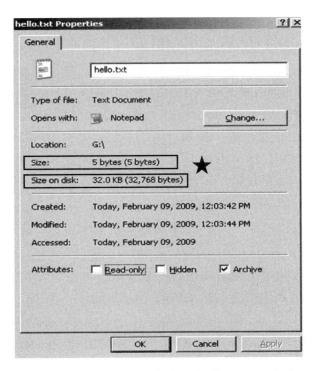

FIGURE 8.11   Document Properties Window for Document hello.txt

In this example, the file "hello.txt" would be allocated 32KB of disk space, regardless of its size. So, a small, 5-byte text document would get the entire 32,768-byte cluster.

As you can imagine, the FAT 16 file system is inefficient in its use of space. What happens to the remaining space? Nothing! It is *allocated space*, as it is part of the cluster assigned to the file "hello.txt," but was not required due to the small size of the file "hello.txt."

The unused space contained within the cluster reserved for "hello.txt" is referred to as *slack space*. It is allocated space but does not contain content from the saved file "hello.txt." The slack space will contain remnants of data that was stored in that allocated cluster previously. (See Figure 8.12.)

For example, say a 29,500-byte document named "Incriminating Evidence. doc" was allocated to that same cluster previously. (See Figure 8.13.) That "Incriminating Evidence.doc" document was sent to the recycle bin and then the recycle bin was emptied, thereby officially making that cluster available or unallocated.

Later, the file "hello.txt" was saved and it was allocated to that same cluster. Being that "hello.txt" is only 5 bytes in size it would only need the first

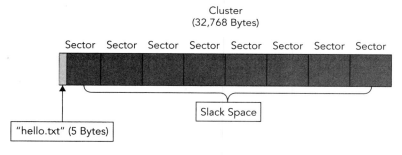

FIGURE 8.12 Slack Space (aka File Slack)

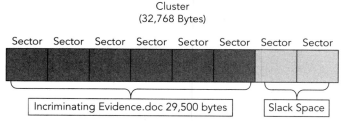

FIGURE 8.13 Incriminating Evidence.doc

five bytes of that cluster in order to contain itself. This would then leave 32,763 bytes of file slack. (See Figure 8.14.)

We determine this by knowing the total number of bytes per cluster (32,768) (i.e., cluster size), less the five bytes for the new file, "hello.txt," giving us the remaining number of bytes left in the original cluster allocated to the file "hello.txt," 32,763 bytes, which is now referred to as slack space.

The previous file saved to the cluster, "Incriminating Evidence.doc" was 29,500 bytes. Much of this file would therefore also remain in what is now file slack.

We determine this by knowing the total number of bytes (29,500 bytes) of the old file, "Incriminating Evidence.doc" less the five bytes of the new file, "hello.txt," giving us 29,495 bytes of slack space, which would contain the remnants of the previous file to occupy this space: "Incriminating Evidence .doc." (See Figure 8.15.)

As you can imagine there may be some worthwhile data contained within the 29,495 bytes of slack space, especially with a document named "Incriminating Evidence.doc."

Slack space can be further broken down into *File Slack* and *Sector Slack*. There are differences but both pertain to the slack space described.

When a file is saved it is allocated to a cluster. As discussed, clusters are comprised of sectors. When saved, a file is saved to the first sector of the cluster. If the file size exceeds the sector size (512 bytes), then it is saved to the next sector, and the next cluster, and the next, and so on and so forth, until the entire file is stored. The unused sectors within a cluster are often referred to as file slack while the unused bytes in a sector are often referred to as sector slack. (See Figure 8.16.)

To continue with our example: 32,768 bytes is our cluster size, less the five bytes of the new file, "hello.txt," equals 32,763 bytes of file slack in this cluster. With 512 bytes as the sector size, less the five bytes of the new file,

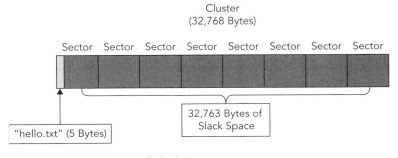

FIGURE 8.14 32,763 Bytes of Slack Space

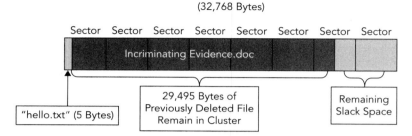

FIGURE 8.15 29, 495 Bytes of Deleted File Remaining in Slack Space

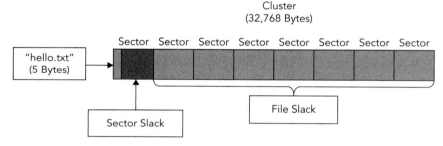

FIGURE 8.16 Sector and File Slack

"hello.txt", we now have 507 unused bytes in the sector, which we refer to as sector slack.

Slack space will be preserved (not overwritten) unless:

1. The file assigned to that allocated space ("hello.txt") is changed and/ or made larger in size, thereby writing to the slack space, (its allocated space).
2. The file, "hello.txt" is deleted from the recycle bin, therefore making the entire cluster available or *unallocated*. This may result in another file being allocated to that cluster. Note—if that new file is the same size or smaller than the previous file ("hello.txt") much of the data contained within the slack space could remain preserved.

 HEX REVIEW NOTE

HEX can be converted to ASCII as seen in a HEX editor. However, not all HEX will appear as text or legible ASCII. Most programming code will not have a human legible ASCII presentation. In fact, the only HEX that will have a legible representation is the HEX value that may be called up by the software code for various display purposes.

For example, when going into Disk Management software and viewing disk partition information, we will see the file system type is FAT 16. How does the computer know to display this information and, more precisely, how does the computer know what to display? The Disk Management programming code will tell the system to go to byte offset 54–58 in the first sector of the partition and display that information in ASCII, "FAT16," as displayed in Figure 8.7. These HEX values do not have a mathematical function; they are used for display purposes. Information that will be displayed will usually be legible in ASCII.

Notice for example the messages in the Volume Boot Record Figure 8.17, "Invalid System Disk," "Disk I/O error," and "Replace the disk, and press any key." This text is retrieved by code and displayed as error messages when there is an error during boot up. It is for this reason it is legible, because it may be called up by code and displayed as a message.

Usually, legible ASCII seen in HEX editors does not perform mathematical calculations or function as programming code; it is simply text that can be extracted and displayed by the system.

DIRECTORY ENTRIES

The second piece of the FAT Filing system, are the *directory entries*. Remember that the FAT filing system consists of three main components:

1. Volume Boot Record
2. Directory Entries
3. File Allocation Table

```
000EB 3C 90 4D 53 57 49 4E 34 2E 30 00 02 40 08 00 02 00 02 00 00 F8 00 01 3F 00 FF 00 3F 00   k<•MSWIN4.0••@•••••••x••?•O•?•
03000 00 86 FA 3F 00 80 00 00 29 6F 03 8C 49 46 41 54 20 20 20 20 20 20 20 20 46 41 54 31 36 20   •••=?•••)o••IFAT     FAT16
06020 20 FA 33 C9 8E D1 BC FC 7B 16 07 BD 78 00 C5 76 00 1E 56 16 55 BF 22 05 89 7E 00 89 4E   ±3I•Q•I(••=•Ev••V·U•••  +• N
09002 B1 0B FC F3 A4 06 1F BD 00 7C C6 45 FE 0F 8B 46 18 88 46 F9 38 4E 24 7D 22 8B C1 99 E8   •1•|=f••=•|FE••-F••Ey8N=}••A•h
12077 01 72 1A 83 EB 3A 66 A1 1C 7C 66 3B 07 8A 57 FC 75 06 80 CA 02 88 56 02 80 C3 10 73 ED   w·r••k:f••|f;• W|u••J••V••C•sm
15033 C9 8A 46 10 98 F7 66 16 03 46 1C 13 56 1E 03 46 0E 13 D1 8B 76 11 60 89 46 FC 89 56 FE   3I F••wf••F••V••F••Q•v•• F| V•
180EB 20 00 F7 E6 8B 5E 0B 03 C3 48 F7 F3 01 46 FC 11 4E FE 61 BF 00 07 E8 23 01 72 39 38 2D   E •wf•••CHws•F|•N•a••hE•r98•
21074 17 60 B1 0B BE D8 7D F3 A6 61 74 39 4E 74 09 83 C7 20 3B FB 72 E7 EB DD BE 7F 7D AC 98   t•`1••X)s&at9Nt •G ;(rgk|>O),•
24003 F0 AC 84 C0 74 17 3C FF 74 09 B4 0E BB 07 00 CD 10 EB EE BE 02 7D EB E5 BE 80 7D EB E0   •p,•@t•<Dt 4•,••M•kn>•}ke>•}k`
27098 CD 16 5E 1F 66 8F 04 CD 19 BE 81 7D 8B 7D 1A 8D 45 FE 8A 4E 0D F7 E1 03 46 FC 13 56 FE   •M•^•f••M•>••}•)• E• N va•F|•V•
300B1 04 E8 C1 00 72 B6 EA 00 02 70 00 B4 42 EE 2D 60 66 8A 00 52 50 06 53 6A 01 68 8B F4   1•hA•rV}•`p•4Bk••†}•BP•S}•}•†E
33074 EC 91 92 33 D2 F7 76 18 91 F7 76 18 42 87 CA F7 76 1A 8A F2 8A E8 C0 CC 02 0A CC B8 01   t|••3Bwv•wv•B•Jwv• z hEL• L8•
36002 8A 56 24 CD 13 8D 64 10 61 72 0A 40 75 01 42 03 5E 0B 49 75 77 C3 03 18 01 27 0D 0A 49   • V}M• d•ar @u•B••Iuwc••••• I
3906E 76 61 6C 69 64 20 73 79 73 74 65 6D 20 64 69 73 6B FF 0D 0A 44 69 73 6B 20 49 2F 4F 20   nvalid system disk0  Disk I/O
42065 72 72 6F 72 FF 0D 0A 52 65 70 6C 61 63 65 20 74 68 65 20 64 69 73 6B 2C 20 61 6E 64 20   error0 Replace the disk, and
45074 68 65 6E 20 70 72 65 73 73 20 61 6E 79 20 6B 65 79 20 0D 0A 00 00 00 49 4F 20 20 20 20   then press any key ••IO
48053 59 53 4D 53 44 4F 53 20 20 20 53 59 53 7F 01 00 41 BB 00 07 80 7E 02 0E E9 40 FF 00 00   SYSMSDOS   SYSU•A,•••••IB0•
510SS AA                                                                                          U•
```

FIGURE 8.17 ASCII Values of HEX Entries in the VBR

Every file and folder/directory is referenced in a separate 32-byte entry called a directory entry. A unique directory entry exists for each file and directory stored on a disk. Each directory entry contains information such as:

1. Names of the file and directory. For example: *"hello.txt."*
2. Time and data metadata.
3. Location—file names have to be linked to the actual data comprising the file and therefore there must be an attribute pointing to where the data actually starts, that is, the starting cluster.
4. Size of the file—its length.

These entries are located in the clusters allocated to the file's parent directory.

Figure 8.18 is an example of the entry for our example document, "Incriminating Evidence.doc," represented in ASCII.

Notice again *each* entry is 32 bytes in length. The total number of directory entries available is determined when volume is formatted and is fixed at 32 sectors within FAT 12/16. So, 32 sectors are allocated for directory entries and each directory entry itself is 32 bytes in length.

The following is a brief overview of the byte offset values of the directory entry in Figure 8.18:

- **Byte Offset 0.** The first character of the file name or status byte. When a file is deleted this character will be replaced with a "~" which tells the system that the space previously occupied by that file is now available, or unallocated. This is an important byte as it is what identifies a file as being deleted, or more appropriately, it identifies the space as unallocated. Note: the rest of the 31 bytes of the directory entry and the actual file remain intact until the space is eventually reallocated and potentially overwritten.
- **Byte Offset 1–7.** File name continued. Here we see a limitation of the FAT file system and it is referred to as Short File Names (SFN). Eight characters reserved for a file name is constrictive to say the least. Well, the file system

Byte Offset	0	1	2	3	4	5	6	7	8	9	10	11	12	13	14	15	16	17	18	19	20	21	22	23	24	25	26	27	28	29	30	31
ASCII	I	n	c	r	i	m	~	1	D	O	C		·		·	N	Q	F	:	I	:	·	·	O	Q	F	:	·	·	·	j	·	·
HEX	49	6E	63	72	69	6D	7E	31	44	4F	43	20	00	8C	4E	51	46	3A	49	3A	00	00	4F	51	46	3A	02	00	00	6A	00	00

FIGURE 8.18 Directory Entry for Document "Incriminating Evidence.doc"

takes this into consideration and appends the file name. The "~" in Byte Offset 6 implies a shortened name.

The 1 in Byte Offset 7 implies that this is the first document to contain those first six characters. For example, say another document was created called "Incrimination Study.doc." It would contain the same first six characters. Because of FATs limitations and in order to differentiate between these documents, FAT would name the second document, "Incrimination Study.doc," as Incrim~2.

- **Byte Offset 8–10.** Three character file extension. Extensions are used mostly by Microsoft Operating Systems and not needed or used by other operating systems. For more information regarding file extensions and types please refer back to Chapter 4.
- **Byte Offset 11.** Attributes—Read only, hidden, and so on.
- **Byte Offset 12–13.** Reserved.
- **Byte Offset 14–17.** Create time and date of file stored as MS_DOS 32-bit timestamp (discussed in Chapter 11).
- **Byte Offset 18–19.** Last accessed, date only, no time.
- **Byte Offset 20–21.** Two high bytes of FAT 32 starting cluster; FAT 12/16 will have zeros.
- **Byte Offset 22–25.** Last written time and date of file again as MS-DOS 32-bit timestamp (discussed in Chapter 11).
- **Byte Offset 26–27.** Starting cluster for FAT 12/16; two low bytes of the starting cluster for FAT 32.
- **Byte Offset 28–31.** Size in bytes of the file. Will be 0 for directories.

 ## FILE ALLOCATION TABLE (FAT)

Remember, the FAT Filing System consists of three main components:

1. Volume Boot Record
2. Directory Entries
3. *File Allocation Table (FAT)*

Here we will discuss and examine this third piece of the FAT filing system. The nomenclature for describing and writing the various FAT types can be shown as either FAT12, for example, with no space, or FAT 12, with a space. Either way is acceptable and used equally.

The FAT can be thought of as a map of all the clusters (a cluster, you will recall, is the smallest unit used to store files) on the hard drive. The FAT contains an entry for each available cluster on the disk.

The FAT tracks which clusters are allocated or unallocated (available or unavailable), tracking those allocated units (or clusters) which contain the file or data. Many times a document may surpass one allocation unit (one cluster) and need to be stored in multiple noncontiguous allocation units, or clusters; it is the FAT that will link these clusters.

The FAT finds the clusters that follow the starting cluster for any given file or directory. As we have discussed, files are not necessarily saved in a physically contiguous manner on the hard drive. It is therefore the job of the FAT to track the sequence of those clusters that will be combined (or *concatenated*) to create the saved file. The FAT also tracks *bad clusters*.

A visual depiction of the FAT is shown in Figure 8.19.

In the FAT filing system, the FAT is by default identified as FAT1. The FAT maintains a spare copy of itself, identified as FAT2, and is stored immediately following the entry for FAT1. The FAT for FAT 12, 16, or 32 begins at a location determined by that drive's structure, and the length of the table depends on the disk size and formatting.

The size of the FAT entries depends upon the version of FAT. In fact, the FAT version (FAT 12, 16, or 32) is named after the amount of bits contained within each entry of the FAT:

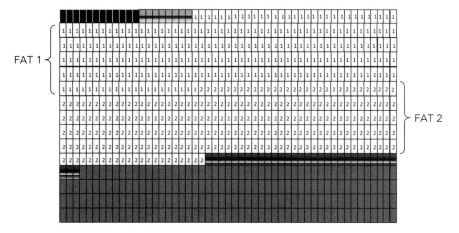

FIGURE 8.19 The File Allocation Table

FAT 12 has 12-bit entries, FAT 16 has 16-bit entries, and FAT 32 has 32-bit entries.

This naturally imposes limitations based upon the number of bits in the FAT, but how? Let's take a closer look at each FAT type.

FAT 12

Each entry is 12 bits in size, and each of these 12-bit entries in the FAT is representative of an actual cluster, the smallest allocation unit on a disk. Table 8.3 tells us how many values or possible outcomes can be achieved with 12 bits.

As we increase the number of bits it may be easier for simplicity and ease of understanding to use a calculator and simply figure 2^{12}. Remember, binary is Base 2!

There are only 4,096 values possible with 12 bits. Therefore, if each entry represents a cluster and there are only enough bits (12) to represent 4,096 unique values, therefore a maximum of only 4,096 clusters can be attained in FAT 12.

Tech Review

A quick review of Base 2 encoding would help to clear up this point. As we discussed previously, we cannot represent the four seasons with only one bit.

TABLE 8.3   Values or Possible Outcomes That Can Be Achieved with 12 Bits

Number of Bits	Possible Number of Values or Outcomes
1	2
2	4
3	8
4	16
5	32
6	64
7	128
8	256
9	512
10	1,024
11	2,048
12	4,096

With one bit we can represent two values, such as on/off, stop/go, or green/red (e.g., 0 = red, 1 = green).

In order to represent four values, as with seasons, we would need a minimum of two bits so that each season can be assigned a unique value (e.g., 00 = spring, 01 = summer, 10 = fall, 11 = winter).

If we were to add a fifth season we would not be able to represent it with a unique two-bit value. We have used up all four binary values possible with two bits. We are essentially dealing with the same problem here. Even if the hard drive has more space, say one *terabyte*, if it was formatted with a FAT 12 filing system it could only contain 4,096 clusters, no more.

If you were not limited by the size in which you could make a cluster then you would theoretically divide the one terabyte drive into 4,096 "chunks" (or data units for example), each "chunk" then being a cluster. Each cluster would be around 200MB in size. Even if this were possible it would be an extremely inefficient use of space. As we have discussed, each file is saved to its own cluster, so each and every file would be assigned 200MB of space. In the end only 4,096 files could be saved to the drive formatted as FAT 12.

Again, there are 4,096 possible outcomes with a 12-bit integer. The outcomes, in this case, represent the amount of clusters possible. If you attempted to add a 4,097th cluster it would be similar to assigning a third value (for example a yellow light) to a 1 bit integer; there can only be two possible values with 1 bit—in our example, red and green (i.e., 0 = red, 1 = green, ? = yellow. There are no values left for yellow).

Actually, there are only 4,084 clusters possible with FAT 12. Certain bits are reserved, which cannot hold data; therefore, in actuality, there is a limitation of just *4,084 files that can be saved in a volume formatted in FAT 12*.

The other flavors of FAT also have their respective size limitations due to FAT restrictions: FAT 16, for example, at 2^{16} can hold only 65,536 clusters maximum. FAT 32, at 2^{32} can accommodate a maximum of 4,294,967,296 clusters. With FAT 12, some of the bits used are reserved, so the actual maximum possible number of clusters would be less.

Within the FAT itself, each 16-bit value in the FAT of a FAT 16 file system will represent one cluster. Likewise, each 32-bit value in the FAT of a FAT 32 file system will represent one cluster. The corresponding decimal equivalent of those binary values (12-, 16-, or 32-bit), as represented within the FAT, are descriptive of a unique cluster.

A brief description of several key values within the FAT are presented in Table 8.4.

TABLE 8.4 Key Values within the FAT

Description	Value
Unallocated	Represented by 0.
Allocated	Value will be represented by the next cluster used by the file.
Last Allocated	The last cluster used by the file. Usually seen with "End of File" HEX values of Fs. Exemption(s): FAT 12—a HEX value greater than HEX value FF8 (12-bit) FAT 16—a HEX value greater than HEX value FF F8 (16-bit) FAT 32—a HEX value greater than HEX value FF FF FF F8 (32-bit)
Bad Cluster	Seen with a HEX value ending in F7: FAT 12—FF7 FAT 16—FF F8 FAT 32—FF FF FF F7

How Does the FAT Work?

A file is called for by file name and path, for example when a user clicks on a document icon saved on the desktop. The storage path leads to the location of the parent directory on the hard drive. It is here that the directory entry for that file is located. The operating system (OS) looks in this parent directory and reads the directory entry.

The directory entry provides the starting cluster (starting physical location on the hard drive) and size of the file. The OS then goes to the starting cluster and begins to read the data. It only reads the data within the cluster up to the size of the file, then the OS stops reading. Any other data in that cluster (this data is what we referred to earlier as slack) is ignored because the length requirements have been met. If the file size surpasses one cluster, then the FAT is necessary in order to link these clusters together (remember, the FAT is necessary whenever a file's size exceeds one cluster).

 ## HOW IS CLUSTER SIZE DETERMINED?

If we multiply the number of bytes per sector by number of sectors per cluster we arrive at the total size of the cluster, in bytes. Thus:

$$(\text{Bytes per sector}) \times (\text{Sectors per cluster}) \text{ or } 512 \times 64,$$
$$\text{which yields a value of } 32{,}768 \text{ bytes per cluster.}$$

A full cluster then, in our example, is 32 KB.

Recall that our document named "hello.txt," discussed previously (see Figure 8.11), was only 5 bytes in length. The cluster size used was 32 KB (as defined by the FAT 16 file system as seen in the Volume Boot Record). Therefore, the document only required (or occupied) one cluster, which was defined by the one, five-byte document occupying a single 512-byte sector, and associated sector slack to fill the unused portion of the first sector and then file slack to fill the unused portions of the remaining sectors, making up the single cluster. (See Figure 8.20.)

So, a file size of 48 KB will need two clusters and therefore the use of the FAT. The 48 KB file will occupy 32 KB of the first cluster and only 16 KB of the second. (See Figure 8.21.)

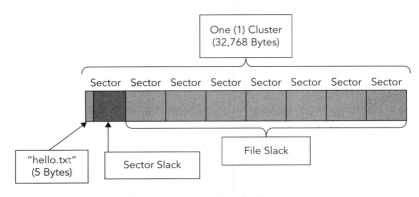

FIGURE 8.20   A 5 KB File Occupying a Single Cluster

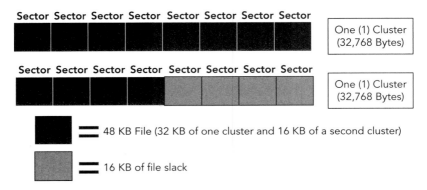

FIGURE 8.21   A 48 KB File Requires More than a Single Cluster

EXPANDED CLUSTER SIZE

For our continued review of clusters, cluster sizes, and how a cluster's size is determined, we took our initial example document "hello.txt" and (a) renamed it to "hello2.txt" and (b) increased its size substantially so that it would need more allocated space (e.g., clusters).

If we browse out to the file and right click on the document to view its properties, we see that its *physical size* of 72.5 KB is now larger than two clusters (64KB) in length. (See Figure 8.22.)

How many clusters does this 72.5 KB document need?

1 cluster = 32 KB—not enough space
2 clusters = 64 KB—still not enough space
3 clusters = 96 KB—enough space to hold a 72.5 KB document

So, as a file's size exceeds one cluster, the FAT automatically allocates additional clusters for the file to occupy, up to a number of clusters sufficient

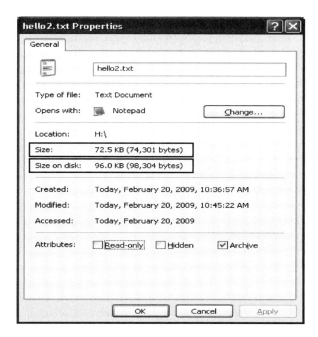

FIGURE 8.22 "hello.txt" Document Showing Larger File Size

to hold the entire file. Very rarely will a file's size be the exact size of a single cluster; this will result in either underutilizing the full, entire cluster or requiring additional clusters.

In either situation, clusters will normally have unused or "leftover" allocated space, not occupied by the file, resulting in both sector and file slack, each of which is of use and value to the cyber forensic investigator.

 ## DIRECTORY ENTRIES AND THE FAT

Let us now look at how the directory entries and FAT work together by examining the FAT directory entry for "hello2.txt" (see Figure 8.23).

Byte Offset	0	1	2	3	4	5	6	7	8	9	10	11	12	13	14	15	16	17	18	19	20	21	22	23	24	25	26	27	28	29	30	31
ASCII	H	E	L	L	O	2			T	X	T		·	/	·	T	T	:		T	:	·	·	+	U	T	:	·	·	=	"	·	·
HEX	48	45	4C	4C	4F	32	20	20	54	58	54	20	18	AF	9C	54	54	3A	54	3A	00	00	AB	55	54	3A	02	00	3D	22	01	00

FIGURE 8.23 FAT Directory Entry for "hello2.txt"

Step 1: Determine Where the File Begins

Q: Why or how does the OS know to go to byte offset 26–27 to determine where the file begins? Why not byte offset 12–13?

A: As we have previously explained, the decision rest in the specific code contained within the OS.

The HEX value at byte offset 26–27, in little endian, remember, is HEX 00 02, which equals the decimal value of 2. Thus, this file begins in cluster 2. From this information provided in the directory entry, the system is able to determine that the file begins at cluster 2. (See Figure 8.24.)

Byte Offset	0	1	2	3	4	5	6	7	8	9	10	11	12	13	14	15	16	17	18	19	20	21	22	23	24	25	26	27	28	29	30	31
ASCII	H	E	L	L	O	2			T	X	T		·	/	·	T	T	:		T	:	·	·	+	U	T	:	·	·	=	"	·	·
HEX	48	45	4C	4C	4F	32	20	20	54	58	54	20	18	AF	9C	54	54	3A	54	3A	00	00	AB	55	54	3A	02	00	3D	22	01	00

FIGURE 8.24 Byte Offset 26–27—Start of "hello2.txt" at Cluster Two

Step 2: Determine the File's Size

Byte offset 28–31 contains the size of the file in bytes. (See Figure 8.25.)

Byte Offset	0	1	2	3	4	5	6	7	8	9	10	11	12	13	14	15	16	17	18	19	20	21	22	23	24	25	26	27	28	29	30	31
ASCII	H	E	L	L	O	2			T	X	T		.	/	.	T	T	:	T	:	.	.	+	U	T	:	.	.	=	"	.	.
HEX	48	45	4C	4C	4F	32	20	20	54	58	54	20	18	AF	9C	54	54	3A	54	3A	00	00	AB	55	54	3A	02	00	3D	22	01	00

FIGURE 8.25 Byte Offset 28–31 Contains the Size of the File in Bytes

Step 3: Determine the Number of Clusters Needed

From our previous discussions on how to determine the necessary cluster size, we know that:

  1 cluster = 32 KB—not enough space
  2 clusters = 64 KB—still not enough space
  3 clusters = 96 KB—is ample enough space to hold a 74KB document.

So, the directory entry tells the system the following information about our example file "hello.txt":

1. Where the file starts.
2. The file's size in bytes.
3. How many clusters to expect (three).

Step 4: Determine Where the File Ends

As we just discussed, with a FAT 16 filing system each cluster is represented by a 16-bit value in the FAT. See Figure 8.26 for a HEX view of the FAT.

FFF8	FFFF	002A	FFFF	FFFF	FFFF	FFFF	FFFF	FFFF	FFFF	FFFF	FFFF	FFFF	FFFF	000F	0010	0011	0012
0013	0014	0015	0016	0017	0018	0019	001A	FFFF	FFFF	FFFF	0029	0000	0000	0000	0000	0000	0000
0000	0000	0000	0000	0000	FFFF	002B	FFFF	0000	0000	0000	0000	0000	0000	0000	0000	0000	0000
0000	0000	0000	0000	0000	0000	0000	0000	0000	0000	0000	0000	0000	0000	0000	0000	0000	0000
0000	0000	0000	0000	0000	0000	0000	0000	0000	0000	0000	0000	0000	0000	0000	0000	0000	0000
0000	0000	0000	0000	0000	0000	0000	0000	0000	0000	0000	0000	0000	0000	0000	0000	0000	0000
0000	0000	0000	0000	0000	0000	0000	0000	0000	0000	0000	0000	0000	0000	0000	0000	0000	0000
0000	0000	0000	0000	0000	0000	0000	0000	0000	0000	0000	0000	0000	0000	0000	0000	0000	0000
0000	0000	0000	0000	0000	0000	0000	0000	0000	0000	0000	0000	0000	0000	0000	0000	0000	0000
0000	0000	0000	0000	0000	0000	0000	0000	0000	0000	0000	0000	0000	0000	0000	0000	0000	0000
0000	0000	0000	0000	0000	0000	0000	0000	0000	0000	0000	0000	0000	0000	0000	0000	0000	0000
0000	0000	0000	0000	0000	0000	0000	0000	0000	0000	0000	0000	0000	0000	0000	0000	0000	0000
0000	0000	0000	0000	0000	0000	0000	0000	0000	0000	0000	0000	0000	0000	0000	0000	0000	0000
0000	0000	0000	0000	0000	0000	0000	0000	0000	0000	0000	0000	0000	0000	0000	0000	0000	0000
0000	0000	0000	0000														

FIGURE 8.26 HEX View of the FAT

The beginning of the FAT contains two special entries, FFF8 and FFFF, reserving clusters 0 and 1. (See Figure 8.27.)

The first cluster available for files is cluster 2. Remember, byte offset 26 and 27 of the directory entry identifies the starting cluster of a file. In our example, "hello2.txt," the starting cluster is 2, which is actually at byte offset 3. (See Figure 8.28.)

Reserved Clusters
Clusters "0" and "1"

FFF8	FFFF	002A	FFFF	FFFF	FFFF	FFFF	FFFF	FFFF	FFFF	FFFF	FFFF	FFFF	FFFF	000F	0010	0011	0012
0013	0014	0015	0016	0017	0018	0019	001A	FFFF	FFFF	FFFF	0029	0000	0000	0000	0000	0000	0000
0000	0000	0000	0000	0000	FFFF	002B	FFFF	0000	0000	0000	0000	0000	0000	0000	0000	0000	0000
0000	0000	0000	0000	0000	0000	0000	0000	0000	0000	0000	0000	0000	0000	0000	0000	0000	0000
0000	0000	0000	0000	0000	0000	0000	0000	0000	0000	0000	0000	0000	0000	0000	0000	0000	0000
0000	0000	0000	0000	0000	0000	0000	0000	0000	0000	0000	0000	0000	0000	0000	0000	0000	0000
0000	0000	0000	0000	0000	0000	0000	0000	0000	0000	0000	0000	0000	0000	0000	0000	0000	0000
0000	0000	0000	0000	0000	0000	0000	0000	0000	0000	0000	0000	0000	0000	0000	0000	0000	0000
0000	0000	0000	0000	0000	0000	0000	0000	0000	0000	0000	0000	0000	0000	0000	0000	0000	0000
0000	0000	0000	0000	0000	0000	0000	0000	0000	0000	0000	0000	0000	0000	0000	0000	0000	0000
0000	0000	0000	0000	0000	0000	0000	0000	0000	0000	0000	0000	0000	0000	0000	0000	0000	0000
0000	0000	0000	0000	0000	0000	0000	0000	0000	0000	0000	0000	0000	0000	0000	0000	0000	0000
0000	0000	0000	0000	0000	0000	0000	0000	0000	0000	0000	0000	0000	0000	0000	0000	0000	0000
0000	0000	0000	0000	0000	0000	0000	0000	0000	0000	0000	0000	0000	0000	0000	0000	0000	0000
0000	0000	0000	0000	0000	0000	0000	0000	0000	0000	0000	0000	0000	0000	0000	0000	0000	0000
0000	0000	0000	0000	0000	0000	0000	0000	0000	0000	0000	0000	0000	0000	0000	0000	0000	0000
0000	0000	0000	0000	0000	0000	0000	0000	0000	0000	0000	0000	0000	0000	0000	0000	0000	0000
0000	0000	0000	0000														

FIGURE 8.27 Beginning of FAT Reserved Clusters 0 and 1

Using a HEX editor and combining the eight-bit HEX characters into pairs, we can more easily visualize each cluster. The first FAT sector (FAT 1), and the third 16-bit HEX character offset is selected here, as shown in Figure 8.28.

FFF8	FFFF	002A	FFFF	FFFF	FFFF	FFFF	FFFF	FFFF	FFFF	FFFF	FFFF	FFFF	FFFF	000F	0010	0011	0012
0013	0014	0015	0016	0017	0018	0019	001A	FFFF	FFFF	FFFF	0029	0000	0000	0000	0000	0000	0000
0000	0000	0000	0000	0000	FFFF	002B	FFFF	0000	0000	0000	0000	0000	0000	0000	0000	0000	0000
0000	0000	0000	0000	0000	0000	0000	0000	0000	0000	0000	0000	0000	0000	0000	0000	0000	0000
0000	0000	0000	0000	0000	0000	0000	0000	0000	0000	0000	0000	0000	0000	0000	0000	0000	0000
0000	0000	0000	0000	0000	0000	0000	0000	0000	0000	0000	0000	0000	0000	0000	0000	0000	0000
0000	0000	0000	0000	0000	0000	0000	0000	0000	0000	0000	0000	0000	0000	0000	0000	0000	0000
0000	0000	0000	0000	0000	0000	0000	0000	0000	0000	0000	0000	0000	0000	0000	0000	0000	0000
0000	0000	0000	0000	0000	0000	0000	0000	0000	0000	0000	0000	0000	0000	0000	0000	0000	0000
0000	0000	0000	0000	0000	0000	0000	0000	0000	0000	0000	0000	0000	0000	0000	0000	0000	0000
0000	0000	0000	0000	0000	0000	0000	0000	0000	0000	0000	0000	0000	0000	0000	0000	0000	0000
0000	0000	0000	0000	0000	0000	0000	0000	0000	0000	0000	0000	0000	0000	0000	0000	0000	0000
0000	0000	0000	0000	0000	0000	0000	0000	0000	0000	0000	0000	0000	0000	0000	0000	0000	0000
0000	0000	0000	0000	0000	0000	0000	0000	0000	0000	0000	0000	0000	0000	0000	0000	0000	0000
0000	0000	0000	0000	0000	0000	0000	0000	0000	0000	0000	0000	0000	0000	0000	0000	0000	0000
0000	0000	0000	0000	0000	0000	0000	0000	0000	0000	0000	0000	0000	0000	0000	0000	0000	0000
0000	0000	0000	0000	0000	0000	0000	0000	0000	0000	0000	0000	0000	0000	0000	0000	0000	0000
0000	0000	0000	0000														

FIGURE 8.28 Cluster 2 at Byte Offset 3—First Cluster Available for Files

The value HEX 002A (or simply HEX 2A) is converted to its decimal equivalent, which equals the value 42. The next piece of this file ("hello2.txt"), since it has exceeded the 32 KB cluster size, is located in cluster 42. Move to sector 42 (offset 43), and we find HEX value is 002B. (See Figure 8.29.)

At byte offset 43, we find the HEX value 002B, and converting this HEX value to its decimal equivalent results in the value of 43. This tells us that the file continues onto cluster 43 (offset 44), one over from cluster 42, at byte offset 43. (See Figure 8.30.)

Cluster 44 is one over and we see it has a HEX value of FFFF. Once again, converting Hex FFFF into its decimal equivalent yields a value of 65,535. Any value greater than FFF8 (decimal 65,528) is interpreted as the end of the file. Given that the value in cluster 44 is 65,535, which is greater than 65,528, this is an indication that the end of the file has been reached.

FFF8	FFFF	002A	FFFF	FFFF	FFFF	FFFF	FFFF	FFFF	FFFF	FFFF	FFFF	FFFF	FFFF	000F	0010	0011	0012
0013	0014	0015	0016	0017	0018	0019	001A	FFFF	FFFF	FFFF	0029	0000	0000	0000	0000	0000	0000
0000	0000	0000	0000	0000	FFFF	002B	FFFF	0000	0000	0000	0000	0000	0000	0000	0000	0000	0000
0000	0000	0000	0000	0000	0000	0000	0000	0000	0000	0000	0000	0000	0000	0000	0000	0000	0000
0000	0000	0000	0000	0000	0000	0000	0000	0000	0000	0000	0000	0000	0000	0000	0000	0000	0000
0000	0000	0000	0000	0000	0000	0000	0000	0000	0000	0000	0000	0000	0000	0000	0000	0000	0000
0000	0000	0000	0000	0000	0000	0000	0000	0000	0000	0000	0000	0000	0000	0000	0000	0000	0000
0000	0000	0000	0000	0000	0000	0000	0000	0000	0000	0000	0000	0000	0000	0000	0000	0000	0000
0000	0000	0000	0000	0000	0000	0000	0000	0000	0000	0000	0000	0000	0000	0000	0000	0000	0000
0000	0000	0000	0000	0000	0000	0000	0000	0000	0000	0000	0000	0000	0000	0000	0000	0000	0000
0000	0000	0000	0000	0000	0000	0000	0000	0000	0000	0000	0000	0000	0000	0000	0000	0000	0000
0000	0000	0000	0000	0000	0000	0000	0000	0000	0000	0000	0000	0000	0000	0000	0000	0000	0000
0000	0000	0000	0000	0000	0000	0000	0000	0000	0000	0000	0000	0000	0000	0000	0000	0000	0000
0000	0000	0000	0000	0000	0000	0000	0000	0000	0000	0000	0000	0000	0000	0000	0000	0000	0000
0000	0000	0000	0000														

FIGURE 8.29 Cluster Continuation at Cluster 42 (offset 43)

FFF8	FFFF	002A	FFFF	FFFF	FFFF	FFFF	FFFF	FFFF	FFFF	FFFF	FFFF	FFFF	FFFF	000F	0010	0011	0012
0013	0014	0015	0016	0017	0018	0019	001A	FFFF	FFFF	FFFF	0029	0000	0000	0000	0000	0000	0000
0000	0000	0000	0000	0000	FFFF	002B	FFFF	0000	0000	0000	0000	0000	0000	0000	0000	0000	0000
0000	0000	0000	0000	0000	0000	0000	0000	0000	0000	0000	0000	0000	0000	0000	0000	0000	0000
0000	0000	0000	0000	0000	0000	0000	0000	0000	0000	0000	0000	0000	0000	0000	0000	0000	0000
0000	0000	0000	0000	0000	0000	0000	0000	0000	0000	0000	0000	0000	0000	0000	0000	0000	0000
0000	0000	0000	0000	0000	0000	0000	0000	0000	0000	0000	0000	0000	0000	0000	0000	0000	0000
0000	0000	0000	0000	0000	0000	0000	0000	0000	0000	0000	0000	0000	0000	0000	0000	0000	0000
0000	0000	0000	0000	0000	0000	0000	0000	0000	0000	0000	0000	0000	0000	0000	0000	0000	0000
0000	0000	0000	0000	0000	0000	0000	0000	0000	0000	0000	0000	0000	0000	0000	0000	0000	0000
0000	0000	0000	0000	0000	0000	0000	0000	0000	0000	0000	0000	0000	0000	0000	0000	0000	0000
0000	0000	0000	0000	0000	0000	0000	0000	0000	0000	0000	0000	0000	0000	0000	0000	0000	0000
0000	0000	0000	0000	0000	0000	0000	0000	0000	0000	0000	0000	0000	0000	0000	0000	0000	0000
0000	0000	0000	0000	0000	0000	0000	0000	0000	0000	0000	0000	0000	0000	0000	0000	0000	0000
0000	0000	0000	0000														

FIGURE 8.30 Cluster Continuation at Cluster 43 (offset 44)

Notice how in our example the file "hello2.txt" is not held (or stored) contiguously upon (across) the hard drive, but instead the file starts in cluster two (2) and skips 40 clusters to cluster 42, and then the file ends at cluster 43 (see Table 8.5).

Imagine for a moment a really long file such as video. This noncontiguous or fragmented file storage can cause inefficiencies, therefore the need for a defragmentation utility. You may have heard some say "defrag your hard drive." Essentially, this defragmentation process attempts to put all the clusters into a contiguous or defragmented state.

TABLE 8.5 Summary of FAT Cluster Values for "hello2.txt"

FAT Cluster Number	HEX Value	Decimal Equivalent
2	002A	42
43	002B	43
43	FFFF	65,535

To decode these four bytes, 3D 22 01 00, as a 32-bit little endian integer, we need to reverse the bytes into 00 01 22 3D, and convert this resulting HEX value into its decimal equivalent. Thus, HEX 00 01 22 3D converted into decimal equals 74,301. Therefore, file size for "hello2.txt" is 74,301 bytes.

FAT FILING SYSTEM LIMITATIONS

The FAT file system has limitations imposed upon it by its various structures; both the FAT and the directory entries pose storage limitations.

FAT Limitations

A FAT 16 file system has 16-bit FAT entries. These 16 bits allow for 65,524 possible outcomes (refer to Appendix 8F: The Power of 2).

How many bytes per sector?

There are 512 bytes per sector.

How many bytes are needed to represent one cluster of a FAT 16 table?

Two bytes or 16 bits (FAT 16). Remember each FAT entry represents one cluster.

How many clusters can be represented by the FAT in one sector?

A total of 256 clusters, determined by halving the 512 bytes per sector, because it takes two bytes to represent one cluster, so 256 clusters can be represented by the FAT in one sector.

How many sectors would the FAT need to track its' potential maximum size?

In order to answer we first need to know what is the maximum size for FAT 16 filing system and how is this determined?

As we have discussed, the maximum potential size of a FAT 16 filing system is 65,536 clusters (really less due to some reserved space, but for our purposes here we will stay with 65,536 clusters). This is its size limitation. Notice this is a cluster limitation, not a byte limitation. The total clusters possible with the FAT 16 file system equals 65,536.

Thus, there are 65,536 clusters total, each needing a unique two-byte entry in the FAT; therefore, only 256 clusters are able to be represented per sector, found by dividing the total number of clusters (65,536 by 256), giving us the number of clusters per sector of 256. Summarizing, 256 sectors are needed to be allocated to the FAT in order to contain the total possible clusters available with a 16-bit file system like FAT 16.

Figure 8.31 depicts a graphical view of the three components of the FAT file system, in addition to identifying two types of "space" found on all disks, wasted space along with allocated space.

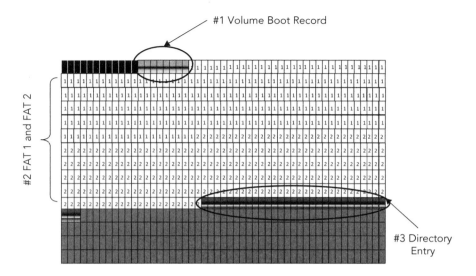

FIGURE 8.31   Three Components of the FAT File System

The legend associated with Figure 8.31 identifies the three components of the FAT, as well as the other areas typically found in the registry.

Note: This is a logical representation of the physical construct on the hard drive. This is only a logical interpretation based on actual physical characteristics of a FAT 16 volume, made by a popular forensic software tool, EnCase by Guidance Software.

FAT Summary

1. Each square represents a single sector or 512 bytes.
2. There are two FATs—for redundancy purposes; they are identical.
3. Each FAT is, as we calculated, 256 sectors long.
4. 256 sectors multiplied by 512 (bytes per sector) equals a FAT of 131,072 bytes.
5. Remember that it takes two bytes to represent one cluster; thus, 131,072 bytes/2 equals 65,536 total possible clusters.
6. Really there are only 65,524 possible clusters, taking into account system reserved clusters.

 ## DIRECTORY ENTRY LIMITATIONS

As we have previously discussed, the FAT imposes limitations on the FAT filing system; with FAT 16 for example only 65,536 clusters are possible. The directory entry poses limitations of its own. Remember from our earlier discussion of the directory entry (FAT 12/16), each entry is 32 bytes in length. The total number of directory entries available is determined when volume is formatted and is fixed at 32 sectors within FAT 12/16.

Remember, one sector contains 512 bytes, one directory entry consists of 32 bytes, and the total sectors reserved for directory entries (in FAT 16 file system) equals 32 sectors. The total number of directory entries is determined as follows:

1. Total sectors reserved for all directory entries equals 32, multiplied by 512 (bytes per sector), which equals 16,384 bytes.
2. Total directory entries therefore is determined by taking the 16,384 (total bytes reserved for directory entries) and dividing that value by 32 (bytes per directory entry), yielding a total of 512 directory entries.

Alternatively, the total directory entries can be determined as such:

How many directory entries are there per sector?

512 (bytes per sector) divide by 32 (bytes per single directory entry) equaling 16 directory entries per sector.

How many total possible directory entries?

16 (directory entries per sector) multiplied by 32 (total sectors assigned for directory entries) equals 512 possible directory entries.

Thus, the limitations of FAT 16! Only 512 directory entries or potential files can be saved regardless of the file's size. FAT 16 would quickly meet its limitations, if not with available storage space in general then in the number of files that could be saved/stored.

Several key concepts of the FAT filing system have been matched with a corresponding analogous companion in Table 8.6.

TABLE 8.6   Library to FAT Comparison

Library Allegory	File Allocation Table
Library	Partition
Card catalog	Filing system
Dewey Decimal System	Filing system type (i.e., FAT 12/16)
Card catalog data	Directory entry data
Book shelving	FAT
Books	Files

 ## SUMMARY

We have gone into great detail and discussed at length the FAT filing system, not so much to get an in-depth understanding of a more or less obsolete filing system, but in order to gain a better understanding of filing systems in general. Also, using the FAT filing system as a backdrop helps explain many important concepts such as allocated space, slack space, endianness, and bit reordering. These concepts are essential in understanding how data is overwritten in the normal saving, deleting, and general processing of information.

Some of these concepts have previously been touched upon, but the discussion here of the FAT filing system brings these critical concepts together. Will understanding the intricacies of FAT be relevant in an investigation? Perhaps and perhaps not, but understanding slack space and allocated space is of extreme importance.

Understanding that a file system exists and having an idea of how file systems operate in general is critical to understanding how data is accessed, stored, changed, deleted, and/or overwritten. Without an understanding of filing systems, how can we understand how a file is deleted, or perhaps more succinctly put, not deleted? When a file is deleted, we discussed how only the first byte within the directory entry is changed to a tilde "~," making that space available for future use, or "unallocated."

However, the rest of the directory entry and the entirety of the file, as demarcated in the FAT, remain. The space is unallocated and ready to be overwritten, but the unallocated and potentially incriminating data remains. These are basic forensic concepts, but some of the most critical and important to grasp!

APPENDIX 8A: PARTITION TABLE FIELDS

Byte Offset	Field Length	Sample Value	Description
00	1 byte	80	Boot Indicator. Indicates whether the partition is the system partition. Legal values are: 00 = Do not use for booting. 80 = System partition.
01	1 byte	01	Starting Head.
02–03	2 bytes	01 00	Starting Sector. Only bits 0–5 are used. Bits 6–7 are the upper two bits for the Starting Cylinder field.
			Starting Cylinder. This field contains the lower eight bits of the cylinder value. Starting cylinder is thus a 10-bit number, with a maximum value of 1,023
04	1 byte	06	This byte defines the volume type.
05	1 byte	0F	Ending Head.
06–07	2 bytes	FF FF	Ending Sector. Only bits 0–5 are used. Bits 6–7 are the upper two bits for the ending cylinder field. Ending Cylinder. This field contains the lower eight bits of the cylinder value. Ending cylinder is thus a 10-bit number, with a maximum value of 1,023.
08–11	4 bytes	3F 00 00 00	Relative Sector. Starting sector for the partition for LBA mode.
12–15	4 bytes	89 7E 9B 1D	Total Sectors. Total number of sectors for LBA mode.

Partition or Volume Type (Offset 4)

01 12-bit FAT primary partition or logical drive.

04 16-bit FAT primary partition or logical drive.

05 Extended partition.

06 32-bit FAT primary partition or logical drive.

07 NTFS primary partition or logical drive.

APPENDIX 8B: FILE ALLOCATION TABLE VALUES

Each 16-bit character in the table of a FAT 16 file system will represent one cluster.

Each 3-bit character in the table of a FAT 32 file system will represent one cluster.

Those values present within the table are as follows:

Unallocated—represented by 0.
Allocated—value will be represented by the next cluster used by the file.
Last Allocated—the last cluster used by the file.

Usually seen with "End Of File" HEX values of Fs.
Although this is not always the case, the rules are:

- FAT 12—a HEX value greater than HEX value FF8 (12 bit)
- FAT 16—a HEX value greater than HEX value FF F8 (16 bit)
- FAT 32—a HEX value greater than HEX value FF FF FF F8 (32 bit)

Bad cluster—seen with a HEX value ending in F7:

- FAT 12—FF7
- FAT16—FF F8
- FAT32—FF FF FF F7

APPENDIX 8C: DIRECTORY ENTRY BYTE OFFSET DESCRIPTION

0   First character of the file name or status byte.

1–7   File name continued.

8–10   Three-character file extension.

11   Attributes—read only, hidden, and so on.

12–13   Reserved.

14–17   Create time and date of file stored as MS-DOS 32-bit timestamp.

18–19   Last accessed, no time.

20–21   Two high bytes of FAT 32 starting cluster; FAT 12/16 will have zeros.

22–25   Last written time and date of file again as MS-DOS 32-bit.

26–27   Starting cluster for FAT 12/16; two low bytes of the starting cluster for FAT 32.

28–31   Size in bytes of the file. Will be 0 for directories.

APPENDIX 8D: FAT 12/16 BYTE OFFSET VALUES*

0–2	At this offset we have assembly jump instruction to bootstrap the code. It is usually 0xEB3C90 or 0xEB5890.
3–10	Offsets from 3–10 contain the OEM id. The OEM id is a string of characters that identifies the name and version number of the operating system that formatted the volume. Some examples of OEM id for different OS versions are: Win95 = MSWIN4.0 Win98 = MSWIN4.1 Win2K / XP = MSDOS5.0
11–12	Bytes per sector. The number of bytes per sector by default is 512, but it can be 1,024, 2,048, or 4,096. As we can see in the figure, the HEX value of 11–12 is 00 02. Needs to be viewed in little endian.
13	Sectors per cluster. It's necessary to have these values in powers of 2 and should always be greater than zero.
14–15	Number of sectors in the reserved area. Fat 12/16 is typically one.
16	Number of FAT tables present. Typically two with FAT 1 and FAT 2. FAT 2 is a duplicate of FAT 1 used for redundancy when FAT 1 is corrupted.
17–18	Maximum number of 32-byte directory entries in the root directory. It is usually 0 for FAT 32 and 512 for FAT 12/FAT 16.
19–20	16-bit integer describing the number of sectors in the partition. If 0, the number of sectors exceeds 65,536. If so, the value is then reflected in byte offset 32–35, a 32-bit integer describing the number of sectors in a partition.
21	Media descriptor which tells whether it is a removable media or nonremovable media. If the value is 0xF8, then it is nonremovable media. If it is 0xF0, then it is removable media.
22–23	16-bit integer describing the number of sectors used by each FAT in FAT 12/FAT 16. Value is zero for FAT 32.
24–25	Sectors per track value. It is usually 63 for hard disk.
26–27	Number of heads value. It is typically 255 for hard disk.
28–31	Number of hidden sectors before the start of the partition. Its value is typically 63 for the first volume on a hard disk.

---

* Steve Bunting and William Wei, *The Official EnCE EnCase Certified Examiner Study Guide* (Indianapolis: John Wiley & Sons, 2006).

32–35	32-bit integer describing the number of sectors in the partition. If 0, the number does not exceed 65,536 and is described as a 16–bit integer in bytes 19–20. Only one of the two (19–20 or 32–35), and not both, must be set to 0.
36	Interrupt drive number; HEX 00 for floppies and HEX 80 for hard drives.
37	Only used by Windows NT; typically set to 0.
38	Extended boot signature to determine the validity of the three fields that follow. If HEX 29, the next three fields are present and valid, otherwise expect HEX 00.
39–42	Volume serial number.
43–53	Volume label in ASCII. This is the label that is given to the user optionally when the volume is created.
54–61	File system type at time of formatting. Shown are ASCII as FAT 12, FAT 16.
62–509	Bootstrap program code and error messages.
510–511	Signature value is two bytes and should be HEX 55AA.

APPENDIX 8E: FAT 32 BYTE OFFSET VALUES*

0–2　At this offset we have assembly jump instruction to bootstrap the code. It is usually 0xEB3C90 or 0xEB5890.

3–10　Offsets from 3–10 contain the OEM id. The OEM id is a string of characters that identifies the name and version number of the operating system that formatted the volume. Some examples of OEM id for different OS versions are:

　　Win95 = MSWIN4.0

　　Win98 = MSWIN4.1

　　Win2K / XP = MSDOS5.0

11–12　Bytes per sector. Number of bytes per sector by default is 512, but it can be 1,024, 2,048, or 4,096. As we can see in the figure, the HEX value of 11–12 is 00 02. Needs to be viewed in little endian.

13　Sectors per cluster. It's necessary to have these values in power of two and should always be greater than zero.

14–15　Number of sectors in the reserved area. Fat 12/16 is typically one.

16　Number of FAT tables present. Typically two with FAT 1 and FAT 2. FAT 2 is a duplicate of FAT 1 used for redundancy when FAT 1 is corrupted.

17–18　Maximum number of 32 byte directory entries in the root directory. It is usually 0 for FAT 32 and 512 for FAT 12/FAT 16.

19–20　16 bit integer describing the number of sectors in the partition. If 0, the number of sectors exceeds 65,536. If so, the value is then reflected in byte offset 32–35, a 32-bit integer describing the number of sectors in a partition.

21　Media descriptor which tells weather it is a removable media or non removable media. If the value is 0xF8, then it is nonremovable media. If it is 0xF0 then it is removable media.

22–23　16-bit integer describing the number of sectors used by each FAT in FAT 12/FAT 16. Value is zero for FAT 32.

24–25　Sectors per track value. It is usually 63 for hard disk.

26–27　Number of heads value. It is typically 255 for hard disk.

28–31　Number of hidden sectors before the start of the partition. Its value is typically 63 for the first volume on a hard disk.

32–35　32-bit integer describing the number of sectors in the partition. If 0, the number does not exceed 65,536 and is described as a

---

*Steve Bunting and William Wei, *The Official EnCE EnCase Certified Examiner Study Guide* (Indianapolis: John Wiley & Sons, 2006).

	16-bit integer in bytes 19–20. Only one of the two (19–20 or 32–35), and not both, must be set to 0.
36–39	32-bit integer which describes the number of sectors used by one FAT (FAT 1/FAT 2) on FAT 32 partition. Bytes 22–23 must be set to 0 for FAT 32.
40–41	A series of values used to describe if the FAT entries are duplicated. If the value is 0 then the FAT is duplicated. If the value is not zero then duplication does not occur.
42–43	The major and minor version numbers of the FAT 32 volume. Usually the values are 0×00 and 0×00 meaning the major number and the minor number of FAT is 0.
44–47	Cluster number where the root directory begins, which is usually 2. Cluster 2 starts immediately after mirror copy of FAT 1, FAT 2 ends.
48–49	Sector number where FSINFO (File System Information) is found. It is generally located at sector 1 and the backup of FSINFO is found at sector 7. FSINFO purpose is to provide information to the Operating System about the number of free clusters available to the system and the location of the next free cluster.
50–51	Sector number for the location of backup boot sector, usually sector 6.
52–63	Reserved, currently not in use.
64	Interrupt driver number. It is HEX 00 for floppies and HEX 80 for hard drives.
65	Not used by any version of windows except for Windows NT. Typically set to 0.
66	Extended boot signature to determine the validity of the three fields that follow. If HEX 0×29, the next three fields (serial number, volume label, file system type) are present and valid. If it is 0×00, then none is available.
67–70	Volume serial number. Every volume has got a serial number which can be seen by using the "vol" command in DOS.
71–81	Volume label in ASCII. If none is give by user then it should show "NO NAME."
82–89	File system type at time of formatting. This is of no use after formatting and can be changed to any arbitrary value.
90–509	Boot strap program code and error messages.
510–511	Signature value; it is of two bytes and should be 0×55AA.

APPENDIX 8F: THE POWER OF 2

2^0	=	1
2^1	=	2
2^2	=	4
2^3	=	8
2^4	=	16
2^5	=	32
2^6	=	64
2^7	=	128
2^8	=	256
2^9	=	512
2^{10}	=	1,024
2^{11}	=	2,048
2^{12}	=	4,096
2^{13}	=	8,192
2^{14}	=	16,384
2^{15}	=	32,768
2^{16}	=	65,536
2^{17}	=	131,072
2^{18}	=	262,144
2^{19}	=	524,288
2^{20}	=	1,048,576
2^{21}	=	2,097,152
2^{22}	=	4,194,304
2^{23}	=	8,388,608
2^{24}	=	16,777,216
2^{25}	=	33,554,432
2^{26}	=	67,108,864
2^{27}	=	134,217,728
2^{28}	=	268,435,456
2^{29}	=	536,870,912
2^{30}	=	1,073,741,824
2^{31}	=	2,147,483,648
2^{32}	=	4,294,967,296
2^{33}	=	8,589,934,592
2^{34}	=	17,179,869,184
2^{35}	=	34,359,738,368
2^{36}	=	68,719,476,736
2^{37}	=	137,438,953,472
2^{38}	=	274,877,906,944
2^{39}	=	549,755,813,888
2^{40}	=	1,099,511,627,776
2^{41}	=	2,199,023,255,552
2^{42}	=	4,398,046,511,104
2^{43}	=	8,796,093,022,208

2^{44}	=	17,592,186,044,416
2^{45}	=	35,184,372,088,832
2^{46}	=	70,368,744,177,664
2^{47}	=	140,737,488,355,328
2^{48}	=	281,474,976,710,656
2^{49}	=	562,949,953,421,312
2^{50}	=	1,125,899,906,842,620
2^{51}	=	2,251,799,813,685,250
2^{52}	=	4,503,599,627,370,500
2^{53}	=	9,007,199,254,740,990
2^{54}	=	18,014,398,509,482,000
2^{55}	=	36,028,797,018,964,000
2^{56}	=	72,057,594,037,927,900
2^{57}	=	144,115,188,075,856,000
2^{58}	=	288,230,376,151,712,000
2^{59}	=	576,460,752,303,423,000
2^{60}	=	1,152,921,504,606,850,000
2^{61}	=	2,305,843,009,213,690,000
2^{62}	=	4,611,686,018,427,390,000
2^{63}	=	9,223,372,036,854,780,000
2^{64}	=	18,446,744,073,709,600,000
2^{65}	=	36,893,488,147,419,100,000
2^{66}	=	73,786,976,294,838,200,000
2^{67}	=	147,573,952,589,676,000,000
2^{68}	=	295,147,905,179,353,000,000
2^{69}	=	590,295,810,358,706,000,000
2^{70}	=	1,180,591,620,717,410,000,000
2^{71}	=	2,361,183,241,434,820,000,000
2^{72}	=	4,722,366,482,869,650,000,000
2^{73}	=	9,444,732,965,739,290,000,000
2^{74}	=	18,889,465,931,478,600,000,000
2^{75}	=	37,778,931,862,957,200,000,000
2^{76}	=	75,557,863,725,914,300,000,000
2^{77}	=	151,115,727,451,829,000,000,000
2^{78}	=	302,231,454,903,657,000,000,000
2^{79}	=	604,462,909,807,315,000,000,000
2^{80}	=	1,208,925,819,614,630,000,000,000
2^{81}	=	2,417,851,639,229,260,000,000,000
2^{82}	=	4,835,703,278,458,520,000,000,000
2^{83}	=	9,671,406,556,917,030,000,000,000
2^{84}	=	1.93E+25
2^{85}	=	3.87E+25
2^{86}	=	7.74E+25
2^{87}	=	1.55E+26

2^88	=	3.09E+26	2^109	=	6.49E+32
2^89	=	6.19E+26	2^110	=	1.30E+33
2^90	=	1.24E+27	2^111	=	2.60E+33
2^91	=	2.48E+27	2^112	=	5.19E+33
2^92	=	4.95E+27	2^113	=	1.04E+34
2^93	=	9.90E+27	2^114	=	2.08E+34
2^94	=	1.98E+28	2^115	=	4.15E+34
2^95	=	3.96E+28	2^116	=	8.31E+34
2^96	=	7.92E+28	2^117	=	1.66E+35
2^97	=	1.58E+29	2^118	=	3.32E+35
2^98	=	3.17E+29	2^119	=	6.65E+35
2^99	=	6.34E+29	2^120	=	1.33E+36
2^100	=	1.27E+30	2^121	=	2.66E+36
2^101	=	2.54E+30	2^122	=	5.32E+36
2^102	=	5.07E+30	2^123	=	1.06E+37
2^103	=	1.01E+31	2^124	=	2.13E+37
2^104	=	2.03E+31	2^125	=	4.25E+37
2^105	=	4.06E+31	2^126	=	8.51E+37
2^106	=	8.11E+31	2^127	=	1.70E+38
2^107	=	1.62E+32	2^128	=	3.40E+38
2^108	=	3.25E+32			

2^128 = 3.40E+38
340,282,366,920,938,000,000,000,000,000,000,000,000

CHAPTER NINE

File Systems—NTFS and Beyond

C HAPTER 9 FURTHER EXAMINES file systems, focusing now on file systems beyond FAT, which are those most likely to be encountered by the cyber forensic investigator.

As technology truly does march to its own beat and is constantly in a state of flux and change, the cyber forensics professional should be attuned to the changes announced by vendors regarding their operating systems and the file system variations that may emerge from any advancement in operating system designs and future release updates to these operating systems.

 NEW TECHNOLOGY FILE SYSTEM

Next up, a review of another Windows file system, the *New Technology File System* (NTFS), whose use started with Windows NT in 1993. Windows XP,

2000, Server 2003, 2008, and Windows 7 also all use later versions of NTFS. The filing system is very complex and to make matters worse there are very little published specifications from Microsoft that describes the "on-disk layout."

What this means is that logical representations of the physical structure of this file system are speculative and very difficult to visualize. It's a good thing our goal here is not an in-depth bit-for-bit analysis of each file system, but instead a more conceptual understanding of file systems in general.

An important concept in understanding the NTFS design is that all data is allocated to files, including the file system itself; the file system files can be located anywhere in the volume, as would a regular file. Therefore, NTFS does not have a normal File System Layout like FAT, as discussed in Chapter 8, where there are areas at the beginning of the volume reserved for these data.

The entire file system is considered a data area, and any sector can be allocated to a file. The only constant within the NTFS file structure is that the first sectors contain the boot sector, similar to the volume boot in FAT.

The New Technology File System (NTFS) contains the following "components":

1. Partition Boot Sector (PBR)—similar to VBR in FAT
2. Master File Table (MFT)—similar to directory entry in FAT
3. $bitmap—similar to the FAT

 PARTITION BOOT RECORD

The Partition Boot Record (PBR) is comprised of 16 sectors, as opposed to one sector with FAT. Typically, however, only eight sectors of the 16 sectors available are used.

Byte offset 0–10 contains jump instructions and the OEM ID (NTFS). OEM is the acronym for Original Equipment Manufacturer, and in NTFS, this is represented by a string of characters that identifies the name and version number of the operating system that formatted the volume.

Figure 9.1 is the first sector of the boot record as seen in a HEX editor. Remember, NTFS allocates the first 16 sectors for the boot "sector."

Byte offset 0–9 is highlighted in Figure 9.1, showing the OEM identifier "NTFS." Byte offset 3–6 in the first sector of the boot sector will contain the ASCII "NTFS" representation of HEX 4E 54 46 53 defining it as such.

Figure 9.2 displays byte offsets 11–63 containing partition parameter information.

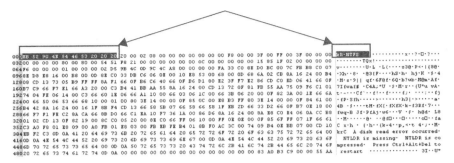

FIGURE 9.1 First Sector of the Boot Record (NTFS)

Byte Offsets 11–63

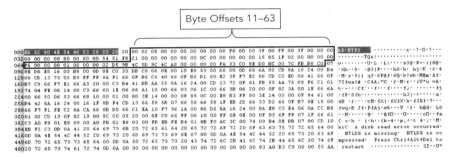

FIGURE 9.2 Byte Offsets 11 through 63 Containing Partition Parameter Information

The reader may wish to review Appendix 8A, Partition Table Fields, for a more in depth look at the data fields and their representation in the PBR.

Table 9.1 lists and describes the field name and decimal value for the contents of byte offsets 11 through 63 of the PBR.

A further look at the PBR will reveal that byte offset 64–509 contains the boot strap code, and byte offset 510–511, by default, and as a control, contains the end of file marker, with a HEX value of 55AA.

MASTER FILE TABLE

The Master File Table (MFT) is the heart of the NTFS file system. It is analogous to the directory entry in the FAT filing systems; it will contain much of the metadata, similar to the card catalogue in our library analogy. The MFT is much

TABLE 9.1 Byte Offsets 11 through 63 of the PBR

Byte Offset	Field Length	Example (HEX)	Field Name	Decimal Value (little endian)
11 & 12	2 bytes	00 02	Bytes per sector	512
13	1 byte	8	Sectors per cluster	8
28–31	4 bytes	3F 00 00 00	Hidden sectors	63
40–47	8 bytes	54 51 F8 21 00 00 00 00	Total sectors	569,921,876
48–55	8 bytes	00 00 0C 00 00 00 00 00	Logical cluster # for the file $MFT	786,432
56–63	8 bytes	15 85 1F 02 00 00 00 00	Logical cluster # for the file $MFT Mirr	35,620,117

like a database as it contains entries to track all data contained within the file system, and in this sense it acts a bit like the FAT. In our comparisons to FAT, the MFT actually has functionalities similar to both directory entries and the FAT. The MFT contains an entry for every file and directory in the partition, including itself, which is named $MFT.

The MFT is scattered throughout the disk structure; it is not contained or constrained to certain specified sectors as are FAT directory entries. Being that the MFT is not confined to predefined sectors, it allows the file system to be dynamic and expand as necessary. It is not bounded or limited to a certain number of files as with FAT filing systems.

Each entry (or record) does however have a fixed length of 1,024 bytes. Being that there are 512 bytes per sector, there are two sectors per MFT entry.

Determining the Location of the MFT

To determine the MFT's starting location we look at byte offset 48–55 (eight bytes) in the Boot Record. The decimal value of these binary values gives us the *Logical Cluster number for the $MFT.*

Figure 9.3 shows the placement of byte offset 48–55, within the PBR, where we would look for the start of the MFT.

Determining the location of the MFT ($MFT) requires a little bit of computer math and remembering our previous discussions on endianness. To start, we identify the HEX values for byte offset 48–55. By looking at Figure 9.3, we

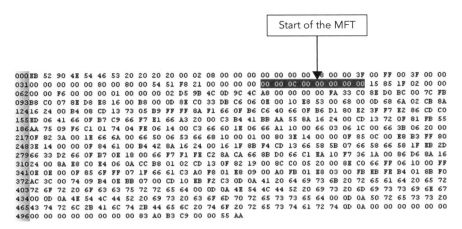

FIGURE 9.3 Byte Offset 48 through 55 and the Start of the MFT

determine that the HEX values for byte offset 48–55 equals HEX 00 00 0C 00 00 00 00 00, which by the way, is in big endian format.

Next, rearrange these HEX values into little endian, resulting in HEX 00 00 00 00 00 00 C0 00 00.

Original in big endian = 00 00 0C 00 00 00 00 00
Convert to little endian = 00 00 00 00 00 0C 00 00
Drop the leading zeros = ~~00 00 00 00 00~~ 0C 00 00

Why are the leading zeros dropped? HEX 00 in decimal equals zero, and just as with any decimal number a zero preceding a number other than zero is usually ignored (e.g., 098 is typically written as simply 98).

Finally, convert the resulting HEX value 0C 00 00 into its decimal equivalent, thereby obtaining a value of 786,432. Thus, confirming the MFT will begin at cluster offset 786,432.

Figure 9.4 shows the first attribute entry in the first sector of the MFT as viewed by a HEX editor.

The MFT views everything about the file as an attribute, metadata and data alike. The first byte of the MFT entry is the standard file record header (see Figure 9.4). The first four bytes of the MFT are combined to form the file Identifier, "FILE." It is this attribute that defines this sector as a record.

In fact, some of the actual data contained within the file will be present within the MFT entry, as it is considered just another attribute. If a file is small,

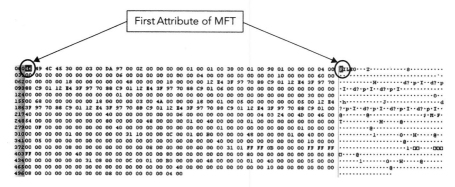

FIGURE 9.4 First Attribute Entry in the First Sector of the MFT

sometimes the entirety of that file is stored within the MFT entry; this is called *resident data.*

A File and Its Attributes

If the file is too large for all its data to be contained within the MFT then the file is allocated to a cluster. The cluster runs are then stored in place of the resident data. Typically, 480 bytes is the maximum length for resident files.

An attribute has two parts:

1. Header—Identifies the attribute: file type, file size, and name. Also, it has flags to identify if the attribute is compressed or encrypted. Header is generic and standard to all attributes.
2. Content—Actual contents of the file for a resident file. Cluster location of file for nonresident files. Content is specific and unique and can be any size.

All file attributes are stored in one of two different ways, depending on the characteristics of the attribute, especially size:

1. Resident Attributes—Attributes that are stored directly within the file's primary MFT record itself. Many of the simplest and most common file attributes are stored resident in the MFT file. In fact, some are required by NTFS to be resident in the MFT record for proper operation. *For example, the name of the file, and its creation, modification, and access date/time stamps are resident for every file.*[1]
2. Non-Resident Attributes—If an attribute requires more space than is available within the MFT record, it then cannot be stored in that record. Instead,

the attribute is placed in a separate location on the disk. A pointer is placed within the MFT that leads to the location of the attribute. This is called non-resident attribute storage.

A letter or package received at the post office can be seen as an analogy. The attribute would be the envelope, box, or storage container. The outside of the container may have your name, address, and possibly the contents written on it. The inside of the box actually contains the contents.[2]

Thus, all items are stored in containers (boxes or envelopes). Containers may be of all sizes and shapes, all with different contents; however, the data written on the outside of the container all contain the same info—name, address, and contents.

In this analogy the header equates to the outside of the box and the content equates to the contents of the box.[3] Readers desiring further information regarding attributes are encouraged to review Appendix 9A, Common NTFS System Defined Attributes.

$Bitmap

Another component of NTFS, which is somewhat similar in functionality to the FAT, is $Bitmap. In comparing NTFS and FAT filing systems it is apparent that the MFT in NTFS actually acts as a directory entry and performs some FAT functionality. As discussed previously, the MFT contains the non-resident attributes that points to where the data is located. This is essentially similar to the role of the FAT.

So what role does $Bitmap perform and how is it similar to the FAT? The $Bitmap is a file that represents cluster allocation within a partition. It identifies if a cluster is allocated or unallocated. Each bit within the $Bitmap represents a cluster. If a bit representing a cluster has a value of zero (in binary), then that cluster is available for use or unallocated; if the bit has a value of one (1), then that cluster is unavailable or allocated.

The $Bitmap does not identify starting locations of files, length of files, cluster size of files, or any data regarding file location or storage. It simply tells the system if the cluster is allocated or unallocated.

 ## NTFS SUMMARY

Explaining the complexities of NTFS is somewhat simplified when building upon an existing understanding of FAT. Both are similar enough to be somewhat analogous. The point of describing either of these systems is to understand how file systems can work in general. By grasping such file system concepts we begin to understand how one file system (such as NTFS) can be much more dynamic and adaptive to growth than another. We also, and perhaps more importantly to the cyber forensic investigator, begin to understand how data are stored.

exFAT

Microsoft's Extended File Allocation Table (exFAT) was released with Windows Vista SP1 (Service Pack One). A file system designed for Flash memory storage and other external devices, ExFAT expands upon the file size, drive size, and directory limitations of older versions of FAT yet maintains the low overhead of FAT.

A robust and complex file system like Windows NTFS allows for relatively efficient storage in extremely large drives. However, the overhead of efficient storage is the consumption of system resources, such as memory and processing power. In systems where resources are limited NTFS is inefficient. The NTFS file system consumes a lot of resources maintaining itself. ExFAT was designed for use in those areas where NTFS is an overkill and inefficient.

There are other filing systems beyond Microsoft's NTFS, exFAT, and FAT. As can be expected, different Operating Systems utilize different filing systems, and as technology advances so too do the functionalities contained within Operating Systems and therefore with File systems. Many of these filing system concepts do not align themselves to the Microsoft filing system paradigm. Slight similarities do exist, being that the end goal is ultimately the same, namely accessing files, but generally the Microsoft filing system is not a model for all file systems.

ALTERNATIVE FILING SYSTEM CONCEPTS

Alternative file systems and the concepts associated with these alternative file systems will be explored in the remainder of this chapter.

Binary Search Tree Filing System

A binary tree is a hierarchical data structure concept used for placing and locating files. Conceptually, in a hierarchical tree data structure things are ordered above or below other things. The tree is made up of *nodes* that are linked together as either parents or children.

The top node of the tree is called the *root*. The nodes directly under another node are referred to as *children*. The nodes directly above another node are called *parents*. Nodes with no children are sometimes called *leaves*. The *Order* of the binary tree is equal to the maximum number of children per node (two with binary trees). The *Depth* of the tree is equal to the length of the path (in number of nodes) from the top root node to the lowest leaf. The search tree size is equal to the total number of nodes.

In a basic binary tree each node can have a maximum of only two children. Within a binary tree structure each node (item in the tree) has a distinct value. Both left and right *subtrees* must also follow binary search tree structure. The left subtree of a node contains only values less than the parent nodes value and the right subtree of a node contains only values greater than the parent nodes value. Again, each node has a maximum of only two children. Figure 9.5 shows a graphical look at a binary tree structure.

For example, in the image in Figure 9.5, the root node 8 is a parent of node 4 and node 11. And likewise, node 4 and node 11 are children of root node 8. The search tree size is 9 nodes; its depth is 3. The leaves are nodes 2, 3, 7, and 14. The left nodes are 4, 2, and 3, and the right nodes are 5, 7, 11, and 15. All nodes except for node 8 are children. Figure 9.6 shows the relationship between the root, parent, and leaves.

The binary tree (b-tree) is a useful data structure for rapidly storing sorted data and rapidly retrieving stored data. It is the relationship between the

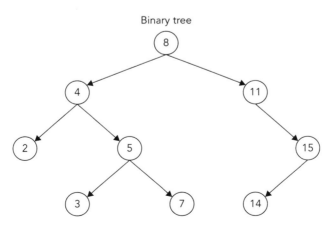

FIGURE 9.5 Binary Search Tree Structure

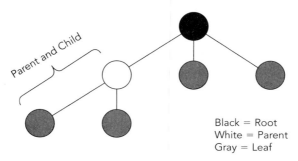

FIGURE 9.6 Binary Tree Relationships

children and the parent node which makes the binary tree such an efficient data structure. It is the leaf on the left that has a lesser key value, and it is the leaf on the right that has an equal or greater key value. As a result, the leaves on the farthest left of the tree have the lowest values, whereas the leaves on the right of the tree have the greatest values. More importantly, as each parent node branches to two other leaves (e.g., children), a new, smaller subset within the binary tree is created. Due to this subdividing process, it is possible to easily access and insert data in a binary tree using search and insert functions recursively called on successive leaves.

The advantage of a binary tree (and variants of b-trees) has to do with disk read efficiencies, the speed of locating and presenting data. As data is called for, records need to be searched in order to locate the data. Searching records takes time. In FAT and NTFS this search can take a lot time (relatively speaking) as the OS searches through what can be the entirety of the file system.

Data in a binary search tree are stored in tree nodes, and must have associated with them an ordinal value or key; these keys are used to structure the tree such that the value of a left child node is less than that of the parent node, and the value of a right child node is greater than that of the parent node. Sometimes, the key and datum are one and the same. Typical key values include simple integers or strings, the actual data for the key will depend on the application.

To perform a search, first start at the root of the tree, and compare the ordinal value of the root to the ordinal value of the node to be located. If the ordinal value is less than the root, follow the left branch of the root, or else follow the right branch. Start the comparison again, but at the branch compare the ordinal value of the child with the node to be located. Traversal of the tree continues in this manner until identifying the node.[4]

The hierarchical index structure of the binary tree allows the search to skip either right or left subtree records at each level. As the search descends the tree, the volume of data needing to be read is quickly reduced.

For the sake of argument say each division within the tree was split 50/50; 50 percent of the records on the left side and 50 percent on the right side. As the search would descend the tree the amount of potential records needing to be searched would drop by half at each layer. The hierarchical index minimizes the number of disk reads necessary to locate a particular record.

To further illustrate this point, assume that the target value of a search is contained within a data set of fictional characters, with the target value identified as Holmes, Sherlock. In this example, the data set will be searched alphabetically, with the objective of identifying the individual record for Holmes, Sherlock (see Figure 9.7).

A B C D E F G H I J K L M N O P Q R S T U V W X Y Z

FIGURE 9.7   Fictional Character Name Data Set

First begin by selecting the middle element of the data set (Figure 9.8), essentially the median, and comparing it against the target value. If the values match it will return success.

A B C D E F G H I J K L M N O P Q R S T U V W X Y Z

FIGURE 9.8   Middle Element of the Data Set

In this example the median value of "M" does not match the "H" of Holmes. If the target value (our example "H") is higher than the value of the median ("M") it will take the upper half of the data set and perform the same operation against it.

Likewise, if the target value is lower than the median value ("M") it will perform the operation against the lower half. (See Figure 9.9.)

A B C D E F G H I J K L M N

FIGURE 9.9   Target Value ("H") Is Higher than the Value of the Median ("M")

Given that the target value (our example "H") is higher than the value of the median ("M"), the search will probe the upper half of the data set. The data set is again split at the median, and the target value ("H") is again compared to the newly established median (which in this second iteration is now, "F"). (See Figure 9.10.)

FIGURE 9.10 Second Iteration Upper Half of Data Set to Be Probed

Given that the target value ("H") is *not* higher than the value of the median ("F"), the search *will not probe* the upper half of the data set (A, B, C, D, E,) but rather the lower half of the remaining date set (G, H, I, J, K, L). (See Figure 9.11.)

FIGURE 9.11 Lower Half of Data Set to Be Probed

Given that the target value ("H") is now higher than the value of the next median value ("I"), the search *will probe* the upper half of the data set (G, H, I) rather than the lower half of the remaining date set (J, K, L). (See Figure 9.12.)

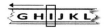

FIGURE 9.12 Binary Search Third Iteration

The binary search process will continue to halve the data set with each iteration, until the value has been found or until it can no longer split the data set. With the fourth iteration the target value "H" is found (see Figure 9.13) and the initial search process terminates.

FIGURE 9.13 Binary Search Fourth Iteration

The same search methodology will begin anew as the data set "H" is probed for an exact match to the target value "Holmes."

B-Tree

A b-tree is conceptually similar to a binary tree in that they are both methods of placing and locating files, but the two are not analogous. The main difference is b-trees are of a higher *order*, meaning nodes can have more than two children. This allows for a record to be found by passing through fewer nodes (the depth of the tree would be less) than if there were only two children per node. The higher order within a b-tree therefore minimizes the number of times a medium or (nodes) must be accessed to locate a desired record. In other words, less writes to the disk speeds up the search process.

Each piece of data stored in a b-tree is called a "key" because each key is unique and can occur in the b-tree in only one location.

A b-tree consists of "node" records containing the keys, and pointers that link the nodes of the b-tree together. Every b-tree is of some "order n," meaning nodes contain from n to $2n$ keys, and nodes are thereby always at least half full of keys. Keys are kept in sorted order within each node. Corresponding lists of pointers are effectively interspersed between keys to indicate where to search for a key if it isn't in the current node. A node containing k keys always contains $k + 1$ pointers.

For example, Figure 9.14 shows a portion of a b-tree with order 2 (nodes have at least two keys and three pointers). Nodes are delimited with ellipses. The keys are city names, and are kept sorted alphabetically in each node. On either side of every key are pointers linking the key to subsequent nodes.

To find the key "Des Moines," we begin searching at the top "root" node. "Des Moines" is not in the node but sorts between "Chicago" and "Hoboken," so we follow the middle pointer to the next node. Again, "Des Moines" sorts between "Denver" and "Detroit" so we follow that node's first pointer down to the next node (marked with an "X").

Eventually, we will either locate the key, or encounter a "leaf" node at the bottom level of the b-tree with no pointers to any lower nodes and without the key we want, indicating the key is nowhere in the b-tree.

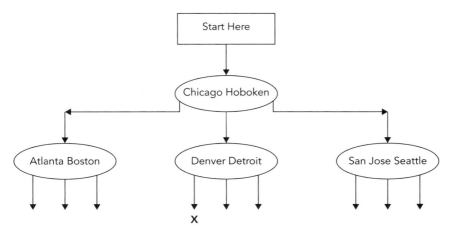

FIGURE 9.14 Portion of a B-Tree with Order 2 (nodes have at least two keys and three pointers)

Searching a b-tree for a key always begins at the root node and follows pointers from node to node until either the key is located or the search fails because a leaf node is reached and there are no more pointers to follow.

Even very large b-trees can guarantee only a small number of nodes must be retrieved to find a given key. For example, a b-tree of 10,000,000 keys with 50 keys per node never needs to retrieve more than four nodes to find any key.[5]

The maximum number of children per node is the order of the tree; b-trees are also binary and therefore can have an order of 32, 64, 128, or more (children per node).

In a tree, the records (data) are stored in locations called leaves. There can be billions of records (leaves). Depth changes as records increase to insure that the b-tree functions optimally for the number of records it contains.

Hierarchical File System

Hierarchical File System (HFS) is the file system used in Apple Macintosh systems. It was introduced by Apple in 1995, replacing their legacy MFS (Macintosh Filing System). Files are referenced with unique file IDs rather than file names; these unique identifiers can be 255 characters long. It uses a b-tree structure, which is a variance of the b-tree file system. As described above, it is this tree data structure that keeps data sorted and allows for quick searches, insertions, and deletions.

UNIX File System

UNIX File System (UFS) is the file system used by the UNIX Operating System, also called Berkeley File System Composition. There is what is called a *"Super-block,"* which contains a "magic number" identifying this as a UFS file system (see Chapter 4 and Appendix 4C for additional information on magic numbers), as well as information describing geometry, statistics, and parameters of drive; functionally, it is similar to Volume Boot Record, which we have detailed in FAT filing systems.

UFS also contains what are called *Inodes*, which contain file attributes (i.e., metadata) that are functionally similar to directory entries. These Inodes are contained within groups called *Cylinder Groups* along with *Data Blocks*, which contain the actual data.

EXT2 and EXT3

EXT are file systems used in many Linux Operating Systems. Linux supports many file systems but EXT is the default file system of most distributions.

EXT3 is a newer version of EXT2; EXT3 adds file system journaling; however, basic construction is the same.

EXT is based on the UFS File System but, as is the case with most things Linux, much of the complexities of UFS were removed, keeping this file system relatively simple. This filing system splits disk space into Block Groups (similar to Cylinder Groups of UFS). The block group sections all contain the same number of blocks, except for the last one, which may contain less depending upon drive size. These blocks are used to store file names, metadata, and file content.

EXT stores all the data relating to a file, unlike FAT or NTFS, which stores metadata in separate locations.

A workable analogy for this filing system would be the theater. The seats in a theater are grouped into sections, just as blocks on a hard drive are grouped into Block Groups. Each section of the theater (block group) is numbered and each section contains the same amount of seats (blocks).

Only the basic layout information of EXT is stored in what is called a Super-block data structure, again comparable to the Volume Boot in FAT. The file content is stored in the blocks, which are groups of consecutive sectors. Blocks in their use here are comparable to clusters. Similar to UFS, the metadata for each file and directory is also stored in the block in a data structure called an inode. The inode has a fixed size and is located within an inode table. There is one inode table per block group.

 ## SUMMARY

Various filing systems and their components may have different names and their physical placement on the drive may vary, but functionally all file systems require similar pieces: those that identify it, those that identify its data, and those that contain the data itself.

We addressed file systems here to explain these components and how data is accessed, stored, deleted, and so on. For the purposes of this text we did not cover each and every file system that a cyber forensics investigator may encounter, nor did we provide the exact bit-for-bit break down of each and every file system—for a good reason.

Books have been written and continue to be written about each of these filing systems and filing system concepts. Existing file systems will evolve and new file systems will develop; we will continue to see this growth in cell phones, iPhones, PDAs, iPads, storage media, and all the new devices to come. What is important for the reader is that by having read this chapter, you now have a better understanding, more confidence, and a greater appreciation of the concepts of file systems and the function they perform.

Technology will continue to evolve, and so must the cyber forensics investigator. As the investigator, you will, in some cases, find yourself potentially drawn to specializing in a certain system type (e.g., Windows, Unix, etc.). As this occurs you will find yourself proficient in one file system type over another. This is the natural evolution of learning and mastering. Within the cyber forensics field, and computers in general, it is next to impossible for a single person to know everything.

Within cyber forensics you will come across investigators with specializations such as the cell phone maharishi, the MAC guru, or the RAID go-to person.

Be confident, you're now one step closer to being the "file systems" guru!

NOTES

1. Charles M. Kozierok, NTFS File Attributes (April 2001), www.pcguide.com/ref/hdd/file/ntfs/filesAttr-c.html.
2. Ibid.
3. Carrier, B., *File Systems Forensic Analysis* (Upper Saddle River, NJ: Pearson Education, 2005).
4. H. Sauro (August 18, 2008), "A simple Binary Search Tree written in C#," www.codeproject.com/KB/recipes/BinarySearchTree.aspx, retrieved December 2010.
5. "B-tree algorithms," Semaphore Corporation, 484 Washington St Ste B PMB 344, Monterey CA 93940-3052, www.semaphorecorp.com/btp/algo.html, used with permission, retrieved December 2010.

APPENDIX 9A: COMMON NTFS SYSTEM DEFINED ATTRIBUTES*

Here's a list of the most common NTFS system-defined attributes:

Standard Information (SI): Contains "standard information" for all files and directories. This includes fundamental properties such as date/timestamps for when the file was created, modified, and accessed. It also contains the "standard" FAT-like attributes usually associated with a file (such as if the file is read-only, hidden, and so on).

Attribute List: This is a "meta-attribute": an attribute that describes other attributes. If it is necessary for an attribute to be made non-resident, this attribute is placed in the original MFT record to act as a pointer to the non-resident attribute.

File Name (FN): This attribute stores a name associated with a file or directory. Note that a file or directory can have multiple file name attributes, to allow the storage of the "regular" name of the file, along with an MS-DOS short filename alias. Stores name in Unicode.

Security Descriptor (SD): The access control and security properties of the file.

Volume Name, Volume Information, and Volume Version: These three attributes store key name, version, and other information about the NTFS volume. Used by the $Volume metadata file.

Data: Contains file data. By default, all the data in a file is stored in a single data attribute—even if that attribute is broken into many pieces due to size, it is still one attribute.

Index Root Attribute: This attribute contains the actual index of files contained within a directory, or part of the index if it is large. If the directory is small, the entire index will fit within this attribute in the MFT; if it is too large, some of the information is here and the rest is stored in external index buffer attributes.

Index Allocation Attribute: If a directory index is too large to fit in the index root attribute, the MFT record for the directory will contain an index allocation attribute, which contains pointers to index buffer entries containing the rest of the directory's index information.

---

* Kozierok, C. (Site Version: 2.2.0 – Version Date: April 17, 2001), "NTFS File Attributes," www .pcguide.com/ref/hdd/file/ntfs/filesAttr-c.html, retrieved November 2011.

Bitmap: Contains the cluster allocation bitmap. Used by the $Bitmap metadata file.

- Similar in function to FAT tables in FAT.
- Contains one bit for each cluster in the partition. Unlike FAT, it tracks cluster allocation only. It does not track cluster runs. If a bit (representing a cluster) has a 1, the cluster is allocated to a file. If the bit (representing a cluster) has a 0, the cluster is unallocated, or available for use. Very simple.

Extended Attribute (EA) and Extended Attribute Information: These are special attributes that are implemented for compatibility with OS/2 use of NTFS partitions.

Most file systems exist to read and write file *content*, but NTFS exists to read and write *attributes*, which can contain file content or header (metadata) content. It's as if NTFS did not differentiate between metadata and regular data (file contents).

Box Analogy

Think about an attribute as a box or storage container. The outside of the container may have your name, address, and contents written on it; the inside is the contents.

The header is generic and standard to all attributes, while the content is a specific type of attribute and can be any size.

Thus, all items are stored in "boxes." Boxes may be of all sizes and shapes with different contents, but the outside all contain the same info: name, address, and contents.

So the header equates to the outside of the box and the content equates to the contents of the box.

CHAPTER TEN

Cyber Forensics

Investigative Smart Practices

T IS IMPORTANT TO SPEND just a moment before proceeding, to discuss the difference, albeit potentially subtle, between "smart" and "best" or even "good" practices.

"Best" or even "good" practices are typically grounded in data, analytical analysis, baselines, perceptions, and practices supported by the actions or results of primarily a single company that catches the eye of an industry, which in turn is then joined by other organizations mimicking or adopting these practices over time, inevitably resulting in the establishment of a "best practice." There seems to be something circular or maybe even incestuous about best practices.

In Chapter 10, the concept of Investigative Smart Practices is introduced. These Investigative Smart Practices are embedded within the sequential "steps" taken during a cyber forensic investigative process.

Smart practices underline the fact that any practice worth such special attention, while also utilizing data and analytical analysis, ought usually to capture the inventiveness required to go beyond "following the pack" to applying independent, logical thought to approaching and solving problems. This means that actions are taken because they are the smartest decisions to make, and steps to take, not simply because others have done so. Smart practices are also defensible on their own and do not rely on "group" approval or acceptance.

Smart practices are employed to help overcome obstacles to innovation. As technology advances and morphs almost daily, the technical challenges and investigative scenarios faced by a cyber forensic investigator will require the implementation and use of smart practices in order to determine a best course of action for the case at hand, which may be a completely different approach or set of actions for the next case. Nonetheless, following a process is integral to the successful investigation of any case.

Remember from the ongoing case: Ronelle Sawyer is investigating whether Jose McCarthy has potentially engaged in the unlawful distribution of his organization's intellectual property to a competitor, Janice Witcome, managing director of the XYZ Company. Ronelle works for a Fortune 500 company named ABC Inc. Ronelle's employer is global, extremely large, and departmentalized. These departments are "siloed" such that each performs a single task and only that task. There are procedures, processes, and guidelines for each and every activity, including cyber forensics.

It is important that Ronelle, as a cyber forensic investigator, follow a defined forensic process. If anything, an investigator should follow those processes set forth by the standard forensic practices adopted by the investigator's organization, department, or agency.

Whatever the forensic process followed, it needs to be followed from the very inception of the investigation, case, or incident all the way to the logical conclusion of the case, investigation, or incident, which can possibly even require the forensic investigator to appear as an *expert witness* in a court of law.

A reminder: As you read through this chapter, you will encounter words that have been *italicized*. These words represent key concepts and are more fully defined by a working definition, which is included within a glossary at the end of the book. Should you desire an explanation of any italicized word, please refer to this glossary.

THE FORENSIC PROCESS

This process, the Investigative Smart Practices, however, need not detail exactly every step-by-step procedure of a cyber forensic investigation, as this could be an exercise in futility; there are so many different directions in which an investigation can evolve, and attempting to follow a specific investigative template or to fit every investigation into the same investigative approach could have disastrous outcomes. Additionally, such procedures would quickly become dated as new investigative technologies are sure to develop.

During the course of our coverage of basic cyber forensic concepts in the previous chapters we occasionally joined Ronelle during her investigation. The actual investigation is only one piece of this investigative process. It may be the piece that pays the bills; however, there are other components to the investigative process that are as equally important. These other pieces may not entail finding the preverbal "needle in the haystack" or the "smoking gun," yet they are equally as important. Why? Any one of the steps done incorrectly, carelessly, or skipped could thwart and invalidate the entire investigation, regardless of the eventual investigative findings.

In general, the cyber forensic investigative process is likely to incorporate a combination of the following initial steps (see Figure 10.1). These Investigative Smart Practices, however, are not necessarily meant to be followed sequentially, nor are they mutually exclusive. As stated, each investigation should be evaluated and processed on its own merits and the steps taken throughout the investigation should be those that ensure an organization or department's cyber forensic investigation procedures are clearly followed, and that there can be no question as to the completeness of the process followed or the accuracy of the evidence collected.

Each forensic case should be considered unique, as each can span the spectrum and diversity of topics: divorce, murder, child molestation, intellectual property theft, employer/employee issues, sexual harassment, cyber extortion, industrial espionage, and the list goes on (it is nearly infinite).

It can be a divorce case based on claims of sexual harassment by an employee. Or perhaps a disgruntled worker steals a copy of his or her employer's strategic marketing plan and offers it for sale to a competitor, or a child makes a new online friend who later turns out to be an adult with previous convictions for solicitation of a minor. Some cases may include more than a single topic; for example, the case may involve an employer investigating an employee's theft of intellectual property and industrial espionage, as is the case with Ronelle's investigation. The possibilities are boundless.

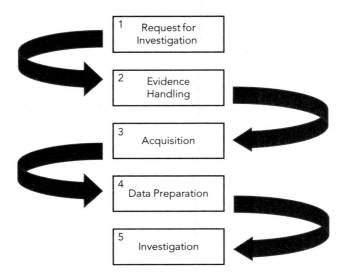

FIGURE 10.1 Generalized Investigation Process Flow

To add to the broad range of investigation types there is also a broad range of investigative practices. Cyber forensic investigators work in all areas and at all levels within society: federal, state, municipal, within law enforcement, at independent small business, and global corporations. Each of these areas is bounded by differing rules, regulations, laws, and procedures. Cyber forensic investigators will face differing hurdles depending upon the organization, state, and even country in which they work.

It is important to remember that forensic investigators are bound by procedures. If an organization has developed written step-by-step procedures, then the organization's investigators are required to follow those steps. The success or failure of a case can be highly dependent upon assuring that the forensic investigator has followed a specific set of written procedures. A savvy lawyer can make an opposing side's forensic investigators look foolish. One could easily imagine the cross-examination dialogue: "If you don't even follow your own procedures how can we be certain you followed existing, required Federal procedures?" In some cases, not following your own written procedures may be comparable to not following the law. Be prepared to follow written forensic procedures.

The process by which procedures can be formulated will be dependent upon the individual organization, taking into consideration any laws that supersede and enjoin the organization to follow these laws. However, there are some general steps or smart practices, guidelines, which should take place and be part of a well-organized cyber forensic investigation. Be advised, these steps may not occur sequentially; some may occur concurrently with other steps, or throughout the entire process.

These Investigative Smart Practices are not the rule but rather suggested smart practices. There may be a situation or an organization that requires additional steps, combines steps, or rearranges the steps shown in Figure 10.1 to a degree; however, skipping a single step or steps or not performing specific steps can lead to potential disaster.

FORENSIC INVESTIGATIVE SMART PRACTICES

Objective: To determine both the validity of the investigative request and to establish the investigative scope.

Step 1: The Initial Contact, the Request

In order for there to be an investigation someone needs to come forward and make a request (see Figure 10.2). Usually there are two opposing parties or sides, the requester and the *target* or *subject*. The subject is the person who is being investigated. Depending upon the case it may be a spouse, co-worker, contractor, or someone in a foreign country that has written some malicious code. The subject could be *labeled* "suspect" but naming him/her as such may be presumptuous or lead to subjectivity.

Usually there is some "document of request," establishing a basis or justification to conduct the investigation. Examples of specific documents that would possibly form the basis for launching an investigation include, but are not limited to, the following:

- Letter of Engagement
- Contract
- Official (Corporate) Request
- Subpoena
- Search Warrant
- Court Order

If there is justification for a specific complaint or reason to investigate, there should also be rules, laws, company policies, procedures, or baselines upon which the investigation request was filed. Again, the specific type of document

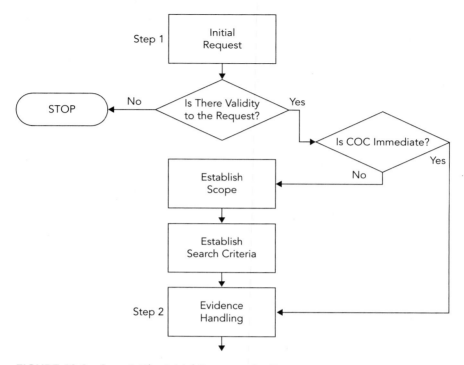

FIGURE 10.2 Step 1: The Initial Contact, the Request

necessary to begin a forensic investigation will depend upon the type of organization and perhaps the type of case.

For example, before a forensic practice in a large corporate environment can begin an investigation, an approval form submitted via the Legal department or Human Resources department may be required. Law enforcement may require a subpoena or search warrant before an investigation may take place. A small independent forensic practice may require a letter of engagement or contract, from a client, before beginning an investigation.

On the other hand, the requester (for example, executive management, a business partner, spouse, or an aggrieved third party) may require the independent cyber forensic investigator to sign a *nondisclosure agreement* (NDA), as he or she will no doubt be made privy to proprietary information. Each of these forensic scenarios is completely different and requires unique handling.

It is here that the legitimacy and scope of the investigation is determined. A judge may determine the legitimacy of a law enforcement investigation by issuing a search warrant, but this isn't so for an internal corporate investigation.

The rules or guidelines for a corporate investigation may not require such stringent controls; perhaps a simple request form approved by the Legal department.

However, the cyber forensic investigator should have advice of legal counsel prior to proceeding with an investigation involving accessing an individual's personal items. In the United States, for example, evidence collection and examination must not violate (as of the writing of this text) the following:

- Fourth Amendment
- Privacy Protection Act
- Electronic Communications Privacy Act

Warrantless workplace searches by private employers rarely violate the Fourth Amendment. So long as the employer is not acting as an instrument or agent of the U.S. Government at the time of the search, and the search is a private search, the Fourth Amendment would not apply (see *Skinner v. Railway Labor Executives' Ass'n*, 489 U.S. 602, 614 [1989]).

The cyber forensic investigator will encounter other unique challenges as well. Does the requester own the system and have the authority to request a forensic investigation? In a divorce does the system requiring investigation belong to the requester's spouse? If so, the forensic investigator may be in violation of privacy laws by performing such an investigation without authority, authorization, court order, etc., and thereby breaking the law. The scope or legitimacy may not always be in the hands of the cyber forensic investigator.

Some additional items that should be addressed prior to beginning a cyber forensic investigation include:

1. Determine whether it is feasible to continue with the investigation based upon information gathered, legitimacy and/or credibility of the complaint, exposure to the organization, and so on.
2. Benefits and/or risks involved in pursuing an investigation.
3. Liabilities and/or risks in not pursuing the investigation.
4. Obligation(s) to pursue (ethical/moral).
5. Are sufficient resources available to successfully carry out the investigation?

It is imperative for the cyber forensic investigator to be provided with the scope of the investigation from management, law enforcement, and so on, or to develop the scope of the investigation based upon the initial evidence presented, violation of law, etc. This may involve an initial meeting in which the requester seeking the cyber forensic investigation provides the forensic investigator with specific parameters of the investigation, the breadth and depth of the intended investigative areas, search criteria, applicable law, etc., thus establishing the scope of the investigation.

At a minimum the search criteria may include several components:

1. Keywords associated with the case being investigated (personnel names, company project code names, competitor names, phrases, etc.).
2. Dates or date ranges during which the act under investigation is reported to have taken place.
3. File types (.docx, .doc, .xls, .pdf, .nef, .tif,.png, .jpg, .wav, .mp4, etc.) associated with the case being investigated.

Some investigators may be strictly bound by this criterion and others may not. Some investigation requests may be general enough such that a broad date range and general file types is all that may be required. A child molestation case performed by law enforcement may not request certain file types, as the investigator may be interested in reviewing any files on the subject's seized hardware.

All data regardless of type may be fair game be it video, images, emails, *Internet artifacts,* or chat transcripts. On the other hand, some cases, involving subpoenas for example, may be strictly bound by exact criterion, such as time and date ranges. Going beyond a certain time or date period would be a violation of the court order (i.e., the subpoena). Again, each case or situation is unique.

In a corporate setting, in which the systems, applications on those systems, and the data all belong exclusively to the organization, there may be more flexibility regarding the investigative process. The organization does however need to advise its employees that the systems belong to the organization as does all its contents and data (notification laws vary in the United States by state; thus, it is important to verify which laws your organization may be required to comply with). An organization will usually present this notification banner to the employee, as a pop-up screen right before login so that the employee has to confirm knowledge of the organization's ownership of the systems and all data on those systems, and accept this condition, in order to successfully log on. This acknowledgment and acceptance by the employee give the organization the right to do whatever it wants to do with their digital property.

This being the case, corporate requests can be (and usually are) as broad and generic as needed (see Figure 10.3).

In our ongoing investigation conducted by Ronelle into the activities of employee Jose McCarthy, company procedure states that all investigation

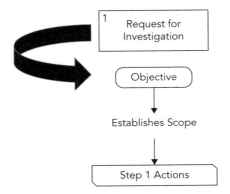

FIGURE 10.3 Step 1: Request for Investigation

requests be routed first through the firm's Legal department. The Legal department decides on the legitimacy of the investigation, and whether to proceed forward or not. The Legal department also decides the scope of the investigation but, being that they do not perform the actual investigation, at times, the specific search criteria necessary for an efficient investigation may not be obtained in such a manner that would best aid Ronelle in her investigations (e.g., the Legal department will likely lack the technical aptitude to ask the best cyber forensic questions).

Senior management within ABC Inc. decided that their initial concerns were warranted and decided to request a full cyber forensic investigation. Procedure dictates HR and Legal approvals. Request was submitted and approved by both departments. The case was then sent down to ABC Inc.'s forensic department and assigned to cyber forensic investigator Ronelle Sawyer as lead investigator.

After further discussions with senior management Ronelle obtained more details involving the case and was able to outline the following investigation scope criteria:

Scope of Investigation

    Date Range—Time period: from employee Jose McCarthy's start date to his termination date—May 10, 2008, to March 26, 2009.

    Keywords—"Janice," "Witcome," and "XYZ." Note: Keywords were not actually supplied with the request but Ronelle was able to create a keyword list from the details provided by management at ABC, Jose's direct manager, and from ABC's general counsel.

    File Types—Documents: word processing and spreadsheets. Ronelle met further with the Legal department to ask if there were specific file types she should focus on, as this information was not initially provided by ABC management and in many cases may be omitted. File types could also be ANY and ALL; once again, each case is different.

The objective in this step is to determine the scope of the investigation. The scope or boundaries begin with determining if the case is legitimate. If it is determined that the case is not legitimate, violates no laws, has no merit, or is not supported by management, then the need or reason for an investigation must be re-examined, as no scope for the investigation has been determined.

This step can be, and depending on the case particulars, may be required to be, shared with others throughout the organization (e.g., Human Resources, IT Security, Operations) or externally to the organization (law enforcement). Ronelle's Legal department determined, based upon the preliminary evidence provided, that the initial case against Jose McCarthy had merit and was legitimate, thus clearing the way to begin the full cyber forensic investigation.

Step 2: Evidence Handling

Objective: To preserve the integrity of the evidence; and being able to prove the integrity of the evidence, in a court of law.

It is at this step of the investigative process that the evidence (typically digital but may also be hard copy) is actually handed off to the cyber forensic investigator. The evidence-handling step occurs continuously while the evidence is in the cyber forensic investigator's possession. Initially it involves the taking possession of evidence, perhaps taking photographs of the evidence, documenting the condition of the evidence, and taking note of any preexisting damage or peculiar markings. Most, if not all, of the cyber forensic investigator's interaction with the evidence can fall under the evidence-handling step. The specific focus of evidence handling, as presented here, is the movement of evidence, typically physical in nature versus electronic (see Figure 10.4).

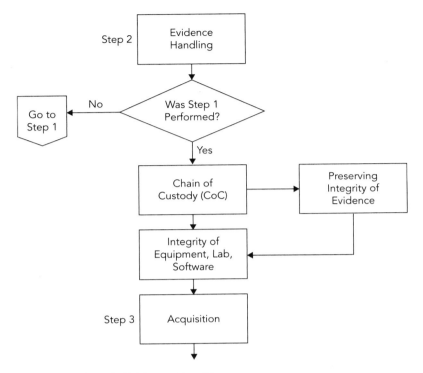

FIGURE 10.4 Step 2: Evidence Handling

Law enforcement is perhaps most obliged, due to specific requirements and legal compliances, to follow stringent evidence handling procedures. For example, some cyber forensic investigators in a corporate environment may skip photographing and documenting irregular markings on hard drives contained within their environment, where this may be a standard procedure by law enforcement professionals.

The cases presented to law enforcement are at times more serious in nature and tend to be criminal versus those cases that may typically arise within a corporate environment. The consequences of mishandling evidence in a criminal investigation are perhaps higher, so therefore the requirements for controls are higher. A general accepted principle in cyber forensics is it is better to be overly cautious; document every step, photograph every piece, take many notes, and so on, rather than being less diligent and failing to document a potentially critical piece of evidence.

Evidence handling is ongoing and occurs throughout the investigation. It includes how the evidence is stored when not being used and how the evidence is handled when being used. Evidence handling can also include the handling of a cyber forensic investigator's equipment and tools. These tools include anything that will connect to, attach to, or otherwise interact with the evidence, software, or hardware. For example, an improperly maintained *hardware write blocker* could possibly short the circuit board on an evidence hard drive. The mishandling of such tools may lead to potential damage or destruction of evidence.

Any equipment the cyber forensic investigator uses to conduct an investigation on the evidence needs to be documented; this includes hardware, software, and connecting media. This equipment should be properly maintained and in working order. Names, versions, upgrades, models, and any other relevant information pertaining to the equipment used (hardware and software) can be considered important and therefore documented per case. As months and perhaps years pass after an investigation, it may not be easy to recall which version of software was used for an investigation.

Later stages of evidence handling, as the case winds down and concludes, may involve returning the evidence to the original owner, if allowed by law. Whenever possession of evidence changes hands, be it upon receipt or return, the *chain of custody* must be upheld.

The chain of custody is the evidence handling procedure that tracks the evidence as it changes possession. Chain of custody usually takes the shape of a form or document of some sort. A form is usually involved because the signatures of those receiving and those relinquishing the evidence are required.

A chain of custody form will usually contain some of the following fields:

- Case number or assignment
- Date
- Time
- Serial/model numbers
- Description fields
- Location

Chain of custody forms take on many appearances. In some cases a form may be broken down into two separate parts:

1. Item description—describes the articles being transferred. This will include serial and model numbers, make, and descriptions (see Figure 10.5).
2. Signatures—Custody transfer—this piece includes the date and time of transfer and the signature of the releaser and the signature of the receiver (see Figure 10.6).

Package #:	Description:			
Make:		Model:	Serial #:	Agency Item #:
Package #:	Description:			
Make:		Model:	Serial #:	Agency Item #:
Package #:	Description:			
Make:		Model:	Serial #:	Agency Item #:

FIGURE 10.5 Chain of Custody Form (Part 1)

Package #'s	Date/Time	Released By	Received By	Reason
	Date	Name/Agency	Name/Agency	
	Time	Signature	Signature	
	Date	Name/Agency	Name/Agency	
	Time	Signature	Signature	
	Date	Name/Agency	Name/Agency	
	Time	Signature	Signature	

FIGURE 10.6 Chain of Custody Form (Part 2)

The key objective of evidence handling is ensuring that data is not altered, manipulated, or changed *in any way* from its originally acquired form, thus the preservation and tracking of the evidence.

Be advised: As explained previously, evidence handling does not necessarily follow the initial request, sequentially. These steps may occur simultaneously, or in some cases chain of custody or the handling of the evidence could occur first. In cases where law enforcement is called to the scene of a crime, these professionals may have to handle and collect evidence well before being directed by the courts as to what needs to be done with the evidence.

The important thing to remember is that *chain of custody needs to occur before, during, and after the transfer of any evidence.* Beginning an initial chain of custody process should not occur after the evidence has been examined, as being able to prove who has had access to the evidence will allow for accountability over the integrity of the evidence. This accountability is an essential step in preserving evidence (see Figure 10.7).

Ronelle received the evidence, in the form of an 80GB hard drive from her Legal department. It was hand delivered in a sealed container. Upon receipt, Ronelle opened the container and found the hard drive and chain of custody form. The form has been filled out and is awaiting Ronelle's signature.

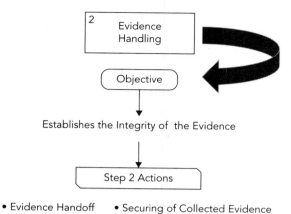

FIGURE 10.7 Step 2: Evidence Handling

Ronelle dated the form, signed her name in the recipient field, and copied it. Ronelle kept the original (for internal records keeping and to verify the audit trail and chain of custody "trail") and returned the copy to the sender for their records. (See Figure 10.8.)

Confidential

Evidence Handling
ABC Inc. Forensic Investigation

Case # 000029

Chain of Custody

Date/Time	From	To	Reason
Date 4/6/09	Name/Organization _LEGAL_ KEVIN SMITH	Name/Organization FORENSICS RONELLE SAWYER	FORENSIC INVESTIGATION
Time 9:30 AM	Signature _Kevin Smith_	Signature _Ronelle Sawyer_	
Date 6/12/09	Name/Organization FORENSICS RONELLE SAWYER	Name/Organization _LEGAL_ KEVIN SMITH	INVESTIGATION COMPLETE EVIDENCE RETURN
Time 4:00PM	Signature _Ronelle Sawyer_	Signature _Kevin Smith_	
Date	Name/Organization	Name/Organization	
Time	Signature	Signature	

FIGURE 10.8 Step 2: Chain of Custody Form—Signature Field

The Legal department filled out the "From" section of the chain of custody document along with a brief description and the serial number of the hard drive; however, the rest of the form was left blank. This is not unusual, as most first responders who are initially responsible for gathering evidence may not have the technical background to go beyond basic macro identification details and may find this a bit too detailed.

Ronelle confirmed that the serial number matched the chain of custody form and the hard drive that was in the container and proceeded to fill out the remaining lines of the custody transfer document, such as the hard drive model and details to describe and identify the hard drive, in the description field. (See Figure 10.9.)

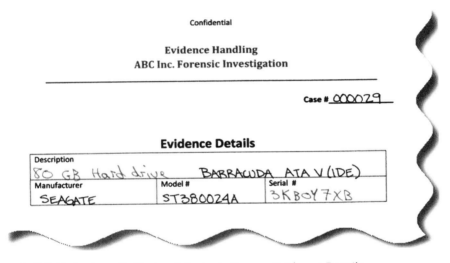

FIGURE 10.9 Step 2: Chain of Custody Form—Evidence Details

After completing the chain of custody documents Ronelle secured the evidence (the hard drive) by sealing it in its container and locking it in a forensic vault, within the forensic lab.

Step 3: Acquisition of Evidence

Objective: Obtain a forensically sound image and preserve the integrity of the original evidence.

The acquisition of evidence generally refers to the imaging of the evidence in a forensically sound manner. A forensically sound manner is one in which the evidence is not altered. Nothing is written, altered, changed, or otherwise modified on the piece of evidence (see Figures 10.10 and 10.11).

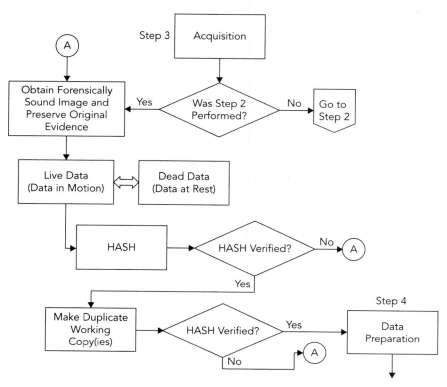

FIGURE 10.10 Step 3: Acquisition Process

The acquisition of evidence can, in theory, fall under the previous evidence handling section. Most if not all of the cyber forensic investigator's interaction with the evidence can fall under evidence handling. As mentioned previously, the evidence handling section discussed the physical movement of evidence and the handing off of evidence, which is the action requiring chain of custody. This line does get blurry.

Consider the case of a live network acquisition. A live network acquisition is one in which an investigator may need to connect to the network of an organization and acquire a system remotely, thereby never actually taking physical possession of the system. However, something needs to be considered, there is a "handing off" of evidence that is occurring, albeit done remotely. In this case, the evidence acquisition and handling would occur simultaneously. Nevertheless, even though these two activities may occur simultaneously, they are still separate activities worth separating for discussion.

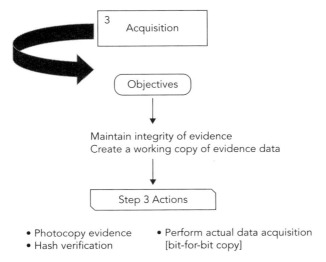

FIGURE 10.11 Step 3: Acquisition Objectives

In the example of a network acquisition, the evidence handling process would imply that the cyber forensic investigator obtain and carry out proper chain of custody through the acquisition of an accurate *IP address* to which to connect to the network. The acquisition "action" would then entail using forensically sound network acquisition software to acquire the system (collect the digital evidence).

Evidence

It is perhaps important to stop for a moment in our discussion of the investigative process to address the various types of evidence which an investigator may encounter

According to the Federal Rules of Evidence, there are three classifications or types of evidence:

1. **Original**. An "original" of a writing or recording is the writing or recording itself or any counterpart intended to have the same effect by a person executing or issuing it. An "original" of a photograph includes the negative or any print there from. If data are stored in a computer or similar device, any printout or other output readable by sight, shown to reflect the data accurately, is an "original."

2. **Duplicate**. A "duplicate" is a counterpart produced by the same impression as the original, or from the same matrix, or by means of photography, including enlargements and miniatures, or by mechanical or electronic re-recording, or by chemical reproduction, or by other equivalent techniques which accurately reproduces the original.

3. **Best evidence.** The *best evidence rule* is a *common law rule of evidence* which can be traced back at least as far as the eighteenth century. In *Omychund v. Barker* (1745) 1 Atk, 21, 49; 26 ER 15, 33, Lord Harwicke stated that no evidence was admissible unless it was "the best that the nature of the case will allow." The general rule is that secondary evidence, such as a copy or facsimile, will be not admissible if an original document exists, and is not unavailable due to destruction or other circumstances indicating unavailability.[1]

Generally, "Best Evidence" states that evidence is best in its most original state. This being the case, it is the cyber forensic investigator's responsibility and priority to keep whatever evidence received in its original (original to the investigator) state. The evidence the cyber forensic investigator received could be a copy of original evidence, but as far as the investigator is concerned the evidence (even though it is a copy and not the original) received is the best evidence. Any changes or alterations to this evidence could have disastrous consequences and may result in the inability to submit in court any of the evidence collected during the investigation. Such a limitation or inability could result in the dismissal of the case and a failure to prosecute a guilty party.

In order to preserve this best evidence it is important that every action taken during the investigative process on will do absolutely nothing to destroy, manipulate, change or alter that evidence in any way. The importance of this cannot be overstated. In step with this mantra, it is also important therefore to be prepared to prove, if required, the integrity of the work in a court of law. Therefore, it is almost equally as critical to document all of the individual steps taken in ensuring the preservation of evidence throughout the investigative process.

In essence, the two main components of evidence acquisition are ultimately preserving evidence and documenting the steps ensuring that preservation.

When acquiring evidence it is imperative to use a *write blocker*. Hardware write blockers are preferred over software write blockers, but each has its appropriate application of use. Write blockers, while allowing data to be copied off of a device, at the same time prevent anything to be written to the

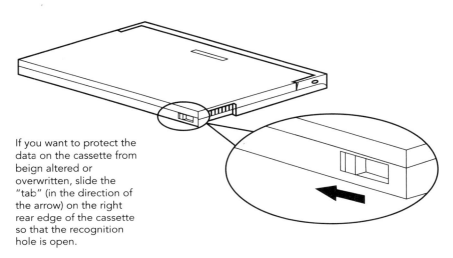

If you want to protect the data on the cassette from beign altered or overwritten, slide the "tab" (in the direction of the arrow) on the right rear edge of the cassette so that the recognition hole is open.

FIGURE 10.12   Write Protecting a Cassette

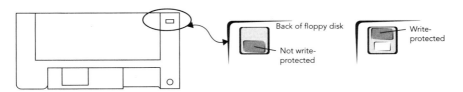

FIGURE 10.13   Write-Protect "Switch" on a Floppy Disk

device. Remember old cassette tapes? You could push in the top tab and prevent overwriting songs contained on the cassette. (See Figure 10.12.)

Floppy disks had something similar, but the lock could be switched on or off, allowing for data to be altered on floppy if one changed his/her mind. (See Figure 10.13.) Nonwritable CDs and DVDs are write blocked.

All these are examples of hardware write blockers. In the forensic field there are many other types of write blockers. At the core of these devices is usually an adapter, which on one end plugs into a source and on the other plugs into a target. (See Figure 10.14.)

The source is the evidence (in our case example, Jose McCarthy's hard drive) and the target is where the evidence will be copied to (a *sanitized drive*).

It is also imperative to acquire bit-for-bit copies or images whenever possible. It is important to understand the difference between a *bit-for-bit image* versus just a copy. Aside from the possibility of altering evidence, a large amount of

FIGURE 10.14 Laptop to IDE Hard Drive Adapter

evidence would be skipped or missed by just copying folders off a system or making a *logical copy*. A bit-for-bit image allows for all of the data contained within the drive to be captured, including the *unallocated space, slack space,* file system structure, and so on. A bit-for-bit is, as the name implies, the copying of every single bit, verbatim, and transplanting each bit onto the target. It is not a logical copy but a *physical copy*, a bit-for-bit copy.

Cyber forensics will not always be performed upon a hard drive; as mentioned, there are network acquisitions to contend with as well as cell phones/ PDA acquisitions, etc. Bit-for-bit copies are not always feasible or in some cases possible. On a corporate file server for example, each employee may be allocated space for saving work files; this space is sometimes referred to as a *Home Directory*. It is a user's personal (for business uses) space on the corporate network. An acquisition of a server containing hundreds of employee's Home Directories may not be warranted.

A logical acquisition of only the specified subject's Home Directory may be the best alternative for acquiring this evidence. The same can be true for corporate email. Many corporate email servers, such as Exchange and Domino (used for Microsoft Outlook and Lotus Notes respectively) bundle their data into large files called PST and NSFs. These file types may be found and residing across enterprise email systems. It may not be necessary to image all the servers or the *array*. Imaging the single file in such a case may suffice. It may be acceptable to mount these files (refer to Chapter 5 for our discussion of mounting files) and image just the components pertaining to the subject under investigation.

Hashing

A hash is usually a mathematical function or algorithm that converts a variable-sized set of data into an invariable, completely random data set. The resulting hash data length is dependent upon the hash type and its intended function. In forensics, uniqueness and distinctiveness is critical, so hash lengths of 128 bits and 256 bits are not uncommon to ensure *evidence uniqueness*.

Hashes are usually displayed in HEX. Each hexadecimal character can encode 4 bits of binary data. (For a refresher of HEX, refer to Chapter 3.) So, a HEX value of 64 characters is equivalent to 256 binary bits. Likewise, a 128 HEX value would represent a 512-bit hash. Although, currently in cyber forensics, a 128-bit hash is sufficient for establishing uniqueness of data.

The uniqueness of hash values is important in cyber forensics such that no two pieces of evidence are identical. Consider fingerprints as an analogy; every person on the planet has unique fingerprints. Matching fingerprints in a crime scene to those of a specific individual would be inconsequential if fingerprints were not unique; 256-bit hash values allow for 2^{256} unique values. (For a refresher on bits and possible values associated with bits review Chapter 1.)

In cyber forensics this uniqueness of the hash values will also ensure *evidence integrity*. To ensure evidence integrity, before the evidence is acquired it is first hashed. The evidence is then acquired and that evidence is hashed a second time. The hash values between the evidence pre-acquisition and post-acquisition need to be identical to ensure evidence integrity.

Any change to the evidence after taking the original hash will cause any subsequent hash to be completely different. Recall hashes are completely random when created, so any alteration of data regardless of scope, amount, or importance of the change will generate a completely new random hash. Any change in the data will completely alter the algorithmic outcome (i.e., the hash value).

Currently, the most commonly accepted legal (read court tried and tested) HASH used is either *MD5* (128-bit hash) or *SHA-1* (160-bit hash). Once the original evidence has been forensically imaged and hashes verified, the original evidence should be properly stored following smart evidence handling procedures. The originally acquired evidence should not be used in the detailed investigation and e-discovery process. Only copies of the evidence, once verified by hashing, should be used, while the originally acquired evidence is locked away.

FIGURE 10.15 Image MASSter Write Blocker

There are a variety of different tools which allow for forensic imaging, some are free and others quite expensive. All forensic tools will usually provide for bit-for-bit imaging and will usually contain a built-in hash verification routine. There is forensic hardware specifically made for forensic imaging, such as Image MaSSter's Solo. There are forensic software suites (software packages with multiple functionality), which allow for imaging as well as other related forensic activities such as HEX editors, drive and file mounting, searching, indexing, *parsing*, and many other tasks. Examples of such forensic suites include Guidance Software's EnCase and Access Data's FTK.

Ronelle received the evidence drive from her Legal department. She followed proper chain of custody procedures and stored the evidence drive in her department's evidence vault. As time permitted Ronelle went to the vault to retrieve the evidence, completed the chain of custody procedure by signing out the evidence, and brought the evidence to her forensic machine. Ronelle acquired her evidence using EnCase Enterprise and ImageMasster's write blocker (see Figure 10.15).

Ronelle opened a new case file in EnCase and connected the evidence drive to her forensic acquisition system via the write blocker. EnCase was able to identify the physical media (i.e., the actual drive removed from Jose's work machine) and mount the drive. An MD5 hash verification of the entire evidence disk was performed, returning the hash value 59a34105247fb3a26e4bc411fea32eb4.

Ronelle used Encase functions to perform a full physical disk acquisition. After the acquisition process completed successfully, without any errors, (according to the EnCase software routine), Ronelle performed another hash verification of the acquired data. The hash values of the original evidence and the forensic image created via Encase matched: 59a34105247fb3a26e 4bc411fea32eb4.

Ronelle then returned the original evidence to the vault and again followed the established chain of custody procedures by checking the evidence back into the vault and recording this on the chain of custody document. Ronelle now has an exact copy of the entire physical disk, which she obtained without altering the original evidence.

Step 4: Data Preparation

Objective: Prepare and identify data for analysis and investigation (see Figures 10.16 and 10.17).

Data preparation can be broken down into two types:

1. Preprocessing
2. Searching

Preprocessing

Preprocessing involves those steps that prepare the evidence before the evidence is searched. Searching the evidence, on the other hand, brings about results, which then need to be investigated.

Mounting

The mounting of the filing systems (see Chapter 5) contained within a piece of evidence is necessary so that the data structure can be viewed, so that the organization of the data can be made apparent. Without mounting the evidence, the simple task of finding a file can be very complex and tedious. Imagine having to manually identify the partition type and then manually *carving* out each and every file by going through each and every byte of the file system. Tedious is an understatement.

Forensic tools (as well as other tools, i.e., operating systems) can quickly mount a drive and its file system, presenting the data in a relatively intuitive manner. Also, more complex files need to be "mounted." ZIP files and other file formats require mounting in order to be readable and therefore searchable.

Recover Deleted Files

Recovery of deleted items involves recovering files from unallocated space. Typically, the tools that recover these files look for file headers and footers,

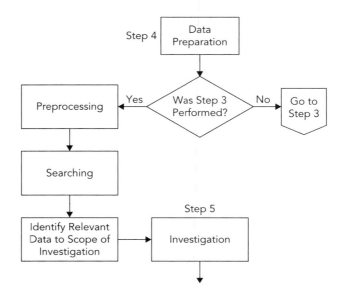

FIGURE 10.16 Step 4: Data Preparation

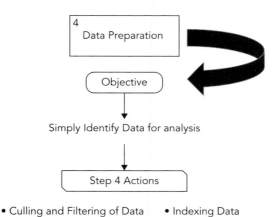

FIGURE 10.17 Step 4: Data Preparation Objectives

thereby requiring a file to be entirely intact. Recall from Chapter 4 that when a file is deleted it is first sent to the deleted items folder. Then, when a file is deleted from the deleted items its space is thereby made available, or unallocated. The file is not moved or magically erased; its space is only made available for some other file to be written to. Until this space is overwritten the data contained within the file is still resident on the drive.

Remember, only the entry in the file system is altered such that retrieval by the operating system is not possible. However, the file system entry is not part of the actual file. The file may be deleted and floating somewhere in unallocated space yet still be completely intact. Forensic tools can locate, identify, and restore these files. Certainly some of the metadata that would normally be seen with a saved file will be missing, but the file itself may be in pristine condition. A file can be partially overwritten and not recoverable in its entirety, however, pieces of that file can still be found and used as evidence.

Verifying

Verifying data ensures the data is what it claims to be. As already discussed, there is the evidence verification process achieved by hash matches; but, here verification implies attempting to uncover a deliberate concealment of evidence. Verifying file types is of great importance as a suspect can quickly and easily rename a file.

For example, is a word document (e.g., .docx) really a word document, or is it an image? Recall from Chapter 4 we discussed files and how files are defined in the file header. Another tedious task for a human would be to go through each and every file checking headers for accuracy. Compounded with having to manually extract or carve out each file, as explained previously, a cyber forensic examination would never end. This file verification function is a functionality contained in most cyber forensic software packages at it is imperative for evidence pre-processing.

Verification also implies verifying if perhaps a partition on a hard drive was deleted. Again, this may be an attempt at concealment. Examining the Master Boot Record (MBR) and Volume Boot Records (VBR) would reveal the presence of any additional partitions, which may not be mounted by the operating system. For a refresher on MBR see Chapter 5 and for VBR see Chapter 8. Forensic software automates this manual task, allowing for a quicker identification of potentially missing partitions.

Indexing

Some forensic tools can index the data contained within a piece of evidence. Essentially, indexing organizes all the data in a "database," which allows for quick search results. Just as Google quickly responds with search results, so too will forensic tools when data is indexed. Google has indexed much of the Internet (websites), allowing for quick search results. If it wasn't for this indexing Google would have to start searching each and every site every time a request was made. The initial indexing, sometimes called crawling, takes some time but the benefits once indexed may be worthwhile. Some time is sacrificed on the front end for some quick searching on the back end.

Searching

Searching essentially involves refining the original evidence into a smaller subset of data which then can be investigated. Searching can be broad in meaning to encompass a wide scope of data, such as data between date ranges or specific file types. It can also imply the actual searching for more exact criteria, such as a keyword. Indexing greatly improves the efficiency of searching when an exact or precise target, perhaps a keyword, is involved.

Filtering may differentiate itself from searching in that it is usually broader in scope, perhaps applying to data falling into a subset. For example, data falling into a certain date range, or all data of a certain file type. Culling is the process of collecting the refined data that is relevant to the investigation. It differs from filtering in that culling usually invokes an eDiscovery effort. It is the collecting of data pertaining to a certain individual or case.

It all still involves refining evidence into a smaller subset. Instead of searching all data within an organization only the data which pertains to the case needs to be searched. For example, searching only the subject's profile involved in the incident instead of all users' profiles contained on a server, or perhaps removing data not within scope (e.g., removing *executables* from a subset).

Searching also applies to finding those pieces of evidence in unallocated space that are no longer part of a file. Much of a file can be overwritten, but sometimes ASCII text, including remnants of sentences or paragraphs, may be recoverable. However you decide to define these terms, in the end, all actions involve the searching for evidence.

Ronelle now has her image in EnCase. She has already verified her image, so she now begins the evidence processing step of the investigation. Ronelle has mounted the image successfully and is able to view the file structure contained on the drive. This implies that the Master File Table (MFT) has not been altered.

Jose McCarthy, in an effort to conceal his actions, created two partitions on his 80 GB hard drive; one in which he used for day-to-day activity and a second he used to store his personal data. When confronted with the possibility of criminal prosecution he quickly deleted the second partition, therefore making it "invisible" to the operating system.

FIGURE 10.18 Hard Drive Label

From the hard drive label (Figure 10.18), Ronelle was able to clearly see that the hard drive is 80 GB, but how would she be able to identify the size of the partition? How would she be able to account for all 80 GB of data?

If the second partition is not identified she may miss a lot of evidence—in this case, all the essential evidence.

As a cyber forensic investigator, Ronelle, by protocol, examined the partition table and noticed the partition of 60 GB. The starting and ending point of that single partition was quickly determined. Without the use of forensic tools, if Ronelle did not have a working knowledge of the specifics and functioning of the Partition Table, how would our investigator be able to explain the missing 20 GB? Identifying the end of the first partition will be helpful to Ronelle in locating the starting point of the deleted partition. Review Chapter 7 for a refresher in identifying partitions.

Finally, the deleted partition was recovered and all those data associated with the second partition was retrieved, accessed, and analyzed. Ronelle has also recovered all deleted files. She verified all file types and then indexed all the contents of the drive.

In our IP theft case, Ronelle Sawyer is investigating whether Jose McCarthy has potentially engaged in the unlawful distribution of his organization's intellectual property to a competitor, Janice Witcome, Managing Director of the XYZ Company.

Ronelle is faced with examining millions of pieces of potential evidential data residing on Jose's hard drive, looking for the proverbial needle in the haystack. Ronelle has filtered all the data from Jose's hard drive to reveal only data that has been created or modified within the scope of the investigation, and the date range (May 10, 2008–March 26, 2009) of the investigation. From the remaining data Ronelle then searched those data for specific keywords related to the case under investigation, namely, "Janice," "Whitcome," and "XYZ."

Step 5: Investigation

Objective: Finding the data that matches the search criteria.

Investigation is the step within the process that finds the data matching the criteria identified in the investigation request. It is this piece that ultimately finds the proverbial smoking gun. Sure, chain of custody done improperly can destroy a case, but without this evidence there might not be a case (see Figures 10.19 and 10.20).

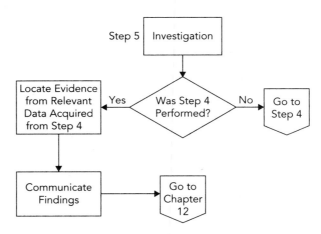

FIGURE 10.19 Step 5: Investigation

Investigations are case specific and ultimately there are infinite avenues from which cases may evolve. Each and every case is different and it may not be necessary to uncover all of the evidence in all of the cases which come across an investigator's desk; however, in some cases, every single stone may need to be overturned.

Ronelle's filtering and searching has returned two documents: "Systemm32.dll" (see Figure 10.21) and a second document named "incriminating evidence.doc." Recall from Chapter 4 that Ronelle identified a file named "Systemm32.dll" (see Figures 4.10, 4.12, and 4.13), which was actually the incriminating document renamed by Jose in an attempt to conceal his activity.

The second document named "incriminating evidence.doc" was located in the second 20 GB deleted partition. The document name, "incriminating evidence," was created solely for the purpose of this text-based case, as naming a document in such an obvious manner would simplify the computer forensics process as well as being outright illogical.

This document appears to contain the evidence that Ronelle's Legal department is seeking.

Let's examine the letter from Jose McCarthy via a HEX editor, shown in Figure 10.22.

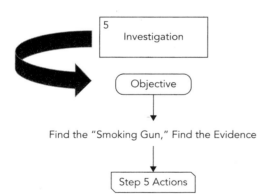

5 Investigation

Objective

Find the "Smoking Gun," Find the Evidence

Step 5 Actions

- Looking for and finding evidence
- Matching criteria as identified in step 1
- Working within scope vs outside scope boundaries (i.e., search criteria)
- Identifying items that may alter your scope
- Identifying when the law may supersede your scope

FIGURE 10.20 Step 5: Investigation Objectives

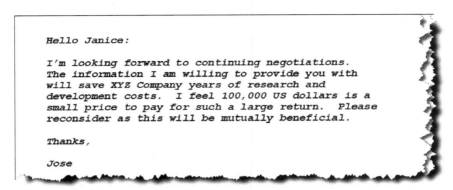

Hello Janice:

I'm looking forward to continuing negotiations.
The information I am willing to provide you with
will save XYZ Company years of research and
development costs. I feel 100,000 US dollars is a
small price to pay for such a large return. Please
reconsider as this will be mutually beneficial.

Thanks,

Jose

FIGURE 10.21   Systemm32.dll and incriminating evidence.doc

```
HexEdit - C:\WINDOWS\system32\SoftwareDistribution\Setup...  _ □ ×
File    Edit   Find   View   About
     0  d0 cf 11 e0 a1 b1 1a e1 00 00 00 00 00 00 00 00  ....
    10  00 00 00 00 00 00 00 00 3e 00 03 00 fe ff 09 00  .........>......
    20  06 00 00 00 00 00 00 00 00 00 00 00 01 00 00 00  ................
    30  26 00 00 00 00 00 00 00 00 10 00 00 28 00 00 00  &...........(...
    40  01 00 00 00 fe ff ff ff 00 00 00 00 25 00 00 00  ............*...
    50  ff ff ff ff ff ff ff ff ff ff ff ff ff ff ff ff  ................
    60  ff ff ff ff ff ff ff ff ff ff ff ff ff ff ff ff  ................
    70  ff ff ff ff ff ff ff ff ff ff ff ff ff ff ff ff  ................
    80  ff ff ff ff ff ff ff ff ff ff ff ff ff ff ff ff  ................
    90  ff ff ff ff ff ff ff ff ff ff ff ff ff ff ff ff  ................
    a0  ff ff ff ff ff ff ff ff ff ff ff ff ff ff ff ff  ................
    b0  ff ff ff ff ff ff ff ff ff ff ff ff ff ff ff ff  ................
    c0  ff ff ff ff ff ff ff ff ff ff ff ff ff ff ff ff  ................
    d0  ff ff ff ff ff ff ff ff ff ff ff ff ff ff ff ff  ................
    e0  ff ff ff ff ff ff ff ff ff ff ff ff ff ff ff ff  ................
    f0  ff ff ff ff ff ff ff ff ff ff ff ff ff ff ff ff  ................
   100  ff ff ff ff ff ff ff ff ff ff ff ff ff ff ff ff  ................
   110  ff ff ff ff ff ff ff ff ff ff ff ff ff ff ff ff  ................
   120  ff ff ff ff ff ff ff ff ff ff ff ff ff ff ff ff  ................
   130  ff ff ff ff ff ff ff ff ff ff ff ff ff ff ff ff  ................
   140  ff ff ff ff ff ff ff ff ff ff ff ff ff ff ff ff  ................
   150  ff ff ff ff ff ff ff ff ff ff ff ff ff ff ff ff  ................
   160  ff ff ff ff ff ff ff ff ff ff ff ff ff ff ff ff  ................
   170  ff ff ff ff ff ff ff ff ff ff ff ff ff ff ff ff  ................
   180  ff ff ff ff ff ff ff ff ff ff ff ff ff ff ff ff  ................
```

FIGURE 10.22   The Letter from Jose McCarthy Shown via a HEX Editor

We can easily see the document file signature, d0 cf 11 e0 (Figure 10.22), which identifies this document as a Word document. So even if this document were to be renamed with a .dll extension, reviewing via the HEX editor would have easily identified this document as a Word document.

Two of Ronelle's keywords ("XYZ" [indentified by HEX 58595a] and "Janice") where identified in the document retrieved from Jose McCarthy's hard

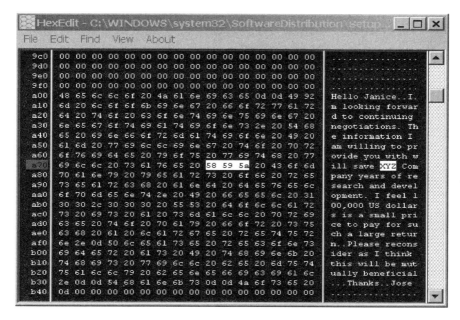

FIGURE 10.23 Identification of Search Word Key Terms

drive (see Figure 10.23). This shows the importance of setting up keywords in such a manner that will ensnare as many real hits as possible. For example, the keyword "Janice Witcome" would not result in a "hit" on the document just reviewed. Understanding human behavior is an important skill when conducting an investigation; as in Ronelle's case, people usually interact on a first name basis.

Ronelle made a startling discovery when examining this document. She noticed some inconsistencies with the document's modified date/time (see Figure 10.24). The created time of "incriminating evidence.doc," as seen by the document properties and viewed via MS Word, do not match the created time of the document when viewed via the filing system metadata. The MS Word document properties can be viewed by right clicking on the document and selecting properties.

The "created time" metadata pulled from the file system shows a create time of 10:10:28. The forensic tool Ronelle is using displays this data. She is unsure how it is being derived and if it is accurate. Ronelle is able to extract the data from the directory entry of the file system as seen in Figure 10.25.

Ronelle understands that such an entry is not an NTFS entry but a FAT entry, and is unsure as to why there is a discrepancy.

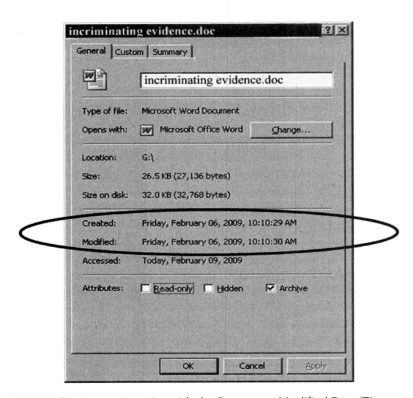

FIGURE 10.24 Inconsistencies with the Document Modified Date/Time

Byte Offset	0	1	2	3	4	5	6	7	8	9	10	11	12	13	14	15	16	17	18	19	20	21	22	23	24	25	26	27	28	29	30	31
ASCII	I	n	c	r	i	m	~	1	D	O	C		•	•	N	Q	F	:	I	:	•	•	O	Q	F	:	•	•	•	j	•	•
Hex	41	53	49	4D	50	4C	7E	31	44	4F	43	20	00	8C	4E	51	46	3A	49	3A	00	00	4F	51	46	3A	02	00	00	6A	00	00

FIGURE 10.25 Extract of the Data from the Directory Entry of the File System

 TIME

Time is an important concept in forensics for more than one reason. As with most topics in forensics, an entire book can be written just on the single concept of time and the relevance of time in an overall investigation.

Stepping back from Ronelle's investigation, time and the role time plays in a cyber forensic investigation will be discussed in Chapter 11. The time discrepancy issue discussed will be further examined to determine why or how this can happen, with a focus on answering the question, "is a hundredth of a second discrepancy important or relevant in a forensic investigation?"

Understanding why this discrepancy exists could be the difference between successfully presenting a case versus looking incompetent during a deposition, or worse, as a testifying expert in court.

 ## SUMMARY

In Chapter 10, we introduced Investigative Smart Practices in a general format to fit most types of forensic organizations and most types of cases. An exact line-by-line instruction set for running a complete cyber forensic investigation is logically impossible to present, as each organization performing a cyber forensic investigation will have their own approaches, procedures, policies, and methods, some dictated by law, others by internal preferences and protocols.

An investigation run by law enforcement, for example, into child pornography versus an internal corporate investigation into the theft of intellectual property may eventually find the evidence necessary to prosecute the guilty; however, the approaches, steps taken, and processes to that end may be entirely different and be supported by completely different protocols and documentation.

It is wise to note that just as peculiar as the differences are between organizations, so too are the differences between cases.

The following Investigative Smart Practices are meant to be broad in scope and used as guidelines:

- **Step 1: Initial Contact/Request.** The validity and scope of the investigative request is established. This function may be performed by someone outside the cyber forensics field. For example, this can be determined by a judge via a court order or perhaps via the HR department within a large organization.
- **Step 2: Evidence Handling.** The integrity of the evidence is preserved throughout the entirety of the case. This process occurs each and every time the evidence is handled. Preserving the integrity of the evidence is vital, as is being able to prove the integrity of the evidence in a court of law.
- **Step 3: Acquisition of Evidence.** This step involves obtaining a forensically sound image of the original evidence. Acquisition of evidence can certainly fall under Step 2, Evidence Handling; however, this step focuses

more precisely on the acquisition of the evidence versus the handling of the evidence during acquisition.

- **Step 4: Data Preparation.** Preparing and identifying data for analysis and investigation. This is the "analyzing" of all data to ensure a valid and complete search. This includes mounting complex files, verifying file types, recovering deleted items, and anything else which would prepare the data for final investigation (Step 5).
- **Step 5: Investigation.** Focuses on finding those data that match specified search criteria. This step tends to be a little more subjective than the others, being that the investigator may need to examine the search results, discard false positives, and identify the critical piece(s) of evidence, which typically is not conveniently named "incriminating evidence.doc."

As is the case with evidence hash values, each case is unique. It is this uniqueness that makes cyber forensics such a challenging field.

 NOTE

1. www.law.cornell.edu/rules/fre/rules.htm#Rule1001.

CHAPTER ELEVEN

Time and Forensics

> The only reason for time is so that everything
> doesn't happen at once.
>
> —*Albert Einstein*

 ## WHAT IS TIME?

Depends on where you look for the answer:

Astronomy: A dimension distinguishing past, present, and future. In relativity, time is portrayed as a geometrical dimension, analogous to the dimensions of space.[1]

Physics: A quantity measuring duration, usually with reference to a periodic process such as the rotation of the Earth or the vibration of electromagnetic radiation emitted from certain atoms.

Classical mechanics: Time is absolute in the sense that the time of an event is independent of the observer.

Philosophy: Time is what clocks measure. We use time to place events in sequence one after the other, and we use time to compare how long events last.[2]

Information technology: A timestamp is a sequence of characters, denoting the date and/or time at which a certain event occurred. A timestamp is the time at which an event is recorded by a computer, not the time of the event itself.

Computer science: Unix time, which describes points in time, is defined as the number of seconds elapsed since midnight proleptic Coordinated Universal Time (UTC) of January 1, 1970, not counting leap seconds.

According to the theory of relativity, it depends on the observer's frame of reference. Time is considered as a fourth coordinate required, along with three spatial coordinates, to specify an event.[3]

Time is a one-dimensional quantity used to sequence events, and to quantify the durations of events and the intervals between them. Time is quantified in comparative terms (such as longer, shorter, faster, quicker, and slower) or in numerical terms using units (such as seconds, minutes, hours, and days).

The reconstruction of events as part of cyber forensics and incident response can involve events from only a single system, as well as events obtained from multiple, geographically separate sources, each with its own clock.

An especially useful technique for event reconstruction is *"time-lining."* Here, discrete events that have a *timestamp* associated with them are ordered into a timeline. Timestamps can be obtained from file system metadata, system logs, or application data. Depending on the source of the events, this can provide a detailed sequence of the events that took place on a system (or multiple ones), allowing an investigator to reconstruct the sequence of events that took place.

When considering timestamps that were recorded by a computing system as evidence in an investigation, several factors need to be considered. The time on a computing system is kept by the system hardware clock and in some cases by an additional software system clock. Depending on the accuracy of these clocks, how they were initialized, and whether they are synchronized, the clock(s) may differ quite considerably from the "real" time. Furthermore, clocks may be misconfigured to be in the wrong time zone or be set to the wrong time, they may be manipulated arbitrarily, and may run fast or slow (*clock skew*).

Time usually just advances. If you have communicating programs running on different computers, time still should advance, even if you switch from one computer to another. Obviously if one system is ahead of the others, the others are behind that particular one. From the perspective of an external observer, switching between these systems would cause time to jump forward and back, a non-desirable effect.

As a consequence, isolated networks may run their own wrong time, but as soon as you connect to the Internet, effects will be visible. Just imagine some e-mail message arriving five minutes before it was sent, and there was a reply two minutes before the message was sent.

NETWORK TIME PROTOCOL

Network Time Protocol (NTP) is an Internet protocol used to synchronize the clocks of computers to some time reference.

NTP provides the mechanisms to synchronize time and coordinate time distribution in a large, diverse Internet operating at rates from mundane to light wave. It uses a returnable-time design in which a distributed subnet of time servers, operating in a self-organizing, hierarchical master-slave configuration, synchronizes local clocks within the subnet and to national time standards via wire or radio.[4]

NTP is designed to produce three products: clock offset, roundtrip delay, and dispersion, all of which are relative to a selected reference clock. Clock offset represents the amount required to adjust the local clock to bring it into correspondence with the reference clock. Roundtrip delay provides the capability to launch a message to arrive at the reference clock at a specified time. Dispersion represents the maximum error of the local clock relative to the reference clock. Since most host time servers will synchronize via another peer time server, there are two components in each of these three products, those determined by the peer relative to the primary reference source of standard time and those measured by the host relative to the peer.

Each of these components is maintained separately in the protocol in order to facilitate error control and management of the subnet itself. They provide not only precision measurements of offset and delay, but also definitive maximum error bounds, so that the user interface can determine not only the time, but the quality of the time as well. The accuracies achievable by NTP depend strongly on the precision of the local-clock hardware and stringent control of device and process latencies.[5]

Like other file attributes, date stamps and timestamps are recorded in the file system in addition to the file. As mentioned, the file system-level date stamps do not interfere with the date stamps that are stored in the file itself.

TIMESTAMP DATA

Timestamp data contained within the file system is metadata (data about data). As we discussed in Chapter 9, this data is stored in the file system records, which in a Windows Operating System would be stored in the Directory Entry if the filing system was FAT or stored in the MFT if the filing system was NTFS. Timestamp data can also be found in other locations such as system logs and application data, for example.

Timestamps are determined by copying the current value of the local clock to a timestamp when some significant event, such as the arrival of a message, occurs. In order to maintain the highest accuracy, it is important that this be done as close to the hardware or software driver associated with the event as possible.[6]

Various programs put their own date and time records in the file contents or meta-tags, like Microsoft Office products and other software. File system level date and time file property do not interfere with the time and date stamps that are stored in the file itself.

Timestamps contained within a system can be introduced in many ways, for example from e-mail headers or HTTP cookie data. So, there may be timestamp data found within a piece of evidence that was introduced from other, external systems.

Timestamp Varieties
- **Creation date and time** is an attribute of a file or a folder that specifies the original creation date and time of that file or folder. When the file or folder is created, or the first time it is saved to a location, creation date and time are recorded in the file system. Ordinarily, this date and time attribute is never changed afterwards since its main purpose is to indicate the original file creation date and time.
- **Last modified date and time** is an attribute of a file or folder that indicates, at the file systems level, when the file or folder was modified the last time. When the file's contents are modified and saved, the last modified date and timestamp is set to correspond with the time at which the changes were made. The purpose of this attribute is to show when the last changes to the file or folder were done.

  Any work with documents, images, and other files automatically alters (modifies) the timestamp of the file. However, in some cases it might be essential to revert a file's last modification date and time back to a particular date and time (e.g., for sorting, recording, logging, or other purposes).

■ **Accessed date** attribute (also called **last accessed date**) indicates on the file systems level when a file was accessed the last time. Last accessed date attribute differs from modification date and file property. While modification date and time indicates when the last changes were made to a file's contents, last accessed date does not necessarily presuppose changes of content. When a file is modified, modification and last accessed dates are set to the same value. However, if the file is only opened for viewing, copied, moved, or—in other words—if the file or folder is used in any way, the last accessed date is changed to the current date.

Any viewing, copying, or moving of the documents, images, and other files automatically alters the last accessed date stamp of the file. Sometimes, last accessed time is changed due to some program's operation with files or folders. It might be antivirus software, which accesses files for virus scanning purpose or Windows Explorer, which extracts an icon from an executable file thus changing the last accessed date.

Resolution of the file last accessed date is one hour for NTFS and one day for FAT. This means that only access hour or day will be recorded for this file property, skipping access minutes or hours accordingly.

For improved file system performance, the last access time update in switched off in Windows Vista by default. Thus, the last access time attribute is set upon creating a file and not changed afterward, even if the file is modified. However, it is possible to enable last access time updates if necessary.[7]

 ## KEEPING TRACK OF TIME

In digital forensic investigations, knowing the correct time when events occurred can be of great importance. This could be because of the need to correlate events from different systems, establish alibis, or to find out when events occurred with respect to events in the real world.[8]

—Brett Tjaden

It is a fundamental design principle that timing must satisfy register setup and hold time requirements. Both *data propagation delay* and clock skew are parts of these calculations. Clocking sequentially adjacent registers on the same edge of a high-skew clock can potentially cause timing violations or even functional failures. Figure 11.1 shows an example of sequentially adjacent

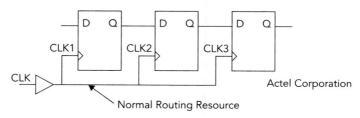

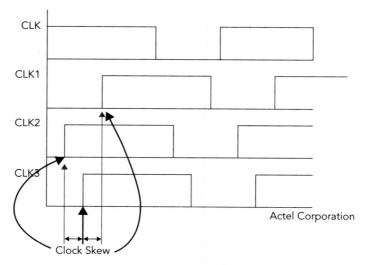

FIGURE 11.1 Sequentially Adjacent Registers with Clock Skew

FIGURE 11.2 Clock Arrival Time Fluctuations in the Circuit of Figure 11.1

registers, where a local routing resource has been used to route the clock signal. In this situation, a noticeable clock skew is likely.

In Figure 11.1, all registers are clocked at the same edge, but the arrival time of the edge is different at each register. Figure 11.2 indicates an example of the clock skew for the circuit shown in Figure 11.1.[9]

The goal in cyber forensic event reconstruction is to sequence all events that are important so that cause-time relationships may be established for an investigation. If all events we need to reconstruct are timestamped by the same system clock, some of the factors discussed above may not matter as the times will differ from "real" time in a consistent manner and a sequence of events can be established.

The possibility of clock manipulation, however, is a factor that always needs to be considered. In particular, when clocks are set back in time an identical time may be recorded for events that occurred before and after the clock change. Furthermore, few computing systems are completely isolated, and external timestamps are introduced in many ways.

For example, information from e-mail headers or HTTP cookie data may play an important role in an investigation, at which point the external and internal timestamps need to be correlated. Also, whenever digital evidence is used to establish or support the point in time when events in the physical world occurred, the timestamps of the systems that are involved need to be translated to this reference time.[10]

> Web servers are generally of more interest to forensic investigations, because timestamps from web servers often can be found on client machines, and HTTP is a widely used protocol in many aspects of computing today.[11]

> —Brett Tjaden

CLOCK MODELS AND TIME BOUNDING: THE FOUNDATIONS OF FORENSIC TIME

When a cyber forensic investigator needs to determine to what time a computer's clock was set at a given time in UTC, or find out at what time a timestamp recorded on a system really occurred, he or she needs to utilize either a clock model or time-bounding techniques.

The clock model introduced by Malcolm Stevens (Unification of Relative Time Frames for Digital Forensics)[12] takes a reference time (usually UTC) as a base, and then the investigator has to specify offsets to the reference time for any clock he or she wishes to describe. These offsets can be dynamic in nature, although Stevens does not elaborate on how to define an offset that changes its value over time.

This model has its strength in showing what values a computer's clock had over time, but to map a host timestamp back to its reference time the inverses of all offsets need to be computed and applied to the timestamp. Furthermore, Stevens neglects the fact that a timestamp value found on a host may map back to the host several times in the reference time, which is a result of a host clock being set back in time.

Time-bounding techniques try to establish a causal order between individual events and thus an overall order of all events on the system. If some of those events can be attributed to a time, it may be possible to define ranges of times when other events must have happened.

Time-bounding techniques will most likely be used in conjunction with a clock model: the model will provide some of the timestamps associated with events while the time bounding technique can be used to verify or disprove that the clock description that is derived for a computer is consistent with the evidence found during the forensic investigation.[13]

MS-DOS 32-BIT TIMESTAMP: DATE AND TIME

The Windows 32-bit time is a time format used by Microsoft in the FAT filing systems for timestamping. We see it in the directory entries, specifically in create times (byte offset 14–17) and last write times (byte offset 22–25).

We clearly see in Figure 11.3 that the ASCII presentation of the create date byte offsets (14–17) [NQF:] is not stored in the way time should be presented.

Dates and time are such that they are mathematical in that they are incremental. Representing such incremental data with ASCII would be difficult and would quickly become cumbersome, as each second in time would need its own binary representation. As we know, time is infinite and we don't have an infinite amount of bits to meet all the possible outcomes to represent time. So, a mathematical approach must be used.

As we can see in Figure 11.3, create date and time is assigned four HEX values or bytes. We know there are eight bits to a byte, so 8(4) = 32 total bits.

MS-DOS date and time values are a 32-bit value that specifies the month, day, year, and time of day (hours, minutes, seconds).

The 32-bit time system operates as two 16-bit values:

- One 16-bit value containing date
- One 16-bit value containing time

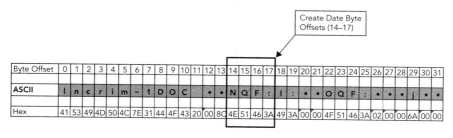

FIGURE 11.3 ASCII Representation of the Create Date Byte Offsets (14–17)

In other words, dates and times are each stored separately in a two-byte binary value. Two 16-bit values = one 32-bit value. Thus, 32 bits are needed to represent date and time.

Therefore, in Figure 11.4:

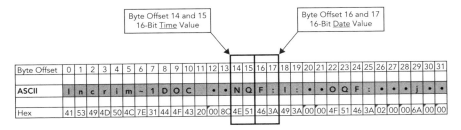

FIGURE 11.4 16-Bit Time and Date Values

Two (2) bytes 4E 51 = 16 bits = Time
Two (2) bytes 46 3A = 16 bits = Date

We mentioned that converting dates and times from HEX to ASCII was not the solution. How about converting the HEX value to its decimal equivalent? Pull out the old scientific calculator.

Converting the HEX values, bytes 4E 51, representing Time, yields the decimal value 20,049. Converting the HEX values, bytes 46 3A, representing the Date value, yields a decimal value of 17,978.

In order to be properly enumerated, both Date and Time require three data fields:

Date = Year, Month, and Day
Time = Hour, Minute, and Second

Note: this timekeeping mechanism works for the purposes as prescribed by Microsoft. Keep in mind, there are many areas where this rather imprecise, broad timekeeping method would have serious shortcomings. Many things in science, medicine, manufacturing, and similar areas require greater precision: milliseconds or microseconds to be tracked.

Obviously, this requirement would have some serious shortcomings in such an environment that records time only to the second, for example. But for its purpose and in its day the MS-DOS 32-bit timestamp was sufficient, and for most people in their day-to-day lives three fields to record the date and three fields for tracking time is more than sufficient.

Even when NTP is utilized, there may be small discrepancies in the clocks between different computers. While the time differences are in the millisecond range this may be a problem if a high degree of accuracy is needed, potentially making time correlation difficult again. For most cyber forensic investigations this may not be important.[14]

We require three separate fields for date yet have only two bytes to do it with, and the same is true for time. Two bytes equates to 16 bits, and 16 bits can be split up to represent three fields (see Figure 11.5).

 ## DATE DETERMINATION

As with time, date is stored as a two-byte binary value. So the date value here, represented by byte offsets 16–17, is HEX 463A (see Figure 11.6).

First, what we need to do is reverse the endianness to little endian as this data is ordered as such. This results in the date represented as HEX 3A46.

Two (2) Bytes 14 and 15 16-Bit Time Value	Hours	Minutes	Seconds
	5 bits	6 bits	5 bits
	01010	001010	01110

Two (2) Bytes 16 and 17 16-Bit Date Value	Year	Month	Day
	7 bits	4 bits	5 bits
	0011101	0010	00110

FIGURE 11.5 Two Bytes, 16 Bits: Three Fields Necessary to Represent Date and Time

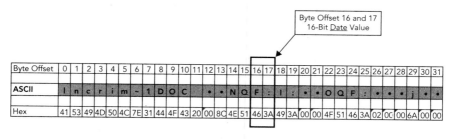

Byte Offset	0	1	2	3	4	5	6	7	8	9	10	11	12	13	14	15	16	17	18	19	20	21	22	23	24	25	26	27	28	29	30	31
ASCII	I	n	c	r	i	m	~	1	D	O	C		•	•	N	Q	F	:	I	:	•	•	O	Q	F	:	•	•	•	j	•	•
Hex	41	53	49	4D	50	4C	7E	31	44	4F	43	20	00	8C	4E	51	46	3A	49	3A	00	00	4F	51	46	3A	02	0C	00	6A	00	00

Byte Offset 16 and 17
16-Bit Date Value

FIGURE 11.6 Date Storage Value 46 3A

TABLE 11.1   Binary Form of HEX 3A46

3	A	4	6
0011	1010	0100	0110

Next we break the HEX values into their raw binary form (i.e., into bits; see Table 11.1).

We need four sets of 4, or two sets of 8, thus 16 total bits (0011101001000110).

Third, the binary number is reordered and divided into three parts representing three date fields: Year, Month, and Day. Let's read on further to see how this is accomplished.

Month

How many months are in one year? 12! How many bits are needed in order to represent 12 individual and separate values?

1 bit = 2 values (on/off light switch example)
2 bit = 4 values (seasons example)
3 bit = 8 values
4 bit = 16 values

Four bits gives us 16 potential values, enough to represent the 12 months of the year.

Day

How many days (maximum) in a month? Again an easy question. Naturally, 31 days is the maximum amount needed. How many bits are needed in order to represent 31 individual and separate values?

1 bit = 2 values
2 bit = 4 values
3 bit = 8 values
4 bit = 16 values
5 bit = 32 values

Five bits gives us 32 potential values, just enough to represent the maximum of 31 days per month.

Year

How many years in an eternity? We have so far assigned nine bits to represent month and day; this leaves us with seven bits to represent year value.

1 bit = 2 values
2 bit = 4 values
3 bit = 8 values
4 bit = 16 values
5 bit = 32 values
6 bit = 64 values
7 bit = 128 values

So we have 128 potential values for year, which is limiting by any calculation. The Microsoft 32-bit time/date formula gets tricky yet again with years. According to MS DOS, the world began on January 1, 1980. The seven-bit binary value is converted to decimal and the resulting value is added to the MS DOS starting year, 1980. The resulting value is then the actual year.

Let's take a look at our example, moving from Table 11.1, and assigning the year, month, and day bits accordingly (see Table 11.2).

Convert the binary values for year, month, and day into their respective decimal equivalents (see Table 11.3).

Remember to find the correct value for year; we must add the decimal value obtained, in this case 29, to the starting Microsoft year value of 1980 (see Table 11.4).

TABLE 11.2 Binary Representation of Year + Month + Day

Year	Month	Day
7 bits	4 bits	5 bits
0011101	0010	00110

TABLE 11.3 Decimal Equivalent of Year + Month + Day

	Year	Month	Day
	7 bits	4 bits	5 bits
Binary	0011101	0010	00110
Decimal	29	2	6

TABLE 11.4 Determining the Correct Decimal Value for Year + Month + Day

	Year	Month	Day
	7 bits	4 bits	5 bits
Binary	0011101	0010	00110
Decimal	29	2	6
ADD MS "World Began in" Value	1980		
HEX Date Value 3A46	**2009**	**2**	**6**

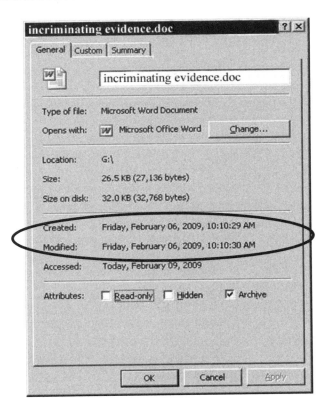

FIGURE 11.7 Incriminating evidence.doc

If we look at document properties (see Figure 11.7), we can verify our year, month, and day findings.

HEX date value 3A46 equals February 6, 2009 (2-6-2009) and HEX time value 4E51 equals 10:10:28 AM.

Having examined how MS-DOS 16-bit date is determined, we now turn our attention to exploring just exactly how the two bytes or 16 bits used to represent time are determined.

 ## TIME DETERMINATION

To determine an exact time, we must first reverse the current endianness of the HEX time from 4E51 (see Figure 11.4, byte offsets 14 and 15) to little endian, so that the data is ordered as such, Time = 514E.

Second, we need to break the HEX values into their raw binary form, into bits. We discussed this previously in Chapter 7 when determining Cylinder Head Sector (CHS) locations. The 32-bit timestamp concept may be complex but all the components and concepts, such as endianness and reordering bits, have already been discussed in previous chapters.

Thus, converting each element of Time, byte offsets 51 and 4E, into their representative binary equivalents results in the binary values of 01010001 and 01001110, respectively.

We need four sets of four, or two sets of eight, resulting in *16 total bits to represent Time.*

Third, the binary number is reordered and divided into three parts representing the three "elements" of time: hours, minutes, and seconds, as shown in Figure 11.8.

As usual, the answer to why this type of arrangement and this particular binary split is that there is code that is written which makes this happen. But why write code to break time up in such a manner? Why a split of five binary bits (hours), six bits (minutes), and five bits (seconds)?

The reasons why have already been discussed in the first chapters of this book. It all has to do with possible outcomes or combinations. As discussed, in order to represent the on or off state of a light switch you would only need one bit—a 1 (On) or 0 (Off). More complex ideas must be represented (e.g., the seasons: winter, spring, summer, and fall).

Two possible outcomes can be represented with one bit, yet there are four seasons. So, in order to present the four seasons you need enough bits to give

HOURS						MINUTES					SECONDS				
0	1	0	1	0			0	0	1	0	1	0	0	1	1	1	0

FIGURE 11.8 Binary Equivalent of Hours, Minutes, Seconds (0101000101001110)

you four possible outcomes. Two bits can give you four possible outcomes: 00, 01, 10, and 11. Now each of those values can be assigned to a season. The same holds true for time. Let's read on further to see how time is calculated and represented.

Hours

How many hours are in one day? Easy, 24! How many bits are needed in order to represent 24 individual and separate values? Remember from our earlier chapters:

1 bit = 2 values (on/off light switch example)
2 bit = 4 values (four seasons example)
3 bit = 8 values
4 bit = 16 values
5 bit = 32 values

Recall binary is Base 2 so everything is squared. Thus, five bits gives us 32 potential values, enough to represent the 24 hours in a day. As a result, 16 total bits to represent time, less five bits for hour, equals 11 bits remaining.

Minutes

How many minutes in an hour? Again, easy: 60 minutes. How many bits are needed in order to represent 60 individual and separate values?

1 bit = 2 values
2 bit = 4 values
3 bit = 8 values
4 bit = 16 values
5 bit = 32 values
6 bit = 64 values

Six bits gives us 64 potential values, enough to represent the 60 minutes of an hour. The 11 bits remaining, less six bits for minutes, equals five bits remaining.

Seconds

How many seconds in an hour? Too easy, 60! How many bits are needed in order to represent 60 individual and separate values?

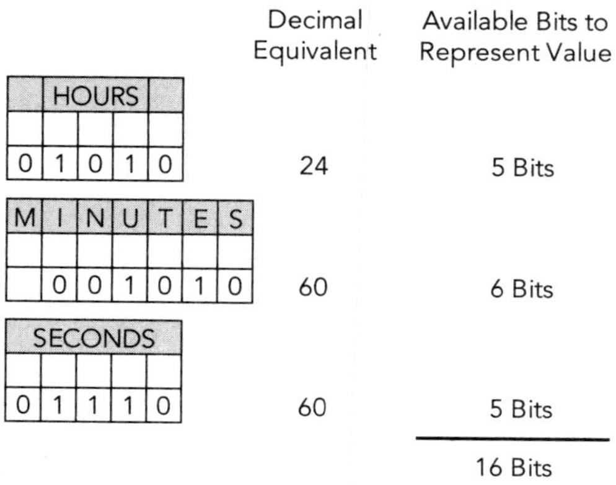

FIGURE 11.9   16 Bits Available to Represent Hours + Minutes + Seconds

1 bit = 2 values
2 bit = 4 values
3 bit = 8 values
4 bit = 16 values
5 bit = 32 values
6 bit = 64 values

Six bits would be needed in order to properly represent the 60 individual seconds within a minute. See Figure 11.9.

But we have only five bits remaining! Whoa, we need six bits. Wait, only five bits left to represent seconds. What happened? How can we accurately represent seconds with only five bits or 32 total potential values? We cannot!

Logically, since there are only five bits remaining, and we need a maximum value of 60, Microsoft uses the value 30 and multiplies by 2, thus giving us our maximum value for seconds. See Figure 11.10.

Microsoft's 32-bit time system essentially rounds up to the nearest even second!

If we break down a day into individual seconds, we find that there are 86,400 seconds in a 24-hour day. A two-byte directory entry for date contains 16 bits. How many possible unique values are there for 16 bits? Answer: 65,536. The deficiency is quickly apparent here too.

Back to our file "Incriminating evidence.doc" (Figure 11.11).

From byte offset 14 and 15, bits 0–4 represent the hour, bits 5–10 represent the minute variable, and bits 11–15 represent the second. (See Table 11.5.)

	Decimal Equivalent	Available Bits to Represent Value	Required Bits to Represent Value
HOURS — 0 1 0 1 0	24	5 Bits	5 Bits
MINUTES — 0 0 1 0 1 0	60	6 Bits	6 Bits
SECONDS — 0 1 1 1 0	60	5 Bits	6 Bits
		16 Bits	17 Bits

FIGURE 11.10 17 Bits Required to Represent Hours + Minutes + Seconds

Byte Offset	0	1	2	3	4	5	6	7	8	9	10	11	12	13	14	15	16	17	18	19	20	21	22	23	24	25	26	27	28	29	30	31
ASCII	I	n	c	r	i	m	~	1	D	O	C				N	Q	F	:	I	:			O	Q	F	:				j		
Hex	41	53	49	4D	50	4C	7E	31	44	4F	43	20	00	8C	4E	51	46	3A	49	3A	00	00	4F	51	46	3A	02	00	00	6A	00	00

FIGURE 11.11 Incriminating Evidence.doc

TABLE 11.5 Decimal Equivalents for HEX 514E

Bits	Bits 0–4	Bits 5–10	Bits 11–15
Binary	0-1-0-1-0	0-0-1-0-1-0	0-1-1-1-0
Decimal	10	10	14
Representation	Hour	Minutes	Seconds

Note: The decimal result (seconds) will need to be multiplied by two (2).

We can see the time, therefore, is 10:10:28 AM. (Note that hours are based on a 24-hour clock, thus, 10 AM is represented by the value 10 and 10 PM would be represented by the value 22, for example.) Don't forget to multiply the seconds, in our example (i.e., 14) times 2 to arrive at the correct value for the "seconds" indicator (i.e., 28).

Since this value is multiplied by two it will always be even, therefore rounded to the closest even second.

If we look at the document properties (see Figure 11.12) we can verify our date and time findings as explained earlier.

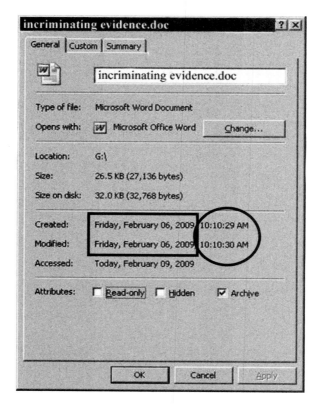

FIGURE 11.12 Incriminating evidence.doc

HEX date value 3A46 equals February 6, 2009 (2-6-2009) and HEX time value 4E51 equals 10:10:28 AM.

 TIME INACCURACY

The Create Time, which we calculated from the data contained within the FAT directory entry for the document incriminating evidence.doc (see Table 11.5), is 10:10:28, yet the properties window, as shown in Figure 11.12, is showing a time of 10:10:29.

The directory entry also contains the date and time that the file was created or last modified.

The time is accurate only to plus or minus 2 seconds because it is stored in a two-byte field, which can store only 65,536 unique values (a day contains

86,400 unique seconds). The time field is subdivided into seconds (five bits), minutes (six bits), and hours (five bits). The date counts in days using three subfields: day (five bits), month (four bits), and year—1980 (seven bits).

With a seven-bit number for the year and time beginning in 1980, the highest expressible year is 2107. Thus, MS-DOS has a built-in Y2108 problem.[15]

The inaccuracy of the windows 32-bit timestamp is clearly apparent here. We are able to see this discrepancy here because the file was accessed from an NTFS partition, the active partition. This file was stored in a FAT16 partition (inactive) but accessed from the active NTFS partition with Windows XP OS.

There is metadata contained within application files such as Microsoft Word, and this allows for the robust, active NTFS file system to retrieve a more exact time.

 ## SUMMARY

In cyber forensic investigations, just as in criminal and medical forensic investigations, knowing the correct time when events occurred can be of great importance. This could be because of the need to correlate events from different systems, establish alibis, or to find out when events occurred with respect to events in the real world.

Clearly, the lack of global agreement on time could potentially hamper forensic investigations in which there is a need for event correlation for events collected from disparate sources, as well as for the correlation of computer events with events in the real world. The large number of hosts that are not synchronized to UTC shows that there is a strong likelihood of event correlation problems when more than one host is involved in a forensic analysis. This is especially true if a high degree of precision is needed for the timestamps.[16]

It should be recognized that clock synchronization requires by its nature long periods and multiple comparisons in order to maintain accurate timekeeping. While only a few measurements are usually adequate to reliably determine local time to within a second or so, periods of many hours and dozens of measurements are required to resolve oscillator skew and maintain local time to the order of a millisecond. Thus, the accuracy achieved is directly dependent on the time taken to achieve it.[17]

Timing inaccuracies are broad and vast. Inaccuracies can be systemwide to NTP server inaccuracies, or system specific due to clock skew. Inaccuracies can be specific to a certain geographical location due to confusing time zones or to a specific operating system's file system, rounding odd seconds to the nearest even second. Discrepancies can be as long as time permits or as short as a second.

This timing inaccuracy is huge when compared to the MS-DOS 32-bit timestamp timing inaccuracy of a second. It is highly unlikely that a timing inaccuracy of a second (as seen in the MS-DOS 32-bit timestamp) would be so pivotal to corroborating someone's innocence (or guilt). One thing time inaccuracies have in common is that they can discredit an expert, such as a cyber forensic investigator.

Opposing counsel could attempt to discredit an investigator for stating inaccuracies in the examination of the evidence (e.g., a file was created at 10:10:28 when in fact it was created at 10:10:29). Can this be explained away? Yes it can.

Could this put some doubt in a juror's mind as to the accuracy of the investigation? *Yes.*

From the following discussion of the importance of time, both to an investigation and to a cyber forensic investigator, in Chapter 12 we will rejoin Ronelle's investigation into the activities of Jose, at the concluding steps of the Investigative Smart Practices process begun in Chapter 10, communicating the findings.

NOTES

1. "Glossary for Extragalactic Astronomy," CalTech, 2005, retrieved November 2010, http://nedwww.ipac.caltech.edu/level5/Glossary/Glossary_T.html.
2. *Internet Encyclopedia of Philosophy*, retrieved November 2010, www.iep.utm .edu/time.
3. *Collins English Dictionary*, HarperCollins, 2003, Retrieved November 2010, www.thefreedictionary.com/time.
4. D. Mills, "RFC1305—Network Time Protocol (Version 3) Specification," Network Working Group, March 1992, retrieved November 2010, www.faqs.org/rfcs/rfc1305.html.
5. Ibid.
6. Ibid.
7. Febooti Software, retrieved October 26, 2010.
8. F. Buchholz and B. Tjaden, "A Brief Study of Time." Reprinted from *Digital Investigation*, 4S 31–42, Elsevier Ltd., Copyright (2007), with permission from Elsevier, retrieved November 2010, www.dfrws.org/2007/proceedings/p31-buchholz.pdf.
9. "Clock Skew and Short Paths Timing," Application Note AC198, Actel Corporation, 2061 Stierlin Court, Mountain View, CA, 94043-4655 USA,

650.318.4200, retrieved November 2010, www.actel.com/documents/Clock_Skew_AN.pdf.

10. Buchholz and Tjaden, "A Brief Study of Time."
11. Ibid.
12. M. W. Stevens, "Unification of Relative Time Frames for Digital Forensics," *Digital Investigation* 1, no. 3 (2005): 225–39.
13. Buchholz and Tjaden, "A Brief Study of Time."
14. Ibid.
15. A. Tanenbaum, A., "Example File Systems," March 8, 2002, retrieved December 2010, www.informit.com/articles/article.aspx?p=25878&seqNum=4.
16. Buchholz and Tjaden, "A Brief Study of Time."
17. Mills, "RFC1305—Network Time Protocol (Version 3) Specification."

CHAPTER TWELVE

Investigation

Incident Closure

I think I did pretty well, considering I started out
with nothing but a bunch of blank paper.

—Steve Martin

T HE EFFORT REQUIRED in the next phases of an investigation is as
systematic and thorough as any of those previously discussed.
Although the process is fairly linear (see Figure 12.1), the "steps" of
the investigative process are not necessarily successive or consecutive; they
may overlap and vary depending upon case. Phases themselves allow for
specific customization suiting various requirements: legal, lawful, corporate,
or otherwise.

FORENSIC INVESTIGATIVE SMART PRACTICES

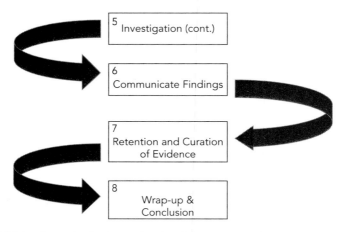

FIGURE 12.1 Steps in the Investigation Process

 ## STEP 5: INVESTIGATION (CONTINUED)

"in•ves•ti•ga•tion"

1. The action of investigating something or someone; formal or systematic examination or research.
2. A formal inquiry or systematic study.

In some circumstances, a cyber forensic investigation could be defined as simply the action of extracting data to meet a given search criteria; something easily accomplished in an automated manner. This definition could certainly apply if under contractual obligation or court order. The "Sherlock Holmes" aspect of an investigation may not always present itself; the investigation may be strictly limited to the search criteria.

At times, a cyber forensic investigator can become over sensitized to the systematic nature and become dependent and eventually reliant upon forensic tools for data extraction. If not inquisitive, Ronelle would not have noticed, or cared to notice, the time discrepancy observed during the investigation. It is this challenging or questioning that, at times, makes up the investigative nature experienced in cyber forensics. This investigative nature is assured with the advances in technology.

Operating Systems are numerous and change frequently, along with constant upgrades, patches, updates, service packs, and so on. An increase in volume and variety of electronic device types also introduces numerous new operating system types and versions. It is this dynamic nature of the field that fuels the need for much investigation.

Many times it is important for the investigator to step back and explore the "rabbit hole" or irregularity (the 32-bit timestamp discrepancy in Ronelle's case, for example) to ultimately be able to explain why such a thing exists. Any exercise in expanding or gaining a better understanding of such an important field is worth exploring.

Now armed with a firm understanding of the time discrepancy, Ronelle feels confident in fully understanding the data she extracted. If requested, Ronelle could examine the data collected and perhaps acquire some additional key words or other search criteria. How an investigator proceeds will vary drastically across the forensic landscape.

Ronelle presented the initial findings to management and suggested new keyword searches. In this circumstance, the Legal department made the decision that they had what they needed and stopped the investigation. The reasons for putting an investigation on hold can vary widely. One major determining factor would include the financial aspect; conducting cyber forensic investigations can be an expensive affair.

 ## STEP 6: COMMUNICATE FINDINGS

The cyber forensic investigator now needs to communicate the results and findings of the investigation, the deliverable being the investigator's report. See Figure 12.2.

The cyber forensic investigator is responsible for accurately and objectively reporting his or her findings and the results of the analysis of the digital evidence examination. Documentation is an ongoing process throughout the examination/investigation; it is important to accurately record the steps taken throughout the digital evidence examination process.

All documentation should be complete, accurate, and comprehensive. The resulting report should be written for the intended audience.

The purpose of the report is to:

1. Deliver the results of search criteria defined in the request.
2. Document the findings in an impartial and accurate manner and provide responsible authority information, to assist in making a determination whether to take corrective, remedial, or disciplinary action.
3. Organize the information so that anyone can read and understand the report without reference to enclosures or other material.

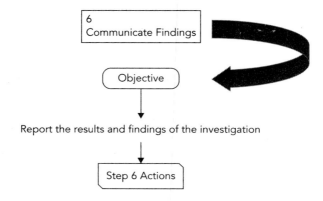

- Objectivity of analysis (report on just the facts)
- Legal requirements, company policy and/or client requirements will direct contents of final report
- Include step-by-step details of the investigation

FIGURE 12.2 Step 6: Communicate Findings

The cyber forensic investigator typically is barred from publishing, distributing or in any manner communicating, independently, the contents of the report to anyone other than authorized persons.

CHARACTERISTICS OF A GOOD CYBER FORENSIC REPORT

Clarity, completeness, objectivity, and accuracy are characteristics of a good report. The report must be clear enough so that others may understand what the writer means. But more than that, it must be written so clearly that others cannot possibly misunderstand the writer's meaning.

Clarity results from a report that contains a concise, systematic arrangement of facts and analysis stated in precise, neutral terms. Completeness dictates that all information a prudent manager reasonably would want to consider before reaching a decision should appear in the report.

Objectivity is arguably the most important trait. An investigator uncovering incriminating data cannot allow him/herself to be swayed, thereby affecting the disposition of the report. Simply put, the investigator cannot "take sides." Lack of objectivity will negatively affect the style and tone of a report. As Sgt. Joe Friday would state, "Just the facts, ma'am."

Accuracy requires there be no errors in reporting facts or identifying people, places, events, dates, documents, and other tangible matters. A good rule of thumb requires asking whether a person who knows nothing about the case could read the report, fully understand what happened, and feel confident in making a decision based on its contents.[1]

Style and Tone

Whether the allegations are sustained or refuted, most reports convey bad news to someone.

Proper style and tone makes the news easier to accept; an inappropriate style or tone impedes acceptance and appropriate resolution. Style varies from one person to another, but a simple, direct approach, void of colorful language, is the most effective way to convey facts.

The tone also should be neutral, not judgmental, convincing in its modesty of language, and not provocative in its descriptions. Style, tone, and clarity must complement one another; each handled well tends to achieve the others.[2]

Analysis

In most investigations, more information is collected than is necessary to reach a conclusion. Some information is redundant; other information is not pertinent to a decision. Sometimes the information is conflicting.

In cases where remedial, disciplinary, or legal action is a possibility, the decision to accept the conclusions in a report is likely to be made only after an examination of all the evidentiary material assembled. So, deciding what information to treat as evidence and how to deal with it in the report is important.

If the report does not appear to fairly address pertinent evidence, its conclusions may be rejected.

Some common issues include:

1. Evidence considered, but not relied upon, should be discussed in the report if it is likely that others would want to consider it or question the completeness of the report were it not mentioned. This is critical when there is conflicting evidence. The failure to discuss and explain why one version of events is relied upon in lieu of competing evidence will cause readers who are aware of the conflicts to question the objectivity of the writer.
2. Evidence that is redundant or repetitive can be summarized when it comes from various sources that present no unique information.
3. The evidentiary analysis must bring together all documentary, physical, and testimonial facts relating to the allegations to reach a conclusion.

The facts relied upon to reach each conclusion should be apparent to the reader. When the applicable standards are themselves vague, or the testimony conflicts, the reasoning that leads to a conclusion is not always apparent. In that case, the analysis in the report must explain to the reader how the investigator reached the conclusion.[3]

 ## REPORT CONTENTS

The investigator's report may consist of a brief summary of the results of the examinations performed on the items submitted for analysis. Again, as with forensic policies, the report will vary drastically between organizations and organization types. A corporate report will have a different audience than one from law enforcement.

The report may include:

- Identity of the reporting agency or requesting department.
- As seen on title page of the exemplar report: "Forensic Investigations, ABC Inc." (see Appendix) This identifies the "author" of the report.
- Case identifier or submission number.
- Unique identifiers are key in tracking anything, for example unique case numbers for help desk support tickets or security incidents.
- Case investigator's name.
- Identity of the submitter.
- Date of receipt.
- Date of report.
- Descriptive list of items submitted for examination, including serial number, make, and model.
- Descriptive list of items used to investigate including both hardware and software.
- Brief description of steps taken during examination, such as string searches, graphics image searches, and recovering erased files.
- Chain of custody documentation/form.
- Results/conclusions.[4]

Ronelle included a copy of the chain of custody (CoC) form with the report, the original remaining with the evidence drive. Ronelle signed the form twice, once upon receipt and once again upon return. Ronelle did not sign the CoC form each time she put it in or took it out of the vault. The evidence vault has its own chain of custody sign in/out form for locking it in the vault or removing it.

When Ronelle eventually returned the evidence drive, the forensic department at ABC Inc. will secure evidence in a vault requiring signatures to check out evidence.

 ## STEP 7: RETENTION AND CURATION OF EVIDENCE

The handling of physical evidence covers a wide variety of activities from the crime scene to the courtroom. In some jurisdictions, this can extend to the period after trial, including the destruction or disposition of evidence.

The evidence should be organized and labeled in such a way as to not alter the evidence and allow it to be easily identified or retrieved at a later date. (See Figure 12.3.)

The complications in handling digital evidence are increased due to the potential for data replication. When presented with original evidence, an investigator will typically make a forensic image from which to investigate, assuming hash verification of course. Being that the evidence is digital in nature, the forensic image can now also be considered evidence.

Retention of evidence used here implies any of the storage, archiving, destruction, or returning of all evidence. This includes the physical as well as the logical: original evidence, forensic images, hard drives, computers,

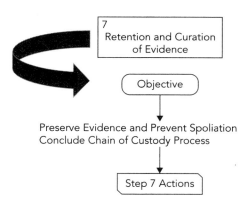

FIGURE 12.3 Step 7: Retention and Curation of Evidence

phones, CDs, tapes, photographs, reports, forensic notes, and so on. Not all case evidence is identical and therefore retention policies may vary between types. For example, after a corporate malware investigation a laptop may be sanitized, reimaged, and returned to the user or perhaps put back into production.

However, the prosecuted in a child pornography case would be wise not to expect a returned laptop. Retention policies will vary even more between different organization types. Also, within the same organization, retention policies for original evidence may vary from those of forensic images or even the final report.

Forensic data retention and archiving policies will depend much upon the type of organization, and may be subjected to existing overriding policies or laws. Depending upon the practice, retention periods can be contractual, corporate policy, or even required by law.

A small, private forensic practice may have in-house policies regarding retention policies unless otherwise specified by contract. All this would have to occur within the boundaries of the law, of course.

Whatever retention is decided upon, the security, organization, and identification of evidence is imperative. The evidence should be stored according to its data classification. If the evidence is confidential then the evidence shouldn't be stored on a file share accessible to all or in an unsecured file cabinet.

When storing digital evidence, the cyber forensic investigator should:

1. Ensure that the digital evidence is inventoried in accordance with the agency's policies.
2. Ensure that the digital evidence is stored in a secure, climate-controlled environment or a location that is not subject to extreme temperature or humidity.
3. Ensure that the digital evidence is not exposed to magnetic fields, moisture, dust, vibration, or any other elements that may damage or destroy it.[5]

Potentially valuable digital evidence including dates, times, and system configuration settings may be lost due to prolonged storage if the batteries or power source that preserve this information fails. Where applicable, those responsible for the transportation of evidence should inform the evidence custodian that electronic devices are battery powered and require prompt attention to preserve the data stored in them.[6]

Early attention to the difficulties in preserving digital information focused on the longevity of the physical media on which the information is stored. Even under the best storage conditions, however, digital media can be fragile and have limited shelf life. Moreover, new devices, processes, and software are replacing the products and methods used to record, store, and retrieve digital information on breathtaking cycles of two to five years.

Given such rates of technological change, even the most fragile media may well outlive the continued availability of readers for those media. Efforts to preserve physical media thus provide only a short-term, partial solution to the general problem of preserving digital information. Indeed, technological obsolescence represents a far greater threat to information in digital form than the inherent physical fragility of many digital media.[7]

If possible, commonly used media (rather than some obscure storage media) should be used for archiving. Access to evidence should be extremely restricted, and should be clearly documented. Controls should be in place to detect unauthorized access to archive storage areas.[8]

While digital evidence obtained as part of a cyber forensic investigation is subject to specific procedures governing its acceptable storage, retention, and archiving, the examination of data retention standards outside of the cyber forensic field can be useful to the forensic investigator in developing comprehensive retention and archiving policies for digital evidence.

ISO 15489:2001

Successful digital curation relies on a robust workflow, which considers the complete lifecycle of a digital resource from inception to disposal or selection for long-term preservation. The development and documentation of policies, responsibilities, authorities, and training schemes for digital resource management is as important as the design and implementation of a system to ingest, manage, store, render, and enable access.

There are many benefits associated with the development, documentation, and adherence to workflow methodologies including the ability to design a system which is effective for all users, the ability to readily comply with legal, regulatory, and standards requirements, asset recognition, and the ability to curate and preserve information over the long term.

ISO 15489:2001 preceded another well-known digital curation workflow standard, OAIS (Open Archival Information Systems Reference Model—ISO 14721:2003). ISO 15489 is considered by many to be more easily understood, as it provides more concrete guidance on the management of records.

Primarily developed for the management of business records, ISO 15489:2001 can be applied to the management of records created by any activity, and is equally applicable to digital or hard copy information.[9]

The standard provides guidance to ensure that records remain authoritative through retention of their essential characteristics: authenticity, reliability, usability, and integrity. It explains how to ensure records are properly curated, easily accessible, and correctly documented from creation for as long as required.[10]

ISO 15489:2001 identifies how systematic management of records can ensure that an organization's, an individual's, or a project's future decisions and activities can be supported through ready access to evidence of actions and past business activities, while facilitating compliance with any pertaining regulatory environments. The need for clearly defined and well-documented records management policies and responsibilities, within an organization or project, along with the benefits which will accrue from development and implementation, is outlined.[11]

Records management processes:

1. Capture
2. Registration
3. Classification
4. Access and security classification
5. Identification of disposition status
6. Storage
7. Use and tracking
8. Implementation of disposition

ISO 14721:2003

ISO 14721:2003 specifies a reference model for an open archival information system (OAIS).

The purpose of this ISO 14721:2003 is to establish a system for archiving information, both digitalized and physical, with an organizational scheme composed of people who accept the responsibility to preserve information and make it available to a designated community.

This reference model addresses a full range of archival information preservation functions including ingest, archival storage, data management, access, and dissemination.

The reference model also:

1. Addresses the migration of digital information to new media and forms the data models used to represent the information, the role of software in information preservation, and the exchange of digital information among archives.
2. Identifies both internal and external interfaces to the archive functions, and identifies a number of high-level services at these interfaces.

3. Provides various illustrative examples and some "best practice" recommendations.
4. Defines a minimal set of responsibilities for an archive to be called an OAIS, and defines a maximal archive to provide a broad set of useful terms and concepts.[12]

The OAIS model described in ISO 14721:2003 may be applicable to any archive. It is specifically applicable to organizations with the responsibility of making information available for the long term. This includes organizations with other responsibilities, such as processing and distribution in response to programmatic needs.[13]

The cyber forensic investigator, while not his/her primary job responsibility, should still keep abreast of the chaining dynamics and requirements in the growing field of digital curation.

 ## STEP 8: INVESTIGATION WRAP-UP AND CONCLUSION

The wrap-up of any investigation is, again, a nonspecific science, meaning that each company, department, or agency will have, by policy, its own procedures and methodology for winding down, wrapping up, closing out, and terminating an investigation. Granted, some actions taken in this final step may be dictated by law, especially if such investigations will be moving beyond an internal disciplinary action taken by company management to prosecution by local, state, or federal authorities.

However, in general there are typically several common tasks, steps or actions that will constitute the final phase of the investigation, which will consume the investigator's time and take him/her away from the actual science of performing cyber forensic analysis and investigation. These tasks and actions, however, are as essential to successfully ending an investigation as the steps taken by the investigator in the early stages of an investigation.

Figure 12.4 summarizes these steps and we discuss each briefly here. The reader should be aware, however, that not every action or task discussed here is performed in every organization or even cohesively in a single step as we have presented here. Many organizations may elect to separate some of the tasks shown in Figure 12.4 into independent steps.

 ## INVESTIGATOR'S ROLE AS AN EXPERT WITNESS

Before briefly discussing what the investigator's role and responsibilities may be as an expert witness, we need first to define, exactly, what is an expert witness?

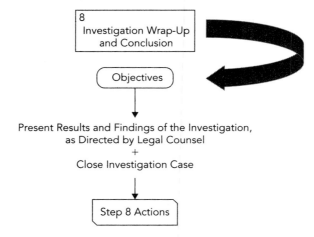

FIGURE 12.4 Step 8: Wrap-Up and Conclusion

According to several real legal type resources, an expert witness and his/her expertise and testimony can be defined as:

1. Testimony in the form of an opinion or otherwise based on scientific, technical, or other specialized knowledge; witness must be qualified, as determined by court. Rule 702, Federal Rules of Evidence (FRE).
2. "Unlike an ordinary witness, an expert is permitted wide latitude to offer opinions, including those that are not based on firsthand knowledge or observation." *Daubert v. Merrell Dow Pharmaceuticals, Inc.*, 509 U.S. 579, 592 (1993).
3. Another key distinction: expert witness, unlike "lay" witness, may answer hypothetical questions based on information presented at or before hearing, including facts and data not admissible in evidence. *Asplundh Mfg. Div. v. Benton Harbor Eng'g*, 57 F.3d 1190, 1202 n.16 (3d Cir. 1995); Rule 703, FRE.

One also has to consider the type of testimony to be given by the cyber forensic investigator (i.e., fact testimony, which is testifying solely as to facts within witness's personal knowledge, or lay opinion testimony, which are opinions or inferences rationally based on witness's own perceptions and not based on scientific, technical, or other specialized knowledge within the scope of Rule 702 [Rule 701, FRE]).[14]

In any case, taking on the role of an expert witness carries with it significant responsibilities as well as risks.

Role of an Expert Witness

The primary role of the expert witness is to provide the finder of fact with reliable evaluations and opinions that are based on scientific, technical, or other specialized knowledge. As explained in Federal Rule of Evidence 702 (Testimony by Experts), expert witness testimony is meant to be substantially useful in assisting the court's understanding of the evidence and facts at issue. To fulfill that role, the expert witness must deliver evaluations that agree with accepted knowledge and experience. Ultimately, it is up to the finder of fact to determine the reliability, relevance, and weight of the expert's testimony.[15]

The lawyer-expert relationship includes a hierarchy and organization that is generally well understood by all involved: the lawyer is in charge of the overall process and provides direction and strategy; the expert evaluates case data and information and presents findings, conclusions, and opinions, in addition to providing technical guidance along the way. This process is simple in appearance only. Litigation that involves the participation of expert witnesses is most often a very complex, lengthy, and tedious process with many variables that can influence the ultimate outcome of a case. Several of the variables are human in nature and often difficult or even impossible to control or predict.[16]

Deposition Steps Prior to Formal Court Presentation

To reign in "bad science," courts are empowered to act as gatekeepers to exclude unreliable or irrelevant expert testimony (*Daubert v. Merrell Dow Pharm., Inc.*, 509 U.S. 579, 589-90 [1993]). This major change in the law has had some of the intended effects but does not appear to have fully solved the problem. In practice, it is indeed very difficult for a court to fulfill the gatekeeper's role fairly and effectively, and the gatekeeper function is not applied consistently across all jurisdictions. For the expert, being "Dauberted" is a serious concern that can negatively affect one's career.

The expert witness is often publicly stigmatized as ethically compromised, considered by some as nothing more than a "hired gun." This stigma is born from misconceptions and from unavoidable human nature. The concept that anyone who charges high hourly rates would say anything to satisfy the paying party, along with a few well-publicized examples of professional misconduct, serve to anchor this stigma.

In reality, the enduring expert witness must demonstrate strong professional and ethical conduct. The typical expert witness may work for the plaintiff in one case and the defendant in another. The expert witness can ill afford to submit erroneous or exaggerated claims and allegations that are contrary to or go beyond what can be supported by the facts in evidence and by sound scientific or technical methodology.

Doing so may ultimately prove ineffective for the case and trigger appeals. Being exposed as unethical could also spell the end of a rewarding professional career. Opinions of the court and transcripts of deposition and trial testimony constitute a public record. That record serves as an effective quality control tool that lawyers and the finders of fact can consult. To succeed as an expert witness, credibility and thoroughness have to complement education and experience.

There are no universal recipes for delivering effective expert testimony or for a successful professional relationship between lawyers and experts. However, there are a few considerations that often matter.

First, for expert testimony, it is important to:

- Prepare extensively and rehearse the testimony with the trial lawyer.
- Present opinions in a simple manner using easy-to-understand language and demonstratives, regardless of how complex the bases for the opinions might be.
- Address the testimony to the finder of fact.
- Limit answers and explanations to the open question.
- In cross-examination, answer only to the open question, using short answers; avoid being dragged into arguing.
- Reserve detailed explanations for redirect to address the critiques that might have been raised in cross-examination.
- Show respect to the court and observe proper decorum.

Second, for a successful lawyer-expert relationship, it is important for the expert to:

- Be the expert, not the lawyer.
- Adapt to the lawyer's personality and modus operandi without compromising work performance and quality.
- Deliver work products on time.
- Keep the lawyer informed of progress, setbacks, and other difficulties.
- Keep track of the budget since it can be a limiting factor.[17]

Securing Access Rights to Case Notes and Related Case Data

All case notes and case data collected and developed by the investigator should be considered first confidential and second proprietary, either of the organization who authorized the investigation or of the entity (local, state, federal) conducting the investigation.

As such, whether as the investigator you are an employee or an independent third-party, it will be essential to ensure that you have addressed the issue of obtaining legal access to all of your case notes, especially if there will be a lapse of time between performing the field-level investigation and the actual presentation of your findings, whether internally to management or in a deposition or court of law.

It is very unlikely that upon completing your investigation there will be an immediate presentation of your findings; there will be a natural time lag between these events. The time lag may depend upon further investigative actions which must be taken by other external entities, a delay to act on the part of management, a backlog of cases preventing immediate response from legal counsel, or a full court docket that delays your appearance as an expert witness in a court of law.

This consideration is critically important, especially as time passes and memories tend to blur and fade, and exact details and critical specifics may only be recalled by reviewing one's case notes. This is an especially important consideration for those investigators who are internal company employees. How would you obtain access to your case notes if you are no longer employed by the same organization under which you conducted your investigation? If, like most investigators, you are working multiple cases simultaneously, you may have many case notes to which you may require access.

As an independent third party, have you, via contract, stipulated that you may retain copies of all case notes pertaining to investigations performed for clients? Do you have the ability to safeguard these documents while they are in your possession? These case notes and the information contained in them may be considered confidential and removal of such material from an organization or client's site without prior written approval may be unlawful or even constitute a breach of contract.

In any situation, as an employee or third-party contracted investigator, the ability to recall critical technical information clearly, concisely, and accurately without hesitation will often times depend on access to one's case notes. Ensuring such access is an important step in the investigator's overall investigative smart practices.

Depending on both the nature and status of the investigation and legal statute, those data seized, collected, and examined by the investigator may be returned to the data's owner, held by the investigative department or agency until the case goes to trial, retained by the cyber forensic investigator, or disposed of and destroyed according to instructions from legal counsel and company policy.

Closing Out Case Files

This step will certainly be guided by department, agency, or company policy. Cases may be closed, for example, based upon a final adjudication in a court of law, decision on the part of management not to take any additional or further action, or advice from legal counsel as to the appropriateness and viability of the evidence collected to withstand a successful presentation at trial.

Once a case is closed and the investigator's files, records, notes, reports, and transcripts have been delivered to the case manager, legal counsel, or management representative, the investigator's responsibility is now complete. Responsibility for the safeguarding, handling, transportation, archiving, and disposition of these files now rests with the recipient.

Whether you are an employee or a third-party contracted investigator, you have one last task to perform, however. You must obtain sign-off from the recipient of:

1. A receipt log, detailing all files, records, notes, reports, and transcripts turned over by the investigator. This receipt log, in addition, should show the case number, recipient's signature, and date.
2. If not a formal internal document, then a letter from the recipient, containing the case number, recipient's signature, and date stating that the case has been officially closed and that there are no outstanding issues or items requiring further action on the part of the investigator.

Post-Investigation Quality Control Assessment and "Lessons Learned"

Investigative smart practices warrant that the overall investigative process should contain an ability to continually look backwards on the process, for evaluative and assessment purposes, with the overall objective of continuous process improvement.

The final step of the investigation process entails, to the degree dictated by organizational policy or mandated by legislation, a quality control and assessment activity.

First, a few definitions are helpful:

- Quality assurance activities include planning for quality management activities and verifying that those activities were carried out.
- Quality control activities include the actual implementation of quality management activities and the documentation thereof.

The quality assessment/control process may or may not be conducted by the cyber forensic investigator, may be conducted independently or via a team review process, and may be preformed internally or through an independently contracted third party. Regardless of the approach, performance of such a review process is essential in ensuring that investigative policies and procedures followed conform to guidelines set forth by legal precedent, management policy, and generally accepted cyber forensic investigative practices and professional due diligence.

A viable quality assessment/control process should specify the organization, procedures, documentation, testing, and methods to be used to provide quality, in accordance with sound investigative policies, guidelines, and proven cyber forensic investigative methodologies.

A typical post cyber forensic investigation program should address, but not be limited to, the following elements:

- Management responsibility
- Investigator responsibility and competencies
- Investigative process and procedures
- Evidence identification, acquisition, traceability, retention, and disposal
- Evidence control
- Inspection, measuring, and testing of forensic diagnostic equipment and software
- Final report documentation, distribution, and control
- Maintenance of assessment records
- Continued investigator training
- Corrective action to policy, procedure, and methodology as required
- Directives for ongoing quality and assessment audits

The ability to substantiate a continuously examined and quality cyber forensic investigative process is essential in establishing and maintaining the ongoing credibility of digital evidence obtained through that process.

 ## SUMMARY

As a cyber forensic investigator your report must communicate all findings in an objective manner, as it may be used in a court of law and you may be called as a witness (expert or not), to defend it. It is better to overdocument than not; thus, always err on the side of caution and overdocument. It is not an insult to a cyber forensic investigator to be called thorough, careful, meticulous, or methodical; this is especially true when you are called to the witness stand.

Deciding what to do with collected evidence after an investigation is closed is a critical issue that must be addressed through well defined, well established, and implemented policies.

Continuous self-assessment of the personnel, processes, procedures, policies, hardware, software, and methodologies used to conduct each cyber forensic investigation is essential in establishing the credibility of evidence brought forth by the cyber forensic investigator, through the investigative process.

 NOTES

1. Office of the Naval Inspector General, Investigations Policy Manual, Chapter 8—Report Writing, July 1995, retrieved September 2011, www.ig.navy.mil/Documents/Downloads%20and%20Publications.htm, used with permission.
2. Ibid.
3. Ibid.
4. Forensic Examination of Digital Evidence: A Guide for Law Enforcement [NCJ 199408], U.S. Department of Justice, Office of Justice Programs, National Institute of Justice, Washington, DC 20531, April 2004, retrieved September 2011, https://www.ncjrs.gov/pdffiles1/nij/199408.pdf.
5. Electronic Crime Scene Investigation: A Guide for First Responders, Second Edition, U.S. Department of Justice Office of Justice Programs National Institute of Justice, U.S. Department of Justice, Office of Justice Programs, 810 Seventh Street N.W., Washington, DC 20531, NCJ 219941, April 2008, retrieved September 2001, www.ncjrs.gov/pdffiles1/nij/219941.pdf.
6. Ibid.
7. Preserving Digital Information Report of the Task Force on Archiving of Digital Information, commissioned by The Commission on Preservation and Access and The Research Libraries Group, May 1, 1996, retrieved September 2011, www.clir.org/pubs/reports/pub63watersgarrett.pdf.
8. D. Brezinski and T. Killalea, "Guidelines for Evidence Collection and Archiving," RFC 3227, The Internet Society, February 2001, retrieved September 2011, http://tools.ietf.org/html/rfc3227.
9. S. Higgins, "ISO 15489," Digital Curation Centre, Appleton Tower, 11 Crichton Street, Edinburgh, EH8 9LE, retrieved September 2011, www.dcc.ac.uk/resources/briefing-papers/standards-watch-papers/iso-15489, used with permission.
10. Ibid.
11. Ibid.
12. H. Bowden, H. "OAIS Reference Model—ISO 14721:2003," The Digital Curation Exchange, University of North Carolina at Chapel Hill, School of Information

and Library Science, November 27, 2009, retrieved September 2011, http:// digitalcurationexchange.org/node/1079.

13. Ibid.

14. "Expert Witnesses: Ethics In Court: DO-07-019a: Attachment to DO-07-019," U.S. Office of Government Ethics 1201 New York Avenue, NW. Suite 500 Washington, DC 20005, retrieved October 2011, www.oge.gov/OGE-Advisories/Legal-Advisories/DO-07-019a--Attachment-to-DO-07-019.

15. R. Hennet, "Working with Lawyers: The Expert Witness Perspective," *Expert Witnesses United States Attorneys' Bulletin* 58, no. 1 (2010), published bimonthly by the Executive Office for United States Attorneys, Office of Legal Education, 1620 Pendleton Street, Columbia, South Carolina 29201, United States, Department of Justice, Executive Office for United States Attorneys Washington, DC, 20530, retrieved October 2011, www.justice.gov/usao/eousa/foia_reading_room/usab5801.pdf, Dr. Remy J-C. Hennet is a Principal at S.S. Papadopulos & Associates, Inc. (SSPA), headquartered in Bethesda, MD; used with permission via discussion with author.

16. Ibid.

17. Ibid.

CHAPTER THIRTEEN

A Cyber Forensic Process Summary

THE NEED FOR COMMUNICATION and information sharing continues to be a driving force of technology. This endeavor began with the dawn of man and continues today. From early cave paintings to stone tablets, to the printing press, to electronically stored data and the Internet, our need and desire to share information continues to grow geometrically.

The ability to communicate electronically has accounted for many of the advancements we have in a society today, along with many conveniences. However, whenever there is good, bad is not far behind; as with everything in life there is a fine balance between good and bad. There is no exception with electronically stored data. Crimes will continue to occur regardless of the technological advancements used by those to perpetrate crimes and those sworn to uphold the law. The difference is the process by which the crimes occur and how they must be investigated.

This book has addressed the process by which data originates, is stored, moved, manipulated, and analyzed to assess its relevance as evidential matter. As with all subjects there must be a logical beginning and similarly, a logical conclusion. Our journey began in Chapter 1 and the root of all electronically communicated information, binary data representation.

 BINARY

In order to properly investigate electronic data or computational communications it is first necessary to understand how we, as a species, attempt to codify our ability to communicate electronically in a world with only two possible states, a world of binary existence.

Binary is a Base 2 encoding scheme which functions well with a two-state paradigm such as electronics. With electronics there are two possible states, on and off. This is the basis for all electronic communications. When stringing these on/offs together complex communications can be achieved, not only for representing the most basic patterns of human communication but also complex alphabetic and numeric patterns, ultimately enabling people to represent entire languages.

The representation of complex language patterns for digital communications began with the primary building block, the bit, represented by either a one (1) or a zero (0). Simply arranging and grouping ones and zeros together allowed for all electronic data representation, from a simple text document to a high definition movie.

Establishing a method of pairing alphabetic characters with the character's binary equivalent produced character codes, which have since evolved into more complex character sets, further allowing us to not only expand our ability to represent a greater range of characters but to also control how computers store, manipulate, and transmit data.

Binary representation of numbers and characters is required when working in a world restricted to only two states of description or existence (e.g., electrical or magnetic). Fortunately for us, our human world is more robust, more colorful, and exists in many states, well beyond that of a binary life. It is also more difficult and time consuming if, as humans, we were required to perform all of our figuring, communicating, and so on, with numbers or letters represented by groups and pairings of 1s and 0s (e.g., 01001000 01100101 01101100 01101100 01101111 instead of "Hello").

BINARY—DECIMAL—ASCII

Converting a binary number into its decimal equivalent is essential for gaining a greater depth of understanding of how data is stored, moved, manipulated, and processed and how this treatment of data is critical to a better understanding of cyber forensics.

A computer only processes binary stored bits, it cannot recognize or process the character "&" in its native form; we humans, on the other hand, do not process binary easily. The middle ground is with decimal values. We can more readily and effortlessly understand the same information, represented and presented in a decimal form.

A decimal value (10 unique decimal characters: 0, 1, 2, 3, 4, 5, 6, 7, 8, and 9) is a mathematical computation of binary, not a visual representation of binary.

The key to converting the binary value to its decimal equivalent is the existence (or lack thereof) of a "current" represented by the binary value of a "0" or a "1" switch or binary character.

If a binary value is present in the placeholder, the value is turned on, represented by the value of one. If no binary values occupies the placeholder, then the value is turned off, which is represented by the value zero.

If the binary switch (or value) is ON (a "1") then the decimal value is ON, meaning it is added or counted when determining the total decimal value. If the binary switch is OFF (a "0"), then the decimal value is not counted or added when determining the total decimal equivalent.

Let's take for example the binary value 01011000, using the information in Figure 13.1.

Go through the binary numbers and if the binary number is 1, bring down the power of two and write it in the corresponding box on the decimal value line. If the binary number is 0, put a 0 in the box. Convert the binary number to a decimal by adding up the decimal value you entered into each box. The sum of the numbers is the decimal equivalent of the binary number.

Binary 01011000 equals a decimal value of 88.

Why bother with converting binary to decimal? Computer processors work with mathematical computations, not letters, symbols, and words, yet humans communicate via letters and words. Thus, a computer needs a way in which to mathematically represent human symbols.

A binary value can be mathematically computed into a decimal value, and a decimal value can be assigned to an ASCII value (human symbols). (See Table 13.1.)

Power	2^7	2^6	2^5	2^4	2^3	2^2	2^1	2^0	
Decimal Equivalent	128	64	32	16	8	4	2	1	
Binary Value	0	1	0	1	1	0	0	0	
									Adding the decimal values
Decimal Value	0	64	0	16	8	0	0	0	0+64+0+16+8+0+0+0=88

FIGURE 13.1   Binary to Decimal Conversion

TABLE 13.1   ASCII Table Snapshot

Binary	Decimal	ASCII Symbol	Description
00110000	48	0	Zero
00110001	49	1	One
00110010	50	2	Two
00110011	51	3	Three
00110100	52	4	Four
00110101	53	5	Five
00110110	54	6	Six
00110111	55	7	Seven
00111000	56	8	Eight
00111001	57	9	Nine

The decimal value is referenced to the corresponding value in the character chart (ASCII or UniCode) by the Operating System (OS) and/or software being used.

Converting binary to decimal is easy when the binary value to be converted is small, but as the binary value increases in size, the numbers can get rather large and tedious.

For example, assume a binary value of 010110000101100101011010. This value may appear daunting, but it is only equivalent to 3 bytes or 24 bits.

If we were to convert this binary string to its decimal value equivalent by turning "on" position values represented by 1s and leaving "off" those position values represented by 0s, our string of numbers would look like this:

010110000101100101011010

off + 4194304 + off + 1048576 + 524288 + off + off + off
+ off + 16384 + off + 4096 + 2048 + off + off + 256
+ off + 64 + off + 16 + 8 + off + 2 + off

When finally totaled, this string of binary values would yield a result of 5,790,042.

The process of deciphering binary values into their decimal equivalent can get very tedious, time consuming, and very expensive, especially if the string of binary values is more than three bytes. Imagine converting a high definition video!

DATA VERSUS CODE

A document or other file has what is sometimes referred to as a header or "code" which is supplemental data placed at the beginning of a block of data being stored or transmitted. In data transmission, the data following the header are called the body. The header, in effect, binds the block of data that follows the header (the body) to the software needed to open it or otherwise access it.

For example, if you create a document using Microsoft (MS) Word, the document cannot be opened using the Adobe Acrobat reader/application. This is because there is code embedded within any document created using MS Word, which tells the operating system that only MS Word (or other compatible software) is needed in order to open the document.

If the code which binds the document to its native software is somehow overwritten or "erased," the software will not be able to reassemble the document into its native format or into a format readable by the user, thereby causing the document to be inaccessible and unreadable by the user.

Some of these data, such as incriminating text (the occurrence of "XYZ" in the case referenced throughout the book, for example), may however still reside in a document, on a disk, or within the hard drive. For a cyber forensic investigator to properly search for a keyword contained within data seized from an entire hard drive (or even from data narrowed down to a specific folder or specific image within a user's hard drive), it is best to use HEX to accomplish this herculean task.

HEX

Hexadecimal, or HEX for short, is strictly a human-friendly representation of binary values.

Viewing data as a HEX representation (or value) allows a cyber forensic investigator to go beyond the application or file. It allows for the viewing of all the data contained within a file including remnants of old or even deleted files.

It is important to understand that not all binary values are convertible into readable ASCII. ASCII is a code, based on the ordering of the English alphabet, and not all data contained within a computer is necessarily text (ASCII) based. There are many programs or software applications that are written in programming code that is not ASCII-based.

This programming code is not meant to be viewed in ASCII, it is meant to perform a function. Recall from our earlier discussions that a computer's functions are all based on math, not the English (nor French, Chinese, Slavic, Greek, Arabic, or any other such) language; code therefore needs to be based on mathematical principles not grammatical ones.

FROM RAW DATA TO FILES

There are hundreds of different formats for data (databases, word processing, spreadsheets, images, video, etc.). There are also formats for executable programs (.exe, .bat, .dll) on different platforms (Windows, Mac, Linux, Unix, etc.). Each format defines how the sequence of bits and bytes are laid out, with ASCII being one of the easiest for humans to decipher or read. A text file is simply a file that stores any text, in a format such as ASCII or UTF-8, with few if any control characters.

There are a wide variety of digital file types containing specific formatting information that allows for file access, storage or "manipulation." This "manipulation" may occur via the operating system itself, or it may occur via a "parent" program installed on the operating system.

A parent program is the program that is used to create, execute, or otherwise access the file. In most cases a file will contain data and its file signature, from which its parent software (or the operating system) will be able to identify and handle its operation. The file signature information is contained in what is sometimes referred to as a "file header." The data contained within a file header is not seen by the casual user, yet is very important for the file to function as designed. It is this data contained within the file header that is used to identify the format of the file.

The value of HEX is apparent when a method to extract the readable data from a file may no longer be feasible, occurring for example when the header information is missing or in some way corrupt. Even though the file is unidentifiable and unable to be opened by native or compatible software, the cyber forensic investigator can search for the binary equivalent of some ASCII representation across the entire hard drive.

The investigator would find this value regardless of modified or missing file signatures. As was discussed previously, many times in the course of normal day-to-day operations and file processing a deleted file and its associated metadata will be partially overwritten, perhaps missing the entire file signature or other important formatting information and even some text. However, if the binary values representing a piece of evidence (e.g., "XYZ") remain within the file's remnants, then they can be found.

 ## ACCESSING FILES

Most files need to be mounted by an operating system (or some software) to be accessed in normal day-to-day use. In order for this to occur an operating system needs to boot up so that it can identify the file structure and location of the file in order to present the data in a readable manner.

The boot process is important, as it is the process of mounting the evidence for which the investigator will investigate. When accessing information on a system, the mounting of the file system is imperative. The importance of the Master Boot Record (MBR) and its contents, such as the partition table (PT), are all relevant bits of information that can have a crucial bearing on the investigation.

A firm understanding of the boot process is necessary if, for nothing else, knowing when evidence is altered and thereby avoiding contaminating evidence by imaging. A cyber forensic investigator, as with any investigator, will at times be responsible for collecting and capturing evidence.

Data can be written to a hard drive (e.g., potential evidence) during the boot process, altering the evidence. Knowing when and how data is altered on a piece of evidence (hard drive or otherwise) is not only important when investigating evidence, but also important when acquiring evidence.

During the boot process of the primary file system (or partition) data is, in most cases, written to the hard drive, such that dates are changed and files are written and altered. It is critical to a sound investigation not to alter evidence for which you have been entrusted to image in a forensically sound manner.

Booting up a computer, in an uncontrolled manner, could very well contaminate the integrity of the data contained within the evidence (hard drive). It would be analogous to a homicide detective stomping through blood splatter at a crime scene. Even if the detective could explain away his/her foot prints, at the very least, the quality of his or her work and competency would be called into question.

 ENDIANNESS

In cyber forensics, how data is stored on a drive is crucial information, as often, the cyber forensic investigator will have to look at raw data (via a HEX editor) for possible evidence, thus; knowing how the information is written to disk, how data are represented and presented physically and logically, is very important.

Understanding the concept of endianness is necessary in order to fully understand how a mathematical based system handles or interprets data, such as whether integers are represented from left to right or right to left.

Not all binary data are treated equally. The way in which binary (HEX, in our view) is handled all depends upon the system architecture, the code. As a system boots it will encounter code that will tell it to execute an instruction set.

Generally, in computing, endianness comes in two flavors: big endian and little endian.

In big endian, the most significant unit (or byte) of a data field is ordered first or left justified. With little endian, however, the least significant unit (or byte) of a data field is ordered first with the most significant byte on the right (i.e., right justified).

Endianness describes how multi-byte data is represented by a computer system and is dictated by the CPU architecture of the system. Unfortunately, not all computer systems are designed with the same Endian-architecture. The difference in Endian-architecture is an issue when software or data is shared between computer systems. An analysis of the computer system and its interfaces will determine the requirements of the Endian implementation of the software.

PARTITIONS

There are subtle differences between volumes and partitions, and sometimes the lines between the two can get fuzzy. Volumes exist at the logical OS level, and partitions exist at the physical, media specific level. Sometimes there is a one-to-one correspondence, but not always.

A partition is a collection of (physically) consecutive sectors and a volume is a collection of (logically) addressable sectors. Herein lies the difference—the data contained within a volume may appear consecutive, but only logically.

A partition is an area of the hard drive that is defined by an entry in the partition table of the MBR, and is recognized system wide. The partition is interpreted by code contained within that same sector, the MBR, and a partition is usually a subdivision. As the name implies it is the process of breaking something larger into smaller pieces.

A volume is an area defined or interpreted by an operating system. A volume is recognized by the operating system and will have a drive letter associated with it. It is often used synonymously with the term drive or disk.

The physical verses logical nature of the partition and volume however are not necessarily always mutually exclusive. The differences or similarities sometimes get fuzzy as they were not created with the idea of the other in mind. In fact, many times they are the same thing.

Perhaps most importantly, a volume contains the file system, which is unique to the operating system and only understood by the specific operating system.

FILE SYSTEMS

A file system is a tool used for storing and retrieving data on a computer. It is the tool that tracks the allocation of the clusters, and it allows for a hierarchy of directories, folders, and files. A file system addresses and manages all the clusters contained within a volume.

A file system is usually defined during the creation of a partition; it is at this point the partition "becomes" a volume. File systems determine how and where files are placed on a hard drive, with the goal of trying to optimize data retrieval speeds. We may know where that document resides logically within a folder structure, but we are oblivious (and justifiably so), as to which specific bits on the hard drive are allocated to this individual document. This is not something the end users need to concern themselves with; however, it is imperative that the file system of the computer knows, otherwise when we click on the Word document icon nothing will happen.

Various filing systems and their components may have different names and their physical placement on the drive may vary, but functionally all file systems require similar pieces—those which identify it, those which identify its data, and those which contain the data itself.

 ## TIME

In cyber forensic investigations knowing the correct time is of great importance. Understanding the timeline of events is imperative in understanding when events occurred with respect to all other events.

Timing inaccuracies are broad and vast. Inaccuracies can be system wide to NTP server inaccuracies, or system specific due to clock skew. Inaccuracies can be specific to a certain geographical location due to confusing time zones or to a specific operating system's file system, rounding odd seconds to the nearest even second.

Time discrepancies can be as long as time permits or as short as a second (or less), as with the MS-DOS 32-bit timestamp timing inaccuracy. It is highly unlikely that a timing inaccuracy of a second (as seen in MS-DOS 32-bit timestamp) would be so pivotal to corroborating someone's innocence; however, one thing time inaccuracies have in common is that they can discredit an expert, especially a cyber forensic expert/investigator!

 ## THE INVESTIGATION PROCESS

An exact line-by-line instruction set for running a complete cyber forensic investigation is logically impossible to present, as each organization performing a forensic investigation will have their own approaches. procedures, policies, and methods—some dictated by law, others by internal preferences and protocols. However, there are general Investigative Smart Practices, which may fit into most types of forensic organizations and most types of cases.

A child pornography investigation run by law enforcement versus an intellectual property theft investigation run by a corporate forensic department may both eventually find the evidence necessary to prosecute the guilty; however, the approaches, steps taken, and processes to that end may be entirely different and be supported by completely different documentation.

As peculiar as the differences are between varying organization types so too are the differences between cases. The Investigative Smart Practices presented in this book are meant to be broad in scope and used as guidelines.

Step 1: Initial Contact/Request

The validity and scope of the investigative request is established. This function may be performed by someone outside the cyber forensics field. For example, this can be determined by a judge via a court order or perhaps via the HR department within a large organization.

Step 2: Evidence Handling

The integrity of the evidence *must be* preserved throughout the entirety of the investigation. This process occurs each and every time the evidence is handled. Preserving the integrity of the evidence is vital, but equally essential is also being able to prove the integrity of the evidence in a court of law.

Step 3: Acquisition of Evidence

This step involves obtaining a forensically sound image of the original evidence. Acquisition of evidence can certainly fall under Step 2, Evidence Handling; however, this step focuses more precisely on the acquisition of the evidence versus the handling of the evidence during acquisition.

Step 4: Data Preparation

Preparing and identifying data for analysis and investigation. This step focuses on "analyzing" data to ensure a valid and complete search. This includes mounting complex files, verifying file types, recovering deleted items, and anything else which would prepare the data for final investigation (Step 5).

Step 5: Investigation

Focuses on finding those data that match specified search criteria. This step tends to be a little more subjective than the others, being that the investigator may need to examine the search results, discard false positives, and identify the critical piece(s) of evidence, which typically is not conveniently named "incriminating evidence.doc."

Step 6: Reporting

Reporting is the means by which the investigation details its findings and communicates them to the client, management, law enforcement, and/or the requestor. Communicating the findings is highly dependent upon organizational structure. A corporate environment may have reporting requirements or templates dissimilar to those in law enforcement, for example.

Some of these steps will occur concurrently while some may occur out of "order." As is the case with evidence hash values, each case is unique. It is this uniqueness that makes cyber forensics such a challenging field.

Step 7: Retention and Curation of Evidence

Evidence retention and curation may fall under the all encompassing "evidence handling" step, yet due to unique issues and complexities it is discussed in its own right. This step involves the post handling of evidence, implying any storage, archiving, destruction, or returning of all evidence. Evidence retention will likely include the handling of all evidence associated with an investigation, be it physical hard drives, digital files, and perhaps the investigator's hand written notes.

As with all steps, requirements are highly dependent upon the type of forensic practice (e.g., law enforcement, corporate, government, private) and may vary from case to case. There will be varying legal, contractual, procedural, financial, and business requirements, which will ultimately set the boundaries for this final evidence handling step.

Step 8: Investigation Wrap-Up and Conclusion

Investigation wrap up is broad in its meaning and covers those post investigation activates loosely structured around defending the cyber forensic investigator's work.

This can occur in the form of being an expert witness in a criminal case, an interview by HR or Internal Audit for a corporate investigation, or perhaps a peer review. This may also include an internal self examination such as "lessons learned" or a quality control assessment.

SUMMARY

Traditional forensics professionals use fingerprints, DNA typing, and ballistics analysis to make their cases. Cyber forensic investigators rely upon various technologies for collecting, examining, and evaluating data in an effort to establish intent, culpability, motive, means, methods, and loss, resulting from crimes conducted by, with, or through any device that is capable of accessing, retrieving, processing, and storing electronic data. The cyber forensic investigator's role is in the discovery, collection, and analysis of data, leading to the identification of digital evidence.

It is our hope that this book has provided you with a solid basis for establishing or expanding an understanding of how raw data are unraveled through a cyber forensic process, resulting in digital evidence.

Appendix
Forensic Investigations, ABC Inc.

Ronelle Sawyer
June 12, 2009
Forensic Report
Case # 000029

Distribution List

Group, Contact Name	Location	Title/Department/ Business Unit
Legal	ABC Inc. Headquarters	Security Operations
HR	ABC Inc. Headquarters	Security Operations

DOCUMENT RELEASE AND CONFIDENTIALITY

This document is proprietary and confidential and has been released only to the persons listed above. It may not be distributed outside the organization without written approval from ABC Inc. Legal department.

1 EXECUTIVE SUMMARY

On April 1, 2009, ABC Inc. Legal department contacted the ABC Inc. Forensic Investigations department regarding the cyber forensic examination of a hard drive belonging to Jose McCarthy. There were suspicions that McCarthy was attempting to sell intellectual property belonging to ABC Inc. to a competitor, XYZ Company. The hard drive used by McCarthy was forensically examined to determine if there were any indications of intellectual property theft.

After careful cyber forensic analysis of McCarthy's hard drive a letter was found showing intent to sell proprietary information.

2 FORENSIC ACQUISITION

2.1 Custody and Storage

On April 6, 2009 Ronelle Sawyer, cyber forensic investigator with ABC Inc., received McCarthy's hard drive for analysis. Ronelle Sawyer performed Chain of Custody with Legal and took possession of the evidence (see the following graphic). Evidence was locked in a security vault until acquisition was performed.

2.2 Forensic Equipment (Hardware, Software, Adapters, etc.) Overview:

Forensic Workstation—Dell Precision T7500 Workstation:
- Windows 7 Professional—64-bit
- CPU—Quad Core Intel Xeon Processor X5687, 3.60GHz, 12M L3, 6.4GT/s
- RAM—12GB, DDR3 RDIMM Memory
- Hard Drive(s)—10,000 RPM Seagate 1 TB SATA drives, RAID 5

Forensic Software:
- Guidance Software's EnCase Forensic v.7.2
- Access Data's FTK v. 3

Other:
- Image Masster Solo-4 Forensic
- Digital Intelligence Ultrablock write blocker
- Evidence duplication—200 GB sanitized Seagate Hard Disk Drive
  - Type—Barracuda ATA (IDE)
  - Model Number—ST360078
  - Serial Number—67DF9R30

2.3 Evidence (Original Evidence) Hard Drive Overview

- 80GB Hard Disk Drive
- Manufacturer—Seagate
- Type—Barracuda ATA V (IDE)

Evidence Handling
ABC Inc. Forensic Investigation

Case # 000029

Evidence Details

Description		
80 GB Hard drive BARRACUDA ATA V (IDE)		
Manufacturer	**Model #**	**Serial #**
SEAGATE	ST3B0024A	3KB0Y7XB

Chain of Custody

Date/Time	From	To	Reason
Date 4/6/09	**Name/Organization** LEGAL KEVIN SMITH	**Name/Organization** FORENSICS RONELLE SAWYER	FORENSIC INVESTIGATION
Time 9:30 AM	**Signature** Kevin Smith	**Signature** Ronelle Sawyer	
Date 6/12/09	**Name/Organization** FORENSICS RONELLE SAWYER	**Name/Organization** LEGAL KEVIN SMITH	INVESTIGATION COMPLETE EVIDENCE RETURN
Time 4:00 PM	**Signature** Ronelle Sawyer	**Signature** Kevin Smith	
Date	**Name/Organization**	**Name/Organization**	
Time	**Signature**	**Signature**	

Chain of Custody Form

- Model Number—ST380024A
- Serial Number—3KB0Y7XB
- MD5 Hash—59a34105247fb3a26e4bc411fea32eb4

2.4 Acquisition and Verification

On April 7, 2009 Ronelle Sawyer, using Image Masster's Solo-4, performed a hash analysis of the evidence hard drive, as described in Section 2.3, which resulted in the following MD5 hash value: 59a34105247fb3a26e4bc411 fea32eb4.

After obtaining the hash value Ronelle obtained a bit-for-bit forensic image of the evidence hard drive using the Solo-4.

The forensic image was captured to a sanitized drive, described in Section 2.2. After this acquisition both the original evidence and the new bit for bit image were both hashed. All MD5 hash values obtained were identical: 59a34105247fb3a26e4bc411fea32eb4.

Upon confirmation of image integrity, Ronelle returned the original evidence drive to the secured forensic evidence vault.

Ronelle created a duplicate drive as the forensic lab's working evidence. Ronelle then connected the duplicate drive to a forensic workstation (described in Section 2.2) via a Digital Intelligence write blocker. Using EnCase Forensic edition 7.2, Ronelle re-acquired the duplicate working copy hard drive in EnCase image file format.

Ronelle divided an 80 GB file into multiple smaller 2 GB pieces for ease of transport, naming these new forensic image files "JoseMcCarthy.E01" through "JoseMcCarthy.E040." Using EnCase, Ronelle hashed the new image and verified the hash match. All future analysis for this case was performed from this image.

Ronelle performed the following preprocessing using EnCase and FTK:

- Opened cases in EnCase and FTK—imported Evidence files "JoseMcCarthy .EOx."
- Hash verification—match.
- Mounted image within EnCase and FTK.
- Verified the system's time and data, which were compared to an external time source synchronized to the U.S. atomic clock—system's time was found to be within five seconds of the actual time.
- Recovered deleted items.
- Verified file types.
- Indexed files.

3 FORENSIC ANALYSIS

Search Criteria:

- **Date Range:** May 10, 2008–March 26, 2009
- **Keywords:**
  - Janice
  - Witcome
  - XYZ
- **File Types:** Any

Searching for criteria above provided two identical documents in separate locations:

1. C:\WINDOWS\system32\SoftwareDistribution\Setup\ServiceStartup\ wups2.dll\7.0.6000.374\systemm32.dll
2. D:\Incriminating Evidence.doc

The text contained in both documents was identical and has been copied here for quick reference:

Hello Janice

I'm looking forward to continuing negotiations. The information I am willing to provide you with will save XYZ Company years of research and development. I feel 100,000 U.S. dollars is a small price to pay for such a large return. Please reconsider as I think this will be mutually beneficial.

Thanks Jose

In uncovering these documents two irregularities were identified:

1. The file named systemm32.dll, located in the system 32 folder created on Friday, February 06, 2009, was actually an MS Word document. Why or how this Word document was stored in the System32 directory and named with a DLL extension cannot be ascertained.
2. The second file, named Incriminating Evidence.doc, was located in a partition that was deleted. This file also was created on Friday, February 06, 2009. Why this partition was deleted cannot be ascertained.

4. CONCLUSION

Two files containing the same text were identified on the hard drive assigned to Jose McCarthy matching the criteria provided. Both files show the same create dates. One file named systemm32.dll, located in the system 32 folder and created on Friday, February 06, 2009, was actually an MS Word document. The second file, named Incriminating Evidence.doc, was located in a partition that was deleted. This file also was created on Friday, February 06, 2009.

Glossary

32-bit register   In computer architecture, a processor register (or general purpose register) is a small amount of storage available on the CPU whose contents can be accessed more quickly than storage available elsewhere.

Typically, this specialized storage is not considered part of the normal memory range for the machine.

Registers are normally measured by the number of bits they can hold, for example, an "8-bit register" or a "32-bit register."

absolute address   An explicit identification of a memory location, peripheral device, or location within a device.

For example, memory byte 413,679, disk drive 1, and sector 451 are absolute addresses.

The computer uses absolute addresses to reference memory and peripherals.

active partition   The partition containing the operating system (OS), which is actively being used. The operating system will actually "boot up" the system/computer.

address   Every byte in a file is assigned a number, called its address, starting at 0 for the first byte of the file, 1 for the second byte, and so on.

allocated   Assigned. Typically refers to disk space (see Allocated space).

Any cluster currently assigned to a file is considered allocated.

allocated space   Space on a storage device (i.e., disk), where the operating system has already written files to.

array   A grouping of similar types of data, referenced as sequential locations. The absolute locations of items in an array may not truly be sequential in a managed memory environment. Some different types are strings and multidimensional arrays.

303

ASCII   Abbreviation for American Standard Code for Information Interchange. A standard code used to store textual characters in memory, in which each character is represented by a unique eight-bit pattern.

asymmetric key encryption   A cryptographic approach that involves the use of asymmetric key algorithms instead of or in addition to symmetric key algorithms.

Unlike symmetric key algorithms, it does not require a secure initial exchange of one or more secret keys to both sender and receiver. The asymmetric key algorithms are used to create a mathematically related key pair: a secret private key and a published public key.

Use of these keys allows protection of the authenticity of a message by creating a digital signature of a message using the private key, which can be verified using the public key.

It also allows protection of the confidentiality and integrity of a message, by public key encryption, encrypting the message using the public key, which can only be decrypted using the private key.

ATA interface   The AT Attachment interface, one of two major standards for connecting storage media devices like hard drives to personal computers (PCs). The opposing standard is SCSI.

PATA is the Parallel ATA specification. Often incorrectly referred to as IDE (Integrated Device Electronics) by a lot of vendors. SATA is the Serial ATA specification.

ATAPI is an extension on the ATA standard for optical media, like CD, DVD, and Blu-Ray.

attribute   For each file (or directory) described in the MFT record, there's a linear repository of stream descriptors (named attributes) packed together in a variable-length record (called an attributes list), with extra padding to fill the fixed 1KB size of every MFT record, and that fully describes the effective streams associated with that file.

b-tree   A balanced search tree in which every node has between $m/2$ and m children, where $m > 1$ is a fixed integer; m is the order.

The root may have as few as two children. This is a good structure if much of the tree is in slow memory (disk), since the height, and hence the number of accesses, can be kept small, say one or two, by picking a large m.

bad clusters   A bad cluster is a hard disk cluster that has been flagged by the file system as being corrupted or damaged in some way and thus will no longer be used for storing data.

base-16 character code   This encoding is the standard case- insensitive HEX encoding and may be referred to as "base 16" or "HEX."

A 16-character subset of US-ASCII is used, enabling four bits to be represented per printable character.

base address   The starting address (beginning point) of a program or table.

basic input/output system (BIOS)   Firmware that can control much of a computer's input/output functions, such as communications with the internal and external media drives (e.g., zip, CD, floppy, etc.) and the monitor. It is also called ROM BIOS.

best evidence rule   The legal doctrine that an original piece of evidence, particularly a document, is superior to a copy. If the original is available, a copy will not be allowed as evidence in a trial.

binary search   A technique for searching an ordered list in which we first check the middle item and—based on that comparison—"discard" half the data. The same procedure is then applied to the remaining half until a match is found or there are no more items left.

binary system   A system of arithmetic used with computers, also called Base 2, that is based on the digits 0 and 1.

bit   Abbreviation for "binary digit." The fundamental storage unit of computer memory, a bit has one of two values: 0 or 1.

bit for bit image   A bitstream image is an exact replica of each bit (or binary digit—the smallest unit of data in a computer) contained in the electronic storage media.

Bitstream images obtained from electronic storage media are essentially a snapshot of the media at that particular point in time.

block cipher   An encryption scheme in which the data is divided into fixed-size blocks (often 64 bits), each of which is encrypted independently of the others.

Complete independence of blocks is cryptographically undesirable, so usually a block cipher will be used in a chaining or feedback mode in which the output from one block affects the way the next is encrypted.

boot sector   Reserved sectors on disk that are used to load the operating system. On startup, the computer looks for the master boot record (MBR) or something similarly named, which is typically the first sector in the first partition of the disk.

The MBR contains a program that reads the partition table which points to the first sector that contains the operating system.

That sector contains another small program that causes the computer to read the operating system.

byte　A group of bits (usually eight bits), which usually represents one character of text data, such as a letter, digit, or special character.

byte offset　A byte offset, typically used to index into a string or file, is a zero-based number of bytes. For example, in the string "this is a test," the byte offset of "this" is 0, of "is" is 5, "a" is 8, and "test" is 10.

This is not always the same as the "character offset." Some characters, such as Chinese ideograms, require two or more bytes to represent. Using ASCII characters only will ensure that the byte offset is always equal to the character offset.

For example, given an array of characters A containing "abcdef," one can say that the element containing the letter c has an offset of 2 from the start of A.

carving (data)　Data carving is an important tool when attempting to recover files from either unallocated drive space, or from a disk that has become very corrupted.

It can be slow, but if a file is critical, it is well worthwhile, and quicker than trying to process by hand.

The process of reassembling computer files from fragments in the absence of filesystem metadata. The carving process makes use of knowledge of common file structures, information contained in files, and heuristics regarding how filesystems fragment data. Fusing these three sources of information, a file carving system infers which fragments belong together.

File carving is a highly complex task, with a potentially huge number of permutations to try. To make this task tractable, carving software typically makes extensive use of models and heuristics. This is necessary not only from a standpoint of execution time, but also for the accuracy of the results.

chain of custody　A legal term that refers to the ability to guarantee the identity and integrity of the specimen from collection through reporting of the test results.

It is a process used to maintain and document the chronological history of the specimen. (Documents should include name or initials of the individual collecting the specimen, each person or entity subsequently having custody of it, the date the specimen was collected or transferred, the employer or agency, specimen number, patient's or employee's name, and a brief description of the specimen.)

A secure chain of custody, together with the analytical techniques used by the investigator to acquire the evidence, leads to the production of a legally defensible report.

character code   A code that pairs a set of natural language characters (such as an alphabet or syllabary, a set of written symbols that represent or approximate syllables, which in turn make up words) with a set of something else, such as numbers or electrical pulses.

Common examples include Morse code, which encodes letters of the Roman alphabet as series of long and short depressions of a telegraph key; and ASCII, which encodes letters, numerals, and other symbols as both integers and seven-bit binary versions of those integers.

child (children)   In a tree, nodes can point to the roots of subtrees. The roots of the subtrees below a given node are the children of that node.

cipher   In cryptography, a cipher (or cypher) is an algorithm for performing encryption or decryption—a series of well-defined steps that can be followed as a procedure.

clock skew   Differences in clock signal arrival times across the chip.

cluster   The logical unit of file storage on a hard disk; it's managed by the computer's operating system.

Any file stored on a hard disk takes up one or more clusters of storage. A file's clusters can be scattered among different locations on the hard disk.

Since a cluster is a logical rather than a physical unit (it's not built into the hard disk itself), the size of a cluster can be varied.

CMOS [complementary metal oxide semiconductor] battery   A battery that maintains the time, date, hard disk, and other configuration settings in the CMOS memory. CMOS batteries are small and are attached directly to the motherboard.

CMOS memory   A small, battery-backed memory bank in a computer that holds configuration settings.

code points   In character encoding terminology, a code point or code position is any of the numerical values that make up the code space.

common law rule of evidence   The best evidence rule is a common law rule of evidence, which can be traced back at least as far as the eighteenth century.

In *Omychund v Barker (1745) 1 Atk, 21, 49; 26 ER 15, 33*, Lord Harwicke stated that no evidence was admissible unless it was "the best that the nature of the case will allow."

The best evidence rule was predicated on the assumption that if the original was not produced, there was a significant chance of error or fraud in relying on such a copy.

compiled program   A "compiler" takes source code and converts it into machine code.

Compilers are simply programs that take text files as input (source code) and through logical processes *do some magic to* produce a single file of executable machine code (program). The result runs on the CPU directly.

compound file   Compound File Binary Format (CFBF), also called Compound File for short, is a file format for storing numerous files and streams within a single file on a disk.

CFBF was developed by Microsoft and is an implementation of Microsoft COM Structured Storage.

compressed file   File that has been electronically "deflated" through proprietary algorithm, to save space and reduce transmission times.

This allows the file to be downloaded faster or more data to be stored on a removable media.

Common compressed file extensions are .ZIP, .RAR, .ARJ, .TAR.GZ, and .TGZ.

concatenated   The operation of joining two character strings end to end.

For example, the strings "snow" and "ball" may be concatenated to give "snowball."

control characters   A code point (a number) in a character set that does not in itself represent a written symbol.

It is in-band signaling in the context of character encoding. All entries in the ASCII table below code 32 (technically the C0 control code set) and 127 are of this kind, including BEL (which is intended to cause an audible signal in the receiving terminal), SYN (which is a synchronization signal), and ENQ (a signal that is intended to trigger a response at the receiving end, to see if it is still present).

The Extended Binary Coded Decimal Interchange Code (EBCDIC) character set contains 65 control codes, including all of the ASCII control codes as well as additional codes, which are mostly used to control IBM peripherals.

The Unicode standard has additional nonprinting characters (i.e., the zero-width non-joiner).

cyber forensics   The use of specialized techniques for recovery, authentication, and analysis of electronic data to determine legal evidence.

cylinder groups   When you create a Unix File System (UFS), the disk slice is divided into cylinder groups, which are made up of one or more consecutive disk cylinders.

The cylinder groups are then further divided into addressable blocks to control and organize the structure of the files within the cylinder group.

Each type of block has a specific function in the file system.

cylinders   Comprises the same track number but spans all such tracks across each platter surface that is able to store data (without regard to whether or not the track is "bad"). Thus, it is a three-dimensional object.

cylinder, sector, head (CHS)   An early method for giving addresses to each physical block of data on a hard drive.

A method of referencing the sectors on a drive as a collection of unique cylinder, head, and sector addresses.

Each block on the drive will have a unique cylinder, head, and sector address.

data block   A physical unit of data that can be conveniently stored by a computer on an input or output device. The block is normally composed of one or more logical records or a portion of a logical record. Synonymous with physical record.

data propagation delay   The length of time data takes to travel from one point on the segment (node) to another point.

decrypt(ion)   Decoding; the activity of making clear or converting from code into plain text; "a secret key or password is required for decryption."

Process of "unscrambling" an encrypted or coded message.

depth   The longest path from the root node to a leaf node.

descendant   Any node that can be reached from the current node by following the children branches.

directory entries   Each entry records the name, extension, attributes (archive, directory, hidden, read-only, system, and volume), the date and time of creation, the address of the first cluster of the file/directory's data, and finally the size of the file/directory.

directory structure   The way an operating system's file system and its files are displayed to the user.

Files are typically displayed in a hierarchical tree structure.

disk array   An arrangement of two or more hard disks, in RAID or daisy-chain configuration, organized to improve speed and provide protection of data against loss.

disk signature   A unique identifier for a disk.

For a master boot record (MBR)-formatted disk, this identifier is a four-byte value stored at the end of the MBR, which is located in sector zero on the disk.

For a GUID partitioning table (GPT)-formatted disk, this value is a GUID stored in the GPT disk header at the beginning of the disk.

.DLL   The DLL file type is primarily associated with "Dynamic Link Library."

A .DLL file is a support file and is used by one or more programs.

As an example, if several parts of a program need to perform the same action that action may be placed into a .DLL file (library) that the various program parts can all use. This saves space and makes it easier when that particular routine needs to be updated.

dwords   bit = ...1 bit...

nibble = 4 bits = 1/2 byte

byte = 8 bits = 2 nibbles

WORD = 2 bytes = 4 nibbles = 16 bits

DWORD = 2 WORDs = 4 bytes = 8 nibbles = 32 bits

QWORD = 2 DWORDs = 4 WORDS = 64 bits

DWORD stands for Double Word

(QWORD for Quad, a prefix meaning 4)

encrypted files   Encrypting File System (EFS) provides the core file encryption technology used to store encrypted files on NTFS file system volumes. Once you encrypt a file or folder, you work with the encrypted file or folder just as you do with any other files and folders.

Encryption is transparent to the user that encrypted the file. This means that you do not have to manually decrypt the encrypted file before you can use it. You can open and change the file as you normally do.

Using EFS is similar to using permissions on files and folders. Both methods can be used to restrict access to data. However, an intruder who gains unauthorized physical access to your encrypted files or folders will be prevented from reading them. If the intruder tries to open or copy your encrypted file or folder he receives an access denied message. Permissions on files and folders do not protect against unauthorized physical attacks.

You encrypt or decrypt a folder or file by setting the encryption property for folders and files just as you set any other attribute such as read-only, compressed, or hidden. If you encrypt a folder, all files and subfolders created in the encrypted folder are automatically encrypted. It is recommended that you encrypt at the folder level. ("Encrypting File System Overview," Windows XP Professional Product Documentation, Microsoft Corp., retrieved February 2010, www.microsoft.com/resources/documentation/windows/xp/all/proddocs/en-us/encrypt_overview.mspx?mfr=true.)

encryption   The transformation of plain text into an apparently less readable form (called ciphertext) through a mathematical process.

The ciphertext may be read by anyone who has the key that decrypts (undoes the encryption) the ciphertext.

encryption key   In cryptography, a key is a piece of information (a parameter) that determines the functional output of a cryptographic algorithm or cipher.

Without a key, the algorithm would have no result.

In encryption, a key specifies the particular transformation of plaintext into ciphertext, or vice versa during decryption.

EPROM   A memory chip that maintains its contents without electrical power, and whose contents can be erased and reprogrammed by removing a protective cover and exposing the chip to ultraviolet light.

evidence integrity (via a hash)   Provides assurance that the original evidence has not been modified or altered from its original state.

evidence uniqueness (via a hash)   Assurance that the evidence is unique onto itself, such that no two pieces of evidence can be identical or similar at the same time or in the same occurrence.

executables   Files that contain a program; that is, a particular kind of file that is capable of being executed or run as a program in the computer.

In a disk operating system or Windows operating system, an executable file usually has a file name extension of .bat, .com, or .exe.

expert witness   A person who is permitted to testify at a trial because of their special knowledge or proficiency in a particular field that is relevant to the case.

An expert witness, professional witness, or judicial expert is a witness, who, by virtue of education, training, skill, or experience, is believed to have expertise and specialized knowledge in a particular subject beyond that of the average person, sufficient that others may officially and legally rely upon the witness's specialized (scientific, technical, or other) opinion about an evidence or factual issue within the scope of his/her expertise, referred to as the expert opinion, as an assistance to the fact-finder.

extended boot record (EBR)   Is a descriptor for a logical partition under the common DOS disk drive partitioning system.

In that system, when one (and only one) partition record entry in the Master Boot Record (MBR) is designated an "extended partition," then that partition can be subdivided into a number of logical drives.

The actual structure of that extended partition is described by one or more EBRs, which are located inside the extended partition.

The first (and sometimes only) EBR will always be located on the very first sector of the extended partition.

extended partition   A construct that is used to partition a disk into logical units.

A disk may have up to four primary partitions or up to three primary partitions and one extended partition. The extended partition may be further subdivided into multiple logical drives.

falseticker   A clock that does not maintain timekeeping accuracy to a previously published (and trusted) standard.

file   Grouping of records each made up of multiple logical segments.

A file is the largest unit of information recognized by the system.

Also a collection of related records treated as a basic unit of storage in a computer system.

file extension   The suffix appended to a file name in the FAT file-naming convention. The extension is optional in some file systems.

The compilers use file extensions to determine the source type of the file.

file format   The way data is organized for a particular kind of file.

Some formats are proprietary and can be read only by the program used to create the file.

Other formats, such as ASCII and rich text format (RTF), are more generic and can be read by many programs.

file header   Supplemental data placed at the beginning of a block of data being stored or transmitted.

In graphics file formats, the header might give information about an image's size, resolution, number of colors, and the like.

file magic number   Bytes within a file used to identify the format of the file; generally a short sequence of bytes (most are two to four bytes long) placed at the beginning of the file.

file share   The process of direct or indirect data sharing on a computer network with various levels of access privilege; also, the process of direct or indirect file transfer via the Internet.

file signature   Data used to identify or verify the content of a file.

file slack   Any space left over between the last byte of the file and the first byte of the next cluster is a form of internal fragmentation called file slack or slack space.

file structure   The format into which a file is arranged by computer so that the information it contains can be retrieved on demand.

file system   A data structure or a collection of files.

The method for storing and retrieving files on a disk. It is system software that takes commands from the operating system to read and write the disk clusters (groups of sectors).

The file system manages a folder/directory structure, which provides an index to the files, and it defines the syntax used to access them (how the "path" to the file is coded).

The physical filesystem is divided first by disk partitions.

The DOS-, Windows-, OS/2-, Macintosh-, and UNIX-based operating systems all have file systems in which files are placed somewhere in a hierarchical (tree) structure. A file is placed in a directory (folder in Windows) or subdirectory at the desired place in the tree structure.

File systems specify conventions for naming files. These conventions include the maximum number of characters in a name, which characters can be used, and, in some systems, how long the file name suffix can be. A file system also includes a format for specifying the path to a file through the structure of directories.

forensic image   Imaging a hard drive is a phrase that is commonly used for preserving the contents of a custodian hard drive or server.

A forensic image is an exact bit for bit copy of the drive to be examined as part of a forensic investigation.

gigabyte (GB)   Equals about 1 billion bytes.

gigahertz (GHz)   One billion (109) cycles or processes in one second.

hardware write blocker   Write blockers are devices that allow acquisition of information on a drive without creating the possibility of accidentally damaging the drive contents. They do this by allowing read commands to pass while blocking write commands, hence their name.

Hardware write blockers can be either IDE-to-IDE or Firewire/USB-to-IDE.

hash values   A hash is a code, calculated based on the contents of a message. This code should have the property that it is extremely difficult to construct a message so that its hash comes to a specific value.

Hashes are useful because they can be attached to a message, and demonstrate that it has not been modified. If a message were to be modified, then its hash would have changed, and would no longer match the original hash value.

HDD   In a personal computer, a hard disk drive (HDD) is the mechanism that controls the positioning, reading, and writing of the hard disk, which furnishes the largest amount of data storage for the PC.

Although the hard disk drive (often shortened to "hard drive") and the hard disk are not the same thing, they are packaged as a unit and so either term is sometimes used to refer to the whole unit.

head   Data is written to and read from the surface of a platter by a device called a head.

Naturally, a platter has two sides and thus two surfaces on which data could be manipulated; usually there are two heads per platter—one on each side, but not always.

headers   The supplemental data placed at the beginning of a block of data being stored or transmitted. In data transmission, the data following the header are called the body.

height   The maximum distance of any leaf from the root of a tree. If a tree has only one node (the root), the height is zero.

HEX editor   A HEX editor is a program that allows you to edit compiled programs and binary data files.

These editors are called HEX editors because they most often present data in hexadecimal format.

Hexadecimal is used because it is easier for most humans than working in binary. In addition, hexadecimal is frequently useful because computers tend to work with eight-bit bytes of information and because ASCII is an eight-bit code (www.tech-faq.com/hex-editor.shtml).

hexadecimal   A numbering system using a base number of 16 and including the 10 decimal digits (zero to nine) along with six alpha digits (A to F).

Thus, a digit is available to represent each of the possible values of a four-bit binary digit.

In computers, HEX numbers are derived from the binary numbers stored on disk and in RAM. The advantage of HEX is that more information can be stored in less space. HEX 00 is the same as decimal 00. However, HEX FF represents decimal 256.

home directory   A file system directory on a multi-user operating system containing files for a given user of the system.

The specifics of the home directory (such as its name and location) is defined by the operating system involved; for example, Windows systems between 2000 and 2003 keep home directories in a folder called Documents and Settings.

inodes   In computing, an inode is a data structure on a traditional Unix-style file system such as UFS.

Each object in the filesystem is represented by an inode.

An inode stores basic information about a regular file, directory, or other file system object.

intellectual property   Intellectual property is divided into two categories:

Industrial property, which includes inventions (patents), trademarks, industrial designs, and geographic indications of source.

Copyright, which includes literary and artistic works such as novels, poems, plays, films, musical works, drawings, paintings, photographs, sculptures, and architectural designs.

Internet artifacts   Cookies, caches, and other temporary Internet files that can contain a wealth of information about the history of a suspect's online activities. Searching these files can be very beneficial to an investigation but can also take a lot of time.

IP address   An electronic identifier for a specific computer or device on the World Wide Web or other (internal or external) electronic network using the TCP/IP protocol. An IP address is a series of four numbers separated by periods ("dots"). Each number is a value from 0 to 255. An example could be 67.234.77.43. "IP" stands for "Internet Protocol."

iteration   To solve a problem by repeatedly working on successive parts of the problem.

kernel   Is the central component of most computer operating systems; it is a bridge between applications and the actual data processing done at the hardware level.

The kernel's responsibilities include managing the system's resources (the communication between hardware and software components).

kilobyte (KB) Equals 1,024 bytes.

leaf (leaves) A node in a tree that has no children.

logical block addressing A method used to address hard disks by a single sector number rather than by cylinder, head, and sector (CHS).

LBA was introduced to support ATA/IDE drives as they reached 504 MB, and Enhanced BIOSs in the PC translated CHS addressing into LBA addressing.

The Master Boot Record is the traditional way of storing partition information about a hard disk, along with some boot code.

That is, the Partition Table is contained inside the MBR, which is stored in the first sector (cylinder 0, head 0, sector 1—or, alternately, LBA 0) of the hard drive.

logical copy A logical copy gets all available active data (including text and multi-media files).

logical file system Refers to a hierarchy of connected directories made of all the files (or disk partitions) that are accessible to the user.

logical folder structure A way in which to store your files:

1. Assists in the orderly storage of your files.
2. Makes it easier to find your files, especially those that are critically important, as well as those you may need to find right away.
3. Aids in managing your files, especially if you need to maintain large volumes of documents.
4. Simpler to archive your files, with a greater likelihood that you won't overlook any files you may want to archive.

magic number A magic number is a number embedded at or near the beginning of a file that indicates its file format (i.e., the type of file it is). It is also sometimes referred to as a file signature.

Magic numbers are generally not visible to users. However, they can easily be seen with the use of a HEX editor.

magnetism Force of attraction or repulsion of a magnetic material due to the arrangement of its atoms.

master boot record (MBR) The first logical sector on a disk, this is (usually) where the BIOS looks to load a small program that will boot the computer.

maximum skew The maximum offset error due to skew of the local clock over the interval determined by NTP.MAXAGE, in seconds.

The ratio <$Ephi~=~roman {NTP.MAXSKEW over NTP.MAXAGE}> is interpreted as the maximum possible skew rate due to all causes.

MD5 Message-digest algorithm meant for digital signature applications where a large message has to be compressed in a secure manner before being signed with the private key.

megabyte (MB) Approximately 1 million bytes.

megaflop One million floating-point operations per second.

metadata Data about data.

In common usage as a generic term, metadata stores data about the structure, context, and meaning of raw data, and computers use it to help organize and interpret data, turning it into meaningful information.

microprocessor Known as the "brains" of the computer, this computer chip contains all the central processing functions of a computer. Also known as the central processing unit (CPU).

MIPS One million instructions per second.

mounted/mounting Is the process of making a file system ready for use by the operating system, typically by reading certain index data structures from storage into memory ahead of time.

The term recalls a period in the history of computing when an operator had to physically place (mount) a magnetic tape or hard disk on a spindle before using it.

multi-partitioned drive Multiple partitions on a single hard drive that appear as separate drives to the operating system.

For example, when you install an operating system like Windows XP, part of the process is to define a partition on the hard drive.

This partition serves to define an area of the hard drive that Windows XP can use to install all of its files. In Windows operating systems, this primary partition is usually assigned the drive letter of "C."

Most operating systems allow users to divide a hard disk into multiple partitions, in effect making one physical hard disk into several smaller logical hard disks.

native format Proprietary file format of a given application. A format which is not intended to be opened by any other application and is usually unsuitable for transferring data from one application to another.

new technology file system   The standard file system of Windows NT, including its later versions Windows 2000, Windows XP, Windows Server 2003, Windows Server 2008, Windows Vista, and Windows 7.

NTFS has a number of advantages over the previous file system, named FAT 32 (File Allocation Table). One major advantage of NTFS is that it includes features to improve reliability.

NTFS has several improvements over FAT and HPFS (High Performance File System) such as improved support for metadata and the use of advanced data structures to improve performance, reliability, and disk space utilization, plus additional extensions such as security access control lists (ACL) and file system journaling.

The new technology file system includes fault tolerance, which automatically repairs hard drive errors without displaying error messages. It also keeps detailed transaction logs, which tracks hard drive errors.

This can help prevent hard disk failures and makes it possible to recover files if the hard drive does fail.

nibble   Sometimes written nybble, it is a four-bit aggregation, or half an octet.

As a nibble contains four bits, there are 16 (2^4) possible values, so a nibble corresponds to a single hexadecimal digit (thus, it is often referred to as a "hex digit" or "hexit").

node   Any element of a tree. Contains some data and potentially has children, which are other nodes in the tree.

nondisclosure agreement (NDA)   Is a legally binding document which protects the confidentiality of ideas, designs, plans, concepts, or other commercial material. Most often, NDAs are signed by vendors, contractors, consultants, and other non-employees who may come into contact with such material.

NTFS partition   NTFS (NT file system; sometimes New Technology File System) is the file system that the Windows NT operating system uses for storing and retrieving files on a hard disk. NTFS is the Windows NT equivalent of the Windows 95 file allocation table (FAT) and the OS/2 High Performance File System (HPFS).

However, NTFS offers a number of improvements over FAT and HPFS in terms of performance, extendibility, and security.

NTFS is the primary file system used in Microsoft's Windows NT, Windows 2000, Windows XP, Windows 2003, Windows Vista, and Windows 7 operating systems.

NTP timestamp   Represented as a 64-bit unsigned fixed-point number, in seconds, relative to 0h on 1 January 1900. The integer part is in the first 32 bits and the fraction part in the last 32 bits.

This format allows convenient multiple-precision arithmetic and conversion to time protocol representation (seconds), but does complicate the conversion to ICMP timestamp message representation (milliseconds). The precision of this representation is about 200 picoseconds.

object linking and embedding (OLE)   Is a technology that allows embedding and linking to documents and other objects developed by Microsoft.

octet   An entity having exactly eight bits.

A series of eight binary digits, they are often formulated or displayed as hexadecimal, decimal, or octal values.

The binary value of all eight bits set (or turned on) is 11111111; equal to the hexadecimal value of FF, the decimal value of 255, and the octal value of 377.

operating system   Operating system (commonly abbreviated to OS, O/S, or kernel) is an interface between hardware and software in a computer system. The software responsible for controlling the overall operation of a multipurpose computer system, including such tasks as memory allocation, input and output distribution, interrupt processing, and job scheduling.

order   (1) The height of a tree. (2) The number of children of the root of a binomial tree. (3) The maximum number of children of nodes in a b-tree. (4) The number of data streams, usually denoted ω, in a multiway merge.

parent   Of a node: the tree node conceptually above or closer to the root than the node and which has a link to the node.

parsing   To analyze or separate (input, for example) into more easily processed components.

partition   Is a logical division on a hard disk drive (HDD).

A "chunk" of space sectioned off of the disk drive. That chunk is then formatted with a file system and assigned a drive letter, at which point it is a volume labeled by its drive letter.

It so happens that the volume is on a partition. You can partition a drive without formatting them; you still have partitions, but no volumes.

partition boot record   A type of boot sector, stored in a disc volume on a hard disk, floppy disk, or similar data storage device, that contains code for booting programs (usually, but not necessarily, operating systems) stored in other parts of the volume.

partition table   A 64-byte data structure that defines the way a PC's hard disk is divided into logical sectors known as partitions.

The partition table describes to the operating system how the hard disk is divided.

Each partition on a disk has a corresponding entry in the partition table.

The partition table is always stored in the first physical sector of a disk drive.

petabyte (PB)   About 1 quadrillion bytes.

petahertz (PHz)   One quadrillion (1015) cycles per second.

Power-On Self-Test (POST)   A self-diagnostic program used to perform a single test of the CPU, RAM and various input/output (I/O) devices. to verify that the computer meets requirements to boot up properly.

If the computer does not pass the POST, you will receive a combination of beeps indicating what is malfunctioning within the computer.

The POST is performed by startup BIOS when the computer is first turned on and is stored in ROM BIOS.

RAID (redundant array of independent disks) array   A way of storing the same data in different places (thus, redundantly) on multiple hard disks. By placing data on multiple disks, I/O (input/output) operations can overlap in a balanced way, improving performance.

Since multiple disks increases the mean time between failures (MTBF), storing data redundantly also increases fault tolerance.

RAM (random access memory)   Memory modules on the motherboard containing microchips used to temporarily hold data and programs while the CPU processes both.

Information in RAM is lost when the PC is turned off.

recursion   A method for solving a problem in which the problem is broken down into a smaller version of itself, which can either be solved explicitly or can be solved recursively.

Registry   A database used by the Windows operating system (Windows 95 and NT) to store configuration information.

The registry consists of the following major sections:

- HKEY_Classes_Root—file associations and OLE information
- HKEY_Current_User—all preferences set for current user
- HKEY_User—all the current user information for each user of the system

- HKEY_Local_Machine—settings for hardware, operating system, and installed applications
- HKEY_Current_Configuration—settings for the display and printers
- HKEY_Dyn_Data—performance data

relative address   A memory address that represents some distance from a starting point (base address), such as the first byte of a program or table.

resident data   To optimize the storage and reduce the I/O overhead for the very common case of streams with very small associated data, NTFS prefers to place this data within the stream descriptor instead of using the MFT entry space to list clusters containing the data; in that case, the stream descriptor will not store the data directly but will just store an allocation map pointing to the actual data stored elsewhere on the volume.

When the stream data can be accessed directly from within the stream descriptor, it is called "resident data."

ROM (read-only memory)   A type of data storage device which is manufactured with fixed contents.

ROM is inherently non-volatile storage—it retains its contents even when the power is switched off, in contrast to RAM.

It is used in part for storage of the lowest level bootstrap software (firmware) in a computer.

root   The node from which all other nodes in the tree descend.

sanitized drive   A hard drive, which has had its contents "erased" via the process of masking information recorded on the hard drive by overwriting the existing information with random, meaningless data.

sector   A specifically sized division of a hard disk drive, optical disc, floppy disk, or other kind of storage medium.

Usually, one sector of a hard disk drive or floppy disk can hold 512 bytes of information. One sector of an optical disc can usually hold 2,048 bytes.

This difference in sector size doesn't imply anything about the difference in possible sizes between hard drives and optical discs—the number of sectors available on the drive or disc determines this.

sector slack   The portion of the slack space from the end of the logical file to the end of the sector (not the cluster) was called RAM slack.

More recently, the term sector slack has been used; both refer to the same portion of the slack space.

SHA-1   Secure Hash Algorithm. Used for computing a condensed representation of a message or a data file specified by FIPS PUB 180-1.

signature word   The two final bytes of the first sector in the MRB, and they are used as a simple validation of the MBR's contents.

slack space   The unused space in a disk cluster. The DOS and Windows file systems use fixed-size clusters. Even if the actual data being stored requires less storage than the cluster size, an entire cluster is reserved for the file.

The unused space is called the slack space.

DOS and older Windows systems use a 16-bit file allocation table (FAT), which results in very large cluster sizes for large partitions.

For example, if the partition size is 2 GB, each cluster will be 32 K. Even if a file requires only 4 K, the entire 32 K will be allocated, resulting in 28 K of slack space.

Operating systems Windows 95 and above resolved this problem by using a 32-bit FAT (FAT 32) that supports cluster sizes smaller than 1K.

stream cipher   A stream cipher encrypts in small units, often a bit or a byte at a time, but unlike a basic block cipher the output corresponding to a given input will depend on where in the message it occurs.

The simplest type of stream cipher uses a complicated function, which retains state, to generate a pseudo-random sequence which is then combined with the input using a simple operation such as bytewise addition.

subject   An individual that can be a witness, but has not been eliminated as a culprit of the investigated activity.

subtree(s)   The tree which is a child of a node.

As the name emphasizes, everything which is a descendant of a tree node is a tree, too, and is a subset of the larger tree.

superblock   A record of the characteristics of a filesystem, including its size, the block size, the empty and the filled blocks and their respective counts, the size and location of the inode tables, the disk block map and usage information, and the size of the block groups.

symmetric key encryption   Are a class of algorithms for cryptography that use trivially related, often identical, cryptographic keys for both decryption and encryption.

The encryption key is trivially related to the decryption key, in that they may be identical or there is a simple transformation to go between the two keys.

The keys, in practice, represent a shared secret between two or more parties that can be used to maintain a private information link.

target   An individual who has been identified as the most likely culprit and is considered to be the focus of the investigation.

terabyte (TB)   About 1 trillion bytes.

terahertz (THz)   One trillion (1012) cycles per second.

time-lining   A sequence of related events arranged in chronological order and displayed along a line (usually drawn left to right or top to bottom). (Chronology: a record of events in the order of their occurrence).

time provider   With respect to the NTP nomenclature, a time provider is a primary reference source, a courier is a secondary server intended to import time from one or more distant primary servers for local redistribution, and a server is intended to provide time for possibly many end nodes or clerks. (Mills, D. (March 1992), "Network Time Protocol (Version 3) Specification, Implementation and Analysis," ftp://ftp.isi.edu/in-notes/rfc1305.txt.)

timestamp   A sequence of characters, denoting the date and/or time at which a certain event occurred.

A timestamp is the time at which an event is recorded by a computer, not the time of the event itself.

In many cases, the difference may be inconsequential: the time at which an event is recorded by a timestamp (e.g., entered into a log file) should be very, very close to the time of the occurrence of the event recorded.

timestamping   Data is usually presented in a consistent format, allowing for easy comparison of two different records and tracking progress over time; the practice of recording timestamps in a consistent manner along with the actual data is called timestamping.

tracks   Are the thin concentric circular strips on a floppy medium or platter surface which actually contain the magnetic regions of data written to a disk drive.

They form a circle and are (therefore) two-dimensional.

At least one head is required to read a single track. All information stored on the hard disk is recorded in tracks.

tree   A data structure accessed beginning at the root node. Each node is either a leaf or a parent, which refers to child nodes.

Trojan   Although Trojan horse programs are categorized as viruses, they are not true viruses, since they do not replicate.

It is a malicious program disguised as something benign, such as a screen saver.

When loaded onto a machine, a Trojan horse can capture information from the system—such as user names and passwords—or could allow a malicious hacker to remotely control the compromised computer.

Trojans are one of the sneakiest of the online risks. They are often downloaded on the back of a free program (freeware) that has some value to the user—a free game, software program, or music, for instance.

truechimer A clock that maintains timekeeping accuracy to a previously published (and trusted) standard.

tuple A particular kind of sequence, written like this: (1, 2, 3), or (C, H, S). Unlike lists, tuples are immutable.

unallocated Not allocated. Typically referring to disk space (see unallocated space).

unallocated space Defined as available disk space that is not allocated to any volume. The area of computer media, such as a hard drive, that does not contain normally accessible data. Unallocated space is usually the result of a file being deleted. When a file is deleted, it is not actually erased, but is simply no longer accessible through normal means.

The space that it occupied becomes unallocated space (i.e., space on the drive that can be reused to store new information). Until portions of the unallocated space are used for new data storage, in most instances, the old data remains and can be retrieved using forensic techniques.

unicode A 16-bit character encoding scheme allowing characters from Western European, Eastern European, Cyrillic, Greek, Arabic, Hebrew, Chinese, Japanese, Korean, Thai, Urdu, Hindi, and all other major world languages, living and dead, to be encoded in a single character set.

volume(s) In the context of computer operating systems, volume describes a single accessible storage area with a single file system, typically (though not necessarily) resident on a single partition of a hard disk.

Similarly, it refers to the logical interface used by an operating system to access data stored on some media using a single instance of a filesystem.

"Volume" can be used in place of the term "drive" where it is desirable to indicate that the entity in question is not a physical disk drive.

volume boot record (VBR) A type of boot sector, stored in a disc volume on a hard disk, floppy disk, or similar data storage device, that contains code for booting programs (usually, but not necessarily, operating systems) stored in other parts of the volume.

On nonpartitioned storage devices, it is the first sector of the device.

On partitioned devices, it is the first sector of an individual partition on the device, with the first sector of the entire device instead being a Master Boot Record (MBR).

witness   An individual that, through sight, sound, touch, smell, and taste or any combination thereof can provide an evidentiary statement as to the investigated activity.

write blocker   A specialized type of computer hard disk controller made for the purpose of gaining read-only access to computer hard drives without the risk of damaging the drive's contents.

write protected   Any physical mechanism that prevents modification or erasure of valuable data on a device. A piece of hardware (or software) that ensures a device that is used to acquire an image cannot write to the suspect media, which could potentially overwrite, damage, or invalidate the data.

zip file   A file that has been compressed, or reduced in size, to save storage space and allow faster transferring across a network over the Internet. To read the information, the file must be uncompressed into its original form.

About the Authors

Albert J. Marcella Jr., PhD, CISA, CISM is president of Business Automation Consultants, LLC, a global information technology and management-consulting firm providing information technology (IT) management consulting and IT audit and security reviews and training for an international clientele.

Dr. Marcella is an internationally recognized public speaker, researcher, author, and workshop and seminar leader with more than 34 years of experience in IT audit, security, and assessing internal controls. An author of numerous articles and 26 books on various IT-, audit-, and security-related subjects, Dr. Marcella's work has appeared in the *ISACA Journal, Disaster Recovery Journal, Journal of Forensic & Investigative Accounting, EDPACS, ISSA Journal, Continuity Insights, The Journal of Applied Business Research*, and *Internal Auditor Magazine*.

Dr. Marcella is the Institute of Internal Auditors Leon R. Radde Educator of the Year (2000) Award recipient. Dr. Marcella has taught IT audit seminar courses for the Institute of Internal Auditors (IIA), and continues to teach a variety of IT and IT audit related programs for the Information Systems Audit and Control Association (ISACA).

Frederic Guillossou, MA, CISSP, CCE has more than eight years' experience working in the Information Security field, including private and corporate sectors. His security experience includes incident response, digital forensics, project management, network security, IPS management, and anti-malware.

Mr. Guillossou has worked in the information security field for a financial institution for much of his career and has familiarized himself with regulatory standards such as PCI, ISO 27001, NIST, SOX, and SEC. He worked closely with in- and outside counsel, fraud investigators, human resource departments, and auditors.

During his career, Mr. Guillossou has investigated the loss of intellectual property, labor/human resource issues, and other internal investigations.

Index

Access Data, 228
Active partition, 96, 97,
        101, 102, 109, 117,
        118, 119, 120
Address:
    HEX editor address panel, 37
    Logical Block Address (LBA),
        130, 132–133
Adobe, 41, 46, 287
Advanced Encryption Standard
        (AES), 65
Apple/Macintosh:
    boot process in, 86
    endian designation by, 117
    file extensions for, 70–72
    file signature information
        for, 76
    file systems of, 152, 153, 202
    hard drive removal from, 91
    operating systems, 44, 76, 86,
        152, 153, 202
ASCII (American Standard
        Code for Information Inter-
        change):
    binary and decimal values
        assigned to, 8–9, 16,
        17, 32–34, 57, 66,
        285–286, 288
    extended, 10–11

HEX equivalent to, 32–34, 55,
        57–58, 66, 77, 154–155,
        161, 248–249, 288
    overview of, 7–9

Bad clusters, 164, 167, 180
Base 2 numbering system, 2–3.
        See also Binary system
Binary system:
    ASCII equivalents to, 8–9,
        16, 17, 32–34, 57, 66,
        285–286, 288
    binary (HEX) editor, 34–39,
        43, 53–57, 66, 98–101,
        117–125, 289
    binary tree filing system,
        196–200
    bits as building blocks of, 4–7,
        165–166, 284
    b-tree filing system, 200–202
    character codes using, 7–13,
        25–42 (*see also* ASCII;
        Hexadecimal characters;
        Unicode)
    decimal equivalents of, 15–24,
        26, 29, 32–34, 252–253,
        285–287
    electricity and magnetism
        relationship to, 3–4

329